Perspectives on
ALFRED HITCHCOCK

Perspectives on
FILM

RONALD GOTTESMAN
University of Southern California
and
HARRY M. GEDULD
Indiana University

Series Editors

Alfred Hitchcock

Photo collection of Ronald Gottesman

❖

Perspectives on
ALFRED HITCHCOCK

❖

edited by

DAVID BOYD

G. K. Hall & Co.
Simon & Schuster Macmillan
New York
Prentice Hall International
London   Mexico City   New Delhi   Singapore   Sydney   Toronto

G. K. Hall & Co.
Simon & Schuster Macmillan
866 Third Avenue
New York, NY 10022

Library of Congress Catalog Card Number: 94-35398

Printed in the United States of America

Printing Number

1 2 3 4 5 6 7 8 9 10

Library of Congress Cataloging-in-Publication Data

Perspectives on Alfred Hitchcock / edited by David Boyd.
    p. cm. — (Perspectives on film)
    Filmography: p.
    Includes bibliographical references (p. –) and index.
    ISBN 0-8161-1603-2
    1. Hitchcock, Alfred, 1899–   —Criticism and interpretation. I. Boyd, David, 1944–   .
II. Series.
PN1998.3.H58P47   1995
791.43'0233'092—dc20   94-35398
                                                                 CIP

Contents

Illustrations follow page 84

Series Editors' Note

This series is devoted to supplying comprehensive coverage of several topics: directors, individual films, national film traditions, film genres, and other categories that scholars have devised for organizing the rich history of film as expressive form, cultural force, and industrial and technological enterprise. Each volume essentially brings together two kinds of critical and historical material: first, previously published reviews, interviews, written and pictorial documents, essays, and other forms of commentary and interpretation; and, second, commissioned writings designed to provide fresh perspectives. Each volume is edited by a film scholar and contains a substantial introduction that traces and interprets the history of the critical response to the subject and indicates its current status among specialists. As appropriate, volumes will also provide production credits, filmographies, selective annotated bibliographies, indexes, and other reference materials. Titles in this series will thus combine the virtues of an interpretive archive and a reference guide. The success of each volume should be measured against this objective.

Professor Boyd's collection has its own logic. After he locates Hitchcock in film history and outlines the salient developments in the history of critical response to his subject, Professor Boyd begins the body of the volume with a wide-ranging interview in which Richard Schickel, always sympathetic but always tough-minded and well-informed, draws Hitchcock out on principles, methods, and basic beliefs, and on particular films and people as well. Hitchcock was notoriously elusive as an interview subject and practiced with consummate skill the fine art of self-propaganda. But by virtue of what he doesn't say as much as by what he does, Hitchcock comes tantalizingly alive in this opening piece. Robin Wood and Thomas Leitch pick up the theme of strategy and allow us to see both visible technical and thematic patterns across the body of Hitchcock's work and the evolving creative imaginations behind them. The remaining essays are "close-ups," and these distinctive and powerfully argued individual essays introduce political, ideological, formal, cultural, and genre issues so central to critical theory over the past decade. Together with the bibliographic, filmographic and other factual information, this collection offers a valuable resource for anyone interested in film and arguably its most popular director. We are delighted that the volume as a whole will raise almost as many questions as it answers. The task of criticism, after all, is neither to praise nor to bury, but to renew.

Ronald Gottesman
Harry M. Geduld

Publisher's Note

Producing a volume that contains both newly commissioned and reprinted material presents the publisher with the challenge of balancing the desire to achieve stylistic consistency with the need to preserve the integrity of works first published elsewhere. In the Perspectives series, essays commissioned especially for a particular volume are edited to be consistent with G. K. Hall's house style; reprinted essays appear in the style in which they were first published, with only typographical errors corrected. Consequently, shifts in style from one essay to another are the result of our efforts to be faithful to each text as it was originally published.

INTRODUCTION

Introduction

DAVID BOYD

In his memoirs, Hume Cronyn recalls listening to Alfred Hitchcock enthusiastically describe how he would go about filming various stories that had captured his interest. Conjuring up the films as he visualised them appearing on screen, Hitchcock would occasionally use images that "were so bizarre, or became so fixed in his mind, that they proved a stumbling block to logic." If anyone had the temerity to question these images, he "would speak derisively of 'the icebox trade.'" This was Hitchcock's term, Cronyn explains, for the kind of people who, having "seen and thoroughly enjoyed a movie, then repaired to somebody's kitchen, raided the icebox, fixed themselves a snack, had a beer, and proceeded to discuss the film they'd just seen." Hitchcock's "contempt for such postmortems," he reports, "was absolute."[1]

Hitchcock's own views on the matter notwithstanding, over the past three or four decades no film maker has been more relentlessly subjected to the attentions of 'the icebox trade'—now institutionalized ('legitimized' might overstate things a bit) as academic film criticism. Not only is the critical literature on his films formidable (now comprising something close to a thousand articles, along with books in English, French, German, Italian, Spanish, Portuguese, Dutch, Polish, Swedish, and Serbo-Croatian), but his work has come to occupy a peculiarly privileged place in film studies. So much so, in fact, that the history of Hitchcock criticism since the 1950s precisely parallels the history of the discipline itself.[2]

By the start of the fifties, filmgoers who were not members of the icebox trade had already long recognized, of course, that Hitchcock was an unusually gifted popular entertainer. Because art and entertainment so often tended, then as now, to be regarded as distinct (and perhaps mutually exclusive) categories, however, his commercial success sometimes seemed to count as evidence against him in the eyes of some critics. Consequently, it was possible for Lindsay Anderson, for instance, to declare unequivocally in 1949 that "Hitchcock has never been a 'serious' director," that his films were "interesting neither for their ideas nor for their characters."[3] Anderson may have been somewhat harsher than most of his contemporaries, admittedly, but he was probably more or less typical of critics of his generation in attributing only relatively modest virtues to Hitchcock.

Anderson was also typical, more particularly, of the British critics of the time in locating those virtues primarily in the films of the thirties, films "in many ways very English, in their humour, lack of sentimentality, their avoidance of the grandiose and the elaborately fake."[4] Other British critics were not always quite so blatant in their chauvinism, but most of them tended, unsurprisingly, to share this view of Hitchcock's move to Hollywood at the end of the thirties as an unfortunate fall from grace; American critics, just as unsurprisingly, tended to treat the films of the forties somewhat more generously. On both sides of the Atlantic, however, it was already becoming clear that Hitchcock's critical fortunes would ultimately be inextricably linked to those of the Hollywood cinema in general.

The critical revaluation of both Hitchcock and Hollywood began in earnest in the early fifties, neither in Britain nor America, however, but rather in France—more specifically, in the pages of *Cahiers du Cinéma*, where the cadre of young film critics who would emerge a few years later as a New Wave in French filmmaking were energetically promoting what quickly, if somewhat misleadingly, became known as the "auteur theory." Actually little more than an attempt to push the interests of the particular film makers, and the particular form of filmmaking, that these critics favored, this so-called theory (François Truffaut, in coining the term, had actually spoken of a "politique des auteurs") maintained simply that there were certain directors who could be regarded as the genuine authors of their films, and that these "auteurs" could be distinguished from mere "metteurs en scène" by the stylistic and thematic coherence of their work as a whole.

Hitchcock was among the first to be admitted into the company of this newly declared elect—not least, perhaps, because he had been so assiduously presenting himself as an "auteur" virtually from the beginning of his career. (Robert E. Kapsis has demonstrated the extent to which his tireless self-promotion contributed to the shaping of his artistic reputation.[5]) Even without these efforts on his own behalf, though, it would have been difficult to deny that his work displayed to a remarkable degree the coherence and distinctiveness demanded of an auteur. Stylistically, Hitchcock's camerawork, his editing, and his handling of sound all deviate radically from the self-effacing norms of the classic Hollywood cinema epitomised by a director like Howard Hawks, and the more obvious features of his personal style (the forward tracking shots, for instance) are so widely known that they could be spoofed by Mel Brooks in his Hitchcock parody, *High Anxiety*, in complete confidence that a popular audience would recognise them. And thematically, the Hitchcock *oeuvre* might well seem not merely coherent, but downright obsessive.

This thematic coherence proved particularly crucial as auteurist criticism, under the growing influence of structuralism, increasingly set as its task the identification of "the hard core of basic and often recondite motifs which, united in various combinations, constitute the true specificity of an author's work."[6] Over the years, various critical formulations of these defining motifs in Hitchcock's case have been advanced, but the earliest, advanced by Eric Rohmer and Claude Chabrol in the first book-length study of Hitchcock's films, published in 1957, remains among the most influential. Characterizing Hitchcock as a specifically Catholic artist—more specifically still, a Jansenist, or Calvinist, obsessed with predestination and original sin—Rohmer and Chabrol identify the quintessential Hitchcockian narrative as based on an exchange, or more generally a sharing, of guilt (a pattern most explicitly and symmetrically worked out, of course, in *Strangers on a Train*). Rohmer and Chabrol's account ends, necessarily, with *The Wrong Man* in 1956, but in a series of three articles in *Cahiers du Cinéma* in 1959 and 1960, and later in a book, much the same approach was extended to the later films, further elaborated, and rendered yet more recondite by Jean Douchet. The final result of the collaborative efforts of Rohmer, Chabrol, Douchet, and the other *Cahiers* critics has been not altogether unfairly described by Penelope Houston as "one of those towering French critical Christmas trees from which may be slung some dazzling illuminations."[7] Other critics (and not only in France) have been busily adding their own ornaments to this tree ever since. If these subsequent critics have generally been somewhat sceptical about the alleged sectarian basis of Hitchcock's thematic obsessions (the director himself, educated by Jesuits, was somewhat bemused to find himself exposed as a closet Jansenist), the emphasis on guilt, the motif of the double, and the tone of moral pessimism quickly became commonplaces of Hitchcock criticism.

Despite the lasting influence of this French criticism of the fifties, however, its Gallic abstractness tended to make it unpalatable to some Anglo-Saxon tastes. Robin Wood, for instance, complained that Rohmer and Chabrol's analyses had "the effect of depriving the films of flesh and blood, reducing them to theoretical skeletons."[8] And it was undoubtedly Wood himself who did most to both naturalize the *auteur* theory in general for Anglo-American readers and, in particular, to define the particular character of Hitchcock as auteur. Despite his reservations about Rohmer and Chabrol, Wood's criticism had unmistakable links with that of the French critics. His own earliest piece on Hitchcock, for instance, first appeared (in French) in the same issue of *Cahiers du Cinéma* as the last installment of Douchet's series.[9]

Wood's more immediate affinities, however, were with various developments in English and American film and literary criticism. Unlike Rohmer and Chabrol, for instance, and very much like Ian Cameron, Victor Perkins, and the other critics associated with the British journal *Movie*, Wood devoted himself primarily to the analysis of character and dramatic structure, rather than to the explication of Christian iconography, and remained more concerned with moral and psychological, rather than with religious and metaphysical, concerns.[10] The influence of the British literary critic F. R. Leavis is also often evident in Wood's relentless moral earnestness, his emphasis on felt experience, and in the language as well as the sheer, breathtaking peremptoriness of his critical judgments: comparing *Vertigo* to *Lamia*, for instance, Wood declares the film "in maturity and depth of understanding, as well as in formal perfection, decidedly superior to Keats' poem."[11] Wood's most important indebtedness, however, is probably to Anglo-American "New Criticism" in general, an indebtedness reflected most clearly in his explicit insistence on organic unity and on the inseparability of content and form:

> The meaning of a Hitchcock film is not a mysterious something cunningly concealed behind a camouflage of "entertainment"; it is there in the method, in the progression from shot to shot. A Hitchcock film is an organism, with the whole implied in every detail and every detail related to the whole.[12]

This might easily serve as a catechism of New Critical articles of belief, and Wood's critical essays on individual films are exemplary specimens of New Critical analysis, able to withstand comparison with the best literary criticism then being published in scholarly journals. The growing acceptance of Film Studies as an academic discipline was due in no small part to such demonstrations that film could be productively subjected to the then-dominant mode of critical analysis.

Wood significantly reoriented the generally accepted critical view of Hitchcock in particular in a number of ways. For one thing, in direct opposition to British critics of the preceding generation like Lindsay Anderson, he insisted that the highpoint of Hitchcock's career was marked not by the films of the thirties, but rather by what he described as the "mature" films of the fifties and sixties. Indeed, although Wood's book was comprehensively entitled *Hitchcock's Films*, it dealt almost exclusively with the period from *Strangers on a Train* (1951) through to *Marnie* (1964), and explicitly argued that "not only in theme—in style, method, moral attitude, assumptions about the nature of life—Hitchcock's mature films reveal, on inspection, a consistent development, deepening, and clarification."[13] Subsequent criticism has certainly not by any means wholly neglected the British films, particularly *The Lodger* (1926), *Blackmail* (1929), and the so-called "thriller sextet" from *The Man Who Knew Too Much* (1934) through to *The Lady Vanishes* (1938). Indeed, Wood himself, in his article in this volume, explores the "relationship of both rupture and continuity" between the British films and the American and discovers both the "basic plot formations" and "all the major elements of Hitchcock's mature style . . . already present in the British work." Critical attention has nevertheless continued to focus very largely on the films of the fifties and to ratify Wood's judgments as to Hitchcock's masterworks: *Strangers on a Train*

(1951), *Rear Window* (1954), *Vertigo* (1958), *North by Northwest* (1959), *Psycho* (1960), and *The Birds* (1963).

If Wood passed on to subsequent critics a Hitchcock canon very different from the one offered by British critics like Anderson, he also handed on a Hitchcockian thematic significantly different from that of French critics like Rohmer and Chabrol. Where they had focused on the metaphysical relationship of man and God, for instance, Wood was concerned with the more immediate emotional and sexual relationships of men and women (later, when he came out as a gay critic, of men and men); and where they had focused on the transfer of guilt as the central narrative pattern, he saw instead a "therapeutic theme, whereby a character is cured of some weakness or obsession by indulging it and living through the consequences." What was probably more important than Wood's identification of this therapeutic process as a recurrent narrative pattern, however, was his further insistence on Hitchcock's "extension of this 'therapy' to the spectator, by means of encouraging the audience to identify," so that "always it is our own impulses that are involved."[14] In directly addressing matters of viewer response in this way, Wood is implicitly responding to one of the recurrent refrains among Hitchcock's detractors and making alleged defect perfection. Rather than denying or apologizing for Hitchcock's manipulation of his audiences, that is, Wood insists upon it and presents the master manipulator as moral teacher.

This emphasis on the importance, and the seriousness, of the affective dimension of Hitchcock's films was quickly taken up by other critics. Leo Braudy, for instance, similarly stresses that Hitchcock's much-vaunted technical skill is not an end in itself, and that "all of Hitchcock's 'techniques' are aimed at destroying the separation between the film and its audience," in an effort to "bring his audience from the detachment of irresponsible spectators to the involvement of implicated participants."[15] Later critics have frequently seen this process as thematized within the films themselves. Robert Stam and Roberta Pearson, for instance, argue that the transformation of the protagonist of *Rear Window* "from distant observer into excited vicarious participant 'allegorises' the transformation engendered in us by the narrative procedures and identificatory mechanisms of Hitchcock's cinema"[16] And Ina Rae Hark, in her analysis of *The Man Who Knew Too Much* and *The 39 Steps* reprinted in this volume, discerns political implications in this characteristic opposition of observation and involvement.

By the end of the sixties, Raymond Durgnat could fairly accurately describe Hitchcock's critics as divided into armed camps: "those for whom Hitchcock is a Master, but a Master of nothing, and those for whom Hitchcock is regularly rather than occasionally a profound and salutary moralist working, not through homily, but through a therapeutic process of involvement."[17] Durgnat himself claimed to offer a middle way between these extremes, acknowledging the overall intelligence and craftsmanship of Hitchcock's films, and their occasional greatness (most clearly in *Psycho*), but denying them any real thematic consistency beyond that of the genres to which they belong. Not many, however, were inclined to follow Durgnat along this supposed middle road. And although occasional critics on both sides of the Atlantic (Penelope Houston in England, for instance, and Charles Thomas Samuels in America) forcefully expressed their continuing doubts about the moral seriousness claimed for Hitchcock's films, the majority of academic film critics, in particular, had clearly adopted either the French or, more frequently, the Anglo-American version of Hitchcock as *auteur*.[18]

If Hitchcock's detractors (such as Anderson, Houston, Samuels, and, in a qualified way, Durgnat) were united in their denial that Hitchcock was really all that different from the common run of commercial film makers, his auteurist champions, French and Anglo-American alike, were conversely united in the conviction that he *was* different—and fundamentally different. For the *Cahiers* critics, the films of an authentic auteur, like Hitchcock, differ from those of a mere *metteur en scène*, not merely in *degree* (in being better crafted, more intelligent, more involving), but in *kind*. Similarly, Wood insists explicitly and at length on the absolute distinction between the affective complexity of Hitchcock's films and what he sees as the pursuit of suspense for its own sake in routine thrillers like *From Russia with Love* and *Whatever Happened to Baby Jane?* For Wood, Hitchcock demands to be seen, not in such questionable company, but rather in the context of the highest of high culture. "One cannot resist invoking Shakespeare," he says at one point.[19] Certainly Wood cannot: In the Introduction alone, invocations of *Measure for Measure*, *Cymbeline*, and *The Winter's Tale* turn up, along with allusions to Spenser, Corneille, Johnson, and Keats. Wood's answer to the question he poses at the beginning of his book—Why should we take Hitchcock seriously?—is obvious: We should take him seriously because his films are like Shakespeare's plays and, equally important, because they are not like (not *at all* like) other Hollywood movies.

The seventies witnessed the emergence of a radically different critical approach, however, which found Hitchcock's films worthy of serious attention, not because of their differences from other Hollywood films, but rather precisely because of their similarities. Like the auteurism of the sixties, this new approach also took its theoretical lead from France, in the work of semiotician Raymond Bellour. As Michael Renov says at the beginning of his article on *Notorious* in this volume (itself an exemplary specimen of this new approach), Bellour's studies of Hitchcock have to be understood as part of a larger "effort to determine the constitutive, systematic elements . . . the highly conventionalised formal and thematic movements of classical American cinema" as a whole. Formally, this project entails an exhaustive tracing of visual repetitions and symmetries, clearly modeled on Roland Barthes' analysis of the codes of classic realist fiction in *S/Z* and conducted with an unprecedented attention to detail (the showpiece of this style of analysis—sceptics would say the *reductio ad absurdum*—is Bellour's 115-page article on *North by Northwest*, more than half of which consists of a shot-by-shot analysis of the cornfield sequence).[20] Thematically, it involves the psychoanalytic understanding of films, as Renov neatly phrases it, as "machines of desire and sexual identification." The formal and thematic projects converge on the notion of "the male gaze" (understood as the gaze of both male characters and male viewers) as the controlling mechanism of identification in classic cinema, a notion taken up and greatly elaborated by Laura Mulvey, who uses *Rear Window* and *Vertigo* as her prime examples in what probably remains the single most influential article in feminist film criticism.[21]

In summary, Bellour's approach might not seem all that different from that of earlier critics. After all, auteurists like Robin Wood also attended to formal repetitions and symmetries, if not so systematically as Bellour, and they too often regarded the treatment of sexual relationships as thematically central to Hitchcock's films. But two factors radically distinguish the new approach from the old. The first is this emphasis, not on what differentiates Hitchcock's work from other Hollywood films in terms both of content and form, but rather on what it shares in common with them. So whether Bellour's elaborate tracing of a "male Oedipal trajectory" through *North by Northwest* is found illuminating or madly over-ingenious, it has to be understood in the light of his insistence that *all* Hollywood films follow a similar trajectory.[22] The second innovation of the new approach is its denial to viewers of that enhanced awareness on which earlier claims for Hitchcock as moral teacher were based. Far from increasing viewers' awareness, in fact, the formal and narrative mechanisms exposed by Bellour allegedly operate precisely to suppress their awareness, so that they can be (in one of the key terms of this approach) *positioned*—positioned specularly by the camerawork and editing, and positioned psychologically and ideologically by the narrative.

For all their differences, though, the New Criticism of the sixties and the *nouvelle critique* of the seventies, what we might call the School of Wood and the School of Bellour, also have a couple of things in common. Both of them posit an essentially passive and homogeneous model of the film viewer. Whether viewers are seen as being morally instructed or ideologically positioned, that is, they themselves apparently have very little to say about the matter, nor does it seem to matter much who they are. And both approaches also offer similarly homogeneous (albeit diametrically opposed) models of Hitchcock's relationship to the conditions of production (generally known, more familiarly, as "the system"). According to the one, he transcends these conditions; according to the other, he is wholly defined by them. But neither alternative leaves much room for variation. And it is precisely the possibility of significant variation within both these areas that has been opened up by the most interesting developments in Hitchcock criticism during the eighties and nineties.

There were some tentative moves in these directions during the previous decade. Michael Renov, for instance, acknowledges that a really adequate account of "the complex processes of identification and spectatorship" could "only be achieved in terms of a material audience experiencing the film in concrete ways." His own account of the operation of these processes in *Notorious*, however, continues for the most part to be predicated on the assumption of a normative male spectatorship, albeit a "fragmented" one. Tania Modleski's *The Women Who Knew Too Much: Hitchcock and Feminist Film Theory*, in contrast, more consistently embraces what Renov terms "the multivalence of spectatorship" by recognizing that "the same scene can elicit very different responses depending on its viewers' experience and values." More specifically, Modleski rejects Laura Mulvey's contention that it is only possible for the female viewer to participate in Hitchcock's films masochistically, and argues that the films actually reveal a deep ambivalence towards femininity, an ambivalence which leaves the female spectator sufficient room of her own within the text to construct a feminist interpretation. Leland Poague provides, in an article on *Blackmail*, a more general theoretical context for this sort of revisionist re-viewing by drawing on the "reception aesthetics" of Hans Robert Jauss to suggest the ways in which the interpretive possibilities available to film viewers are historically determined.[23] As it happened, the re-release of Hitchcock's so-called "missing films" in the early eighties provided an object lesson in this process: Seen again 25 years after its original release, *Vertigo*, for instance, now seemed a very different film to many critics, less a romantic mystery than an essay on sexual politics.

No doubt these various efforts to redefine the relationship between Hitchcock's films and their viewers are largely a response to the recent empowering of the viewer (or reader) in critical theory generally, and in theories of radically different kinds. George Toles, for instance, describes in an article on *Rear Window* as "critical allegory" the ways in which Marxist, deconstructionist, and feminist interpretations can all shift part of the responsibility for the construction of meaning onto the viewer.[24] But at least some of these developments are also an attempt to respond to something specific to Hitchcock's films. Thomas Leitch argues in *Find the Director and Other Hitchcock Games*, for instance, that the director's cameo appearances are symptomatic of the way in which his films erode "the customary distinction between story and discourse to create a no-man's-land not adequately described by communication, psychoanalytic, or mimetic theories of narrative." As an alternative, Leitch proposes that the films be regarded as rule-governed games that "do not inscribe passive, unconscious cultural constraints but rather engage audiences on a conscious, contractual, elective basis by providing a distinctive pleasure." Whatever its limitations, this sort of account surely represents a considerable advance in sophistication over the view of Hitchcock as "the Pavlov of film makers, playing on the international reflex."[25]

If recent work of this sort offers a more heterogeneous and specific account of the reception of Hitchcock's films, other scholars have been similarly refining and complicating our understanding of the contexts in which the films were produced. The seminal work in this area has been Tom Ryall's *Alfred Hitchcock and the British Cinema*, which simultaneously revives and displaces the debate over Hitchcock's status as artist or entertainer by demonstrating that he was, in actual fact, a genuine hybrid from the beginning, "a marooned figure, too businesslike and commercial to be an 'artist,' yet too 'artistic' to be fitted comfortably into the British entertainment cinema of the time."[26] He presents "a particularly striking example of a professional film maker working within the commercial film industry but with a set of interests and concerns which intersect with areas of the film culture that implicitly rejected the commercial cinema," specifically the "minority film culture of the Film Society, the development of the specialised film journal, the 'art' cinemas of Europe which sprang into being in the 1920's, and the British documentary film movement of the 1930's."[27] Although Ryall confines his attention to the British films, his findings have direct implications for the view fostered by Bellour, Mulvey, and others that the American films are exemplary specimens of classical Hollywood narrative. "Although the primary formal and stylistic influence on Hitchcock was the classical American cinema," he argues, "the experimental qualities in his films which link them to the 'art' cinemas of Europe make for an off-centred relationship between them and mainstream classical cinema."[28]

Although nothing approaching the scope of Ryall's book has as yet been attempted on the social, cultural, and industrial contexts of Hitchcock's work in Hollywood, there have been a number of useful and illuminating studies recently of particular aspects of the production process. In the light of these studies, it is becoming increasingly difficult to take very seriously the picture that Hitchcock himself liked to offer to reporters and interviewers of the master at work, slumped in his director's chair, indifferent to those around him, every detail already anticipated in the screenplay and storyboards, wearily going through the tiresome business of transferring on to celluloid the film already completed in his head. The Hitchcock who emerges from Stephen Rebello's journalistic account of the making of *Psycho*, for instance, is a canny Hollywood producer as well as director, a "player," as actively involved in making deals as in framing shots.[29] And what remains of the pure auteurist view of the director as the only begetter of his films (a view obligingly endorsed by Hitchcock himself in interviews) has been seriously called into question by studies of the often crucial contributions made by such collaborators, offscreen and on, as David Selznick, Bernard Herrmann, Cary Grant, and James Stewart.[30]

Illuminating as this historical research often is, however, it seems unlikely to provide an ultimate solution to what Raymond Durgnat dubbed "the strange case of Alfred Hitchcock." Tom Ryall optimistically endorses David Bordwell's claim that the "historicising of textual analysis" will permit criticism to "break free from the endless process of open reading based upon 'the sterile notion of the self-sufficient text.'"[31] This hope that the historically contextualized text will prove any more susceptible to interpretive closure than the supposedly self-sufficient text is itself, however, scarcely borne out by history. Research such as Ryall's further complicates, rather than simplifies, our understanding of Hitchcock's films by revealing the ways in which they were subject to shaping by factors in addition to the director's vision, and the degree to which—like dreams, to which they are so often compared—they are therefore complexly overdetermined. Like dreams, too, they seem endlessly to demand interpretation, and endlessly to elude it.

This book makes no attempt to survey the entire field of Hitchcock criticism. All of its contents were first published within the past 20 years, most of them within the past ten, and they were selected, not only for their intrinsic interest, but also as representative of some main currents in recent writing about Hitchcock.

Hitchcock made himself freely available for interviews throughout his career, but very early in his career developed a public persona that generally permitted him to conceal more than he revealed. His interview with Richard Schickel, however, is something of an exception: Some familiar anecdotes do get retold yet again, but an unusually candid and thoughtful Hitchcock also emerges. The other two items in the "Overviews" section provide contrasting characterizations of the coherence of the Hitchcock oeuvre, Robin Wood emphasising the stories, or "plot formations," and Thomas Leitch the storytelling, the narrative "games" in which the director invites his viewers to participate. The items in the "Close-Ups" section take a more detailed look at eight particular films, focusing on three issues: Tania Modleski and Michael Renov present radically different views of the sexual politics of Hitchcock's films; Ina Rae Hark and R. Barton Palmer offer political and metafictional perspectives, respectively, on their reflexivity; and Royal S. Brown and Lesley Brill remind us (unfashionably, but nevertheless illuminatingly) that, although these films do undoubtedly reward examination within their immediate social and cultural context, they also deserve to be seen as part of much older narrative traditions.

I am grateful to Professor Ronald Gottesman for his advice and for generously supplying publicity stills from his collection.

NOTES

1. Hume Cronyn, *A Terrible Liar: A Memoir* (New York: William Morrow, 1991), 205–206.

2. The secondary literature is exhaustively surveyed in Jane E. Sloan, *Alfred Hitchcock: A Guide to References and Resources* (G.K. Hall, 1993).

3. Lindsay Anderson, "Alfred Hitchcock," *Sequence* 9 (Autumn 1949), reprinted in *Focus on Hitchcock*, ed. Albert J. LaValley (Englewood Cliffs: Prentice-Hall, 1972), 58.

4. Ibid., 54.

5. See Robert E. Kapsis, *Hitchcock: The Making of a Reputation* (Chicago: University of Chicago Press, 1992), Chapters Two and Three.

6. G. Nowell-Smith, "Cinema and Structuralism," *Twentieth Century Studies*, no.3 (1970): 133.

7. Penelope Houston, "Alfred Hitchcock," in *Cinema: A Critical Dictionary*, ed. Richard Roud (London: Secker and Warburg, 1980), 488.

8. Robin Wood, *Hitchcock's Films Revisited* (New York: Columbia University Press, 1989), 62.

9. Robin Wood, "Psychoanalyse de *Psycho*," *Cahiers du Cinema* 19, no. 113 (November 1961): 1–6.

10. For some exemplary instances of the *Movie* approach, see Ian Cameron, "Hitchcock and the Mechanics of Suspense" and "Hitchcock 2: Suspense and Meaning" in *The Movie Reader*, ed. Ian Cameron (New York: Praeger, 1972): 26–34, and V. F. Perkins, *Film as Film: Understanding and Judging Movies* (Baltimore: Penguin Books, 1972).

11. Wood, *Hitchcock's Films Revisited*, 66; Wood explicitly acknowledges the influence of Leavis in *Personal Views: Explorations in Film* (London: Gordon Fraser, 1976), 69–75.

12. Ibid., 62.

13. Ibid., 64.

14. Ibid., 71–72.

15. Leo Braudy, "Hitchcock, Truffaut, and the Irresponsible Audience," *Film Quarterly* 21, no.4 (Summer 1968): 22, 24.

16. Robert Stam and Roberta Pearson, "Hitchcock's *Rear Window*: Reflexivity and the Critique of Voyeurism," *Enclitic* 7 (1983): 136–145, reprinted in *A Hitchcock Reader*, ed. Marshall Deutelbaum and Leland Poague (Ames, Iowa: Iowa State University Press, 1983), 205.

17. Raymond Durgnat, *The Strange Case of Alfred Hitchcock or the Plain Man's Hitchcock* (Cambridge: MIT Press, 1974), 39.

18. Penelope Houston, "The Figure in the Carpet," *Sight and Sound* 32 (Autumn 1963): 159–165; Charles Thomas Samuels, "Hitchcock," *American Scholar* 39, no. 2 (Spring 1970): 295–304.

19. Wood, 65. (All references to *Revisited*)

20. Raymond Bellour, "Le Blocage Symbolique," *Communications*, No. 23 (1975): 235–350.

21. Laura Mulvey, "Visual Pleasure and Narrative Cinema," *Screen* 16, no. 3 (Autumn 1975):31–39.

22. Janet Bergstrom, "Alternation, Segmentation, Hypnosis: Interview with Raymond Bellour," *Camera Obscura*, No. 3–4 (1975): 93.

23. Leland Poague, "Criticism and/as History: Rereading *Blackmail*," in *A Hitchcock Reader*, op. cit.

24. George E. Toles, "Alfred Hitchcock's *Rear Window* as Critical Allegory," *boundary 2*, 16, no. 2–3 (Winter–Spring, 1989): 225–246.

25. Penelope Houston, "Alfred Hitchcock," op. cit., 488.

26. Tom Ryall, *Alfred Hitchcock and the British Cinema* (Urbana: University of Illinois Press, 1986), 183.

27. Ibid., 169.

28. Ibid., 182.

29. Stephen Rebello, *Alfred Hitchcock and the Making of Psycho* (New York: Dembner, 1990).

30. Leonard J. Leff, *Hitchcock and Selznick* (New York: Weidenfeld & Nicholson, 1987); Royal S. Brown, "Herrmann, Hitchcock, and the Music of the Irrational," *Cinema Journal*, 21, no. 2 (Spring 1982): 14–49; James Naremore, *Acting in the Cinema* (Berkeley: University of California Press, 1988), 213–238, 239–261.

31. Ryall, page 1, quoting David Bordwell, "Textual Analysis Etc," *Enclitic*, No. 10–11 (1981–82): 125, 135.

OVERVIEWS

Hitchcock on Hitchcock: An Interview

RICHARD SCHICKEL

Alfred Hitchcock's fears and anxieties dominate his imagination and the conduct of his daily life, just as, more lightly and artfully expressed, they dominate his films. Now seventy-five years old, and active as ever professionally, he continues to arrange his existence so that nothing untoward—the sort of mischance that so often propels his protagonists into danger—will happen to him. As he has often said, he has never learned to drive a car in order to obviate the possibility of receiving a traffic ticket. Indeed, unless he is shooting a picture or is out promoting one, he rarely ventures away from home or office, which is a bungalow at Universal City studios in the San Fernando Valley. A chauffeured car deposits him there in the morning, he nips quickly through a side door and does not emerge again until quitting time. The studio commissary is not a hundred yards away, but lunch is brought in and served in a spacious dining-*cum*-conference room a few steps from his desk. (Lunch, incidentally, is extremely modest considering his girth and his reputation as a gourmet —lean steak or broiled sole, salad and coffee; no bread, potatoes or dessert.) Once a week, when they're both in town, Lew Wasserman, head of mighty MCA—of which Universal is the major subsidiary—takes lunch with Hitchcock and he, like the rest of the world, beats a path to the director's door.

Behind that door one finds a well-ordered world. The director's office is dominated by an extraordinarily large desk with a tooled-leather top. It is extremely neat, with a few trimly stacked papers and perhaps some books of film criticism and theory on it—along with a well-thumbed European railway timetable, which he employs to plan imaginary journeys to exotic places. When he does travel, it is rarely to unfamiliar locales. New York, London, Paris—these are on his beat, but when he goes to them—he always stays in the same room in a hotel he has frequented for years and, once ensconced, encourages people to visit him in the hotel so he does not have to chance the streets more than is absolutely necessary. As for the rest of his office furnishings, they combine to give the impression of being modeled on the library of an English country home, or perhaps the writing room of a London club. There is a profusion of leather-covered sofas and easy chairs, breakfront bookcases containing, among other items, the books on which he has based some of his films as well as other mystery

Reprinted from *The Men Who Made the Movies* (New York: Atheneum, 1975), 271–303.
Copyright © 1976, Richard Schickel.

and suspense tales he has obviously considered. Across from his desk is a comic painting of Mount Rushmore—site of the famous climax in *North by Northwest*—with Hitchcock's face worked in among the American presidential visages there. Elsewhere in the bungalow are offices—empty when we shot our interview —here writers, production managers and other functionaries can establish themselves when Hitchcock is preparing or shooting a film. The draperies are closed against the California sun, the air-conditioner thrums steadily, and in the world capital of casual attire, the director wears a funereal black suit, a white shirt whose starched collar inevitably starts to curl up by day's end and a conservative narrow tie.

In short, he has gone to every effort to create a serene, stable, *traditional* atmosphere around him. He has done so because, even though he is one of the few film directors who are truly household names, even though he has more control over his career than almost any other director (absolutely free choice over projects, final cut of the finished film), even though he is wealthy, he remains prey to the phobias and fantasies of his childhood. Indeed, it is because he is so closely in touch with them, and because they are to greater or lesser degree common to so many of us, that his films have through the years exercised such consistent mass appeal. Acrophobia, agoraphobia, claustrophobia—these have been recurring motifs in his films from the beginning. And, of course, there is his overriding preoccupation, which is a form of paranoia: Hitchcock has time and again returned to the "wrong man" theme, in which an innocent individual is wrongly accused of some crime and is nightmarishly pursued by the police or some other agency of the state which normally we would turn to in search of peace if not justice, and also by the true miscreants trying to silence him. What makes that preoccupation so compelling to the rest of us is the implication that the protagonist, though he may not be guilty of the crime he has been accused of, is indeed guilty of something. That may not be an indictable offense, it may be (as it is with Tippi Hedren in *The Birds*) only the crime of indifference. Or insensitivity. Or nothing more than membership in the human race, for Hitchcock was raised a Catholic and there is no question that he believes we are all tainted by something like Original Sin. And though he never comments directly on the matter, one can speculate that he believes he is as guilty as the next man of some vague imperfection for which he deserves punishment.

Hence his cautious life-style. Hence the careful way he covers his tracks in his movies, making sure his tormented heroes and heroines are bright and witty and handsome, so that the heavy—not to say tragic—themes of his best work don't spoil our identification with them or interfere with the entertainment values of the pictures. Hence the dazzling yet subtle technique which so entrances sophisticated viewers, who might otherwise speculate more deeply on his meanings. Hence—and this is perhaps the most interesting revelation one gains by spending some time with him—

the almost entirely fictional persona he has created for himself: the jolly fat man with the macabre, punning sense of humor.

He put that one over on us when he was host of the "Alfred Hitchcock Presents" television series in the 1950s. An appealing characterization, it served to hide from the public the fact that he is a serious artist who has a craving (constantly checked) to be taken seriously. The problem was, I think, that he calculated that this desire (a perfectly reasonable one, after all) might interfere with the popularity of that art; if people saw that he did not create it in an entirely larkish spirit, they might start to probe a little more deeply and thus find themselves discomfited by films they had taught themselves (with a little help from the master) to take lightly. Certainly, few in the general public—and not many critics outside the film quarterlies—perceived the general darkening of tone in his films once he had left behind the genial little English comedy thrillers and passed through the overdressed, perhaps excessively psychoanalytic, certainly more romantic Selznick phase. However, such great works of the 1950s and 1960s as *Strangers on a Train, Rear Window, The Wrong Man, Vertigo, North by Northwest* and, climactically, *Psycho* and *The Birds* were much more ambiguous, pessimistic and richer in meaning than most of what had gone before. (*Shadow of a Doubt*, which Hitchcock has said is his favorite film, would be the one film of his earlier career that I would rank with these in complexity and ambition.)

Be that as it may, Hitchcock has favored most interviewers from the popular media with nothing more than re-runs of his television personality. On the other hand, he has been exhaustive, and entirely sober, about technique with François Truffaut as well as with scholarly and well-prepared interviewers from the more serious film journals, from whose writing has grown—especially among younger critics and filmmakers—an increasing regard for him as a film artist in recent years. It would appear that he is attending to his "image" with the journalists, his posterity with the students. Happily, he chose to put me and my film crew with the latter group—doubtless because we were representing public television—and so we came away with an interview of considerable duration (thirteen camera rolls) in which he spoke earnestly about technique and, to the limited extent that he chooses to, about his view of the world.

BEGINNINGS

I think it would be interesting to talk about fear and how it first came to one. Psychiatrists will tell you if you have certain sort of psychological problems [and] you can trace them back to, say, your childhood, all will be released. And, of course, I don't believe this to be true at all. If you go back and trace the origins of when you were first scared as a child, I suppose the earliest thing I can think of is when my father, who was a wholesale and retail fruit and greengrocer at the time, sent me with a note to the local chief of police, who glanced at the little piece of paper and then led me along a corridor and I was locked in a cell for five minutes. Then he let me out and said, "That's what we do to naughty boys." I always think it was the clang of the door which was the potent thing—the sound and the solidity of that closing cell door and the bolt. But it hasn't altered the fact, even though I can trace that episode so many years ago, that I'm still scared of policemen. In fact, I don't drive a car on the simple fact that if you don't drive a car you can't get a ticket. I mean, the getting of a ticket, to me, is a rather suspenseful matter.

I think somebody once said to me: "What's your idea of happiness?" And I said, "A clear horizon, no clouds, no shadows. Nothing." But being given a ticket is a cloud on one's personal horizon, and this was brought home very, very forcibly to me when I was at college,[1] a Jesuit college called St. Ignatius. It may be that I was probably born with a sense of drama because I tend to dramatize things, and at college the method of punishment was rather a dramatic thing. If one had not done one's prep, the form master would say, "Go for three." Well, going for three, that was a sentence, and it was a sentence as though it were spoken by a judge. And the sentence then would be carried out by another element, which would mean a special priest in a special room, with the help of a rather old-fashioned sort of strop for sharpening razor blades, only it was made of gutta-percha, which is a soft black rubber. And the awful part about this to, say, a little boy of ten was that, having been sentenced, it was up to him when he should take it. He could take it at the first morning break, lunchtime, mid-afternoon or the end of the day. And always it was deferred until the end of the day. And then you'd go into this room and the priest would enter your name in a book and then grab the hand that was to be punished and lay this thing in. Never more than three on one hand because the hand became numb and it was no good putting four on the hand because a fourth one you'd never feel it. So then they started on the other hand. And if, by chance, the crime was so great that you were sent for twelve, I mean, that would be for a terrible crime of some kind, you could have only six a day and then the other six the following day. Well, this was like going to the gallows. And the other interesting thing— and one almost compares it with the crowds that used to watch public executions—was that if one went into this particular room, outside the door a number of the boys would gather and listen for these loud thwacks and then wait and look to see what kind of expression the culprit had on his face as he emerged. Yes, they were voyeurs. But I don't think that when one emerged you were aware of them, really. That was the least important factor. The most important factor was this making up your mind when to go, when to have your head removed, shall we say. I think it's a most horrible kind of suspense.

DEGRADATION AS PUNISHMENT

The degradation really occurs when the persons being charged with an offense are, for the first time in their lives, removed into a world to which they've been totally unaccustomed. As I showed in *The Paradine Case*, the most degrading moment, but it was a true moment, was when the wardress, the woman guard, went through Alida Valli's hair and put her fingers through the hair and let it down. This beautifully coiffed head, you see, already was degraded and reduced. You know, it's like the medieval sort of stories when a woman is going to have her head chopped off and the scissors [are] going through the hair to lay bare the neck; [that] is another degrading moment.

If I may digress while we're on the subject of head removing I read some long time ago a fascinating story about a Chinese executioner who was able to wield a sword so skillfully that there was an occasion when a victim mounted the steps onto a platform and the executioner was slightly behind him. And the victim said, "Mr. Executioner, please don't keep me standing here in agony. Why don't you do your work?" And the executioner said, "My dear sir, please nod your head slightly."

But going back to the degradation thing—I once saw a picture of the head of the New York Stock Exchange going to jail handcuffed to a criminal, and by contrasting their clothes and general demeanor it was a weird thing to see a man of such eminence as this going off to jail.

I've always thought that the handcuff thing was almost a kind of a fetish. If you notice, any press photographer around a courthouse will try and get the picture of the man in handcuffs. There's some strange appeal that it has, and just in the same way the man who is handcuffed tries to cover them up. He'll even take his topcoat and hang it over his hands. It's almost a symbol of reduction, as it were, to the lowest form. It's like a chain on a dog, you know? And it's always been, and that's why in *The 39 Steps*, used in a different context as a comedy thing, it nevertheless had a fascinating effect on audiences—the fact that the man and woman were handcuffed together. And it sort of brought out all kinds of thoughts in their minds; for example, how do they go to the toilet was one natural, obvious question. And the linking together is a kind of—I think it relates more to sex than to anything else.

EVIL AS DISORDER, DISORDER AS EVIL

If you take your bourgeois family and then the element of the bizarre comes into it, like one of the members of the family gets into trouble, you can pretty well say that that family—if it all comes out that either the daughter or son is a murderer—that family's life is ruined for good and all. When I was working in the city of London, they had a social club and as part of the activities of the club we were given the opportunity to learn to dance—waltzing or what have you. I suppose I was about eighteen or nineteen at the time, and a middle-aged gentleman taught me to waltz. Three or four years later his daughter [Edith Thompson] was not only arrested as a murderess but was hanged as well. Now the whole family— the mother, the father, the sister —they were practically isolated from society. There's no question that one is very definitely fascinated by this [kind of material] because if one does stories, we'll say, about policemen or about criminals, they're professionals, so there's no—how shall we say?— dramatic counterpoint. Or there is one, but it's not good enough for me. The color contrast is not [the same as] where you have the laymen suddenly placed in a bizarre situation, whether it's people being hijacked in a plane or being in some disaster like the *Titanic*. When I first came to America the film I was going to do was the story of the *Titanic*. And they changed it to *Rebecca*. But I can remember researching the whole of the *Titanic* thing and as I researched it I wanted to epitomize visually what the sinking of this great big ship meant to ordinary passengers and I thought of one idea which might express the whole thing. That would be to show, after you've shown the iceberg rip away under the water—three-hundred-feet-long gash, I think it took—go to the smoke room, you see, because it was about eleven at night, eleven forty it occurred, where men are playing cards. And all I wanted to do was to do a closeup of a glass of Scotch and soda, but the level of the liquid in the glass was slowly changing. And that to me said all I wanted to say: Here are ordinary people playing cards, unaware of what's really happening. How long will it be before they realize? Will a man glance at that glass and see that the level of the liquid is changing? So that really is the prime example of taking the complete bizarre and putting it among the ordinary people.

But this is [another] point. These situations are so familiar that you have to put into them unfamiliar pieces of activity so that it makes the whole of the activity fresh. You can't take [an ordinary] street. That's not enough. But the Statue of Liberty, Mount Rushmore, the Washington Memorial . . . Or, if you like, a chase through the House of Representatives—you see, jumping across the Speaker's desk. I mean, these are the symbols [of order].

Imagine. Imagine the Queen reading the government speech, which she does when she formally opens Parliament in England. She goes to the House of Lords and stands before a throne and she reads a speech written by the Prime Minister of the day. Well, this is all terribly formal. [But] the Members of Parliament, you see, are called to the bar of the House of Lords, they have no seats, they all stand. Well, imagine the Queen reading [and] a voice from the back shouting: "Liar!" It's a dreadful thought; it's lése majesté, of course. I don't know what the penalty for shouting at the Queen might be, but these [ideas] occur for one because you take symbols of complete order and throw into it the element of disorder.

Evil is complete disorder, although common in practice. I don't think you can say that evil is bizarre, because there are so many gradations of evil. Whether it's filching a small coin, thievery as such, or saying bad things about somebody which are not true. Evil is a pretty, pretty broad spectrum, really.

There was a thing on TV the other day—an interview with two con-demned men—they'd murdered six people. There the element of evil was exemplified by their attitudes—the complete lack of remorse, they didn't even apologize. They were almost giggling over it. And that struck me as being the epitome of evil.

But going back—we talked about the House of Representatives and the man jumping up and running around. If you take an average courtroom which is dealing with evil, examining it, processing it, the interesting thing, the contrapuntal thing, is the remark of the usher, and he says, "Order in court." You see. As though it was a special thing, that in court they only had disorder. And I must, to give an example of this, tell you a story that Ben Hecht once told me. He was a famous reporter at the time in Chicago and he was in court and the accused got up and jumped on the bench and stabbed the judge. Well, there was certainly disorder in that court immediately. And the interesting thing was it was such an unusual thing, this piece of evil coming out in the court itself, that everybody was petrified. All the reporters stopped. But Ben Hecht noticed one reporter was scribbling away. No one else had written a thing. And he saw the man call for a messenger and he gave the messenger his copy. And Hecht stole it. And he looked to see what the man had written, with the idea of copy-ing that himself. "The judge has been stabbed. The judge has been stabbed. The judge has been stabbed." It was a repetition of the one sen-tence. It was a fascinating example of the bizarre.

THE OMNIPRESENCE OF EVIL

There's that scene outside the church in *Shadow of a Doubt*[2] that really at the time gave an indication that the sheltered life in the town of Santa Rosa, where this young girl lived, may have been her world but it wasn't *the* world. Outside there, there were many other things happening. And of course unfortunately, you see, today to a great extent evil *has* spread, every little town has had its share of evil. It's like the town near where we live in northern California, Santa Cruz. You would have felt that this was a [quiet] little seaside resort town and yet they had the most bizarre murder. I don't think the man has been sentenced yet, he may have been—killed five people and tied them up and threw their bodies into a pool. Then you go further north in California and there's this man who killed twenty-five farm workers. So we can't say there is somewhere to hide. I would say, you know, if we take a period [around] the turn of the century, before

World War I, the world was very placid in many ways. And if one country had a conflict with another, they didn't immediately go to war. They sent a gunboat. And all the gunboat did was to go and anchor off the other country's coast, but not do anything. I think they had a word for it. It was called "gunboat diplomacy." Well, that today would be looked upon as ridiculous because you don't just wag a finger any more and say, "Be careful, other country, or else."

MURDER AND THE ENGLISH

One is often asked, "Why do you have a predilection for crime?" and my answer has always been that that is typically an English thing. The English for some reason seem to have more bizarre murders than any other country, and in consequence literature used to treat crime fiction on a very high level—unlike America, where crime literature is second-class literature. If you go back to Conan Doyle, Chesterton—they were all interested in crime as a source of literature. And I think the British more than anyone else are interested in themselves in this, right up to Agatha Christie. I know that one used to read in the English newspapers of a famous trial in progress at the Old Bailey and among the spectators was Sir George Somebody, a famous actor or a novelist was there. And it's like the moors murders. They had a case where a young boy and a girl kidnapped little children and put them to death and turned on a tape recorder so that the cries of anguish from these children were recorded and they used to play them back. Well, when the trial came on, the famous actor Emlyn Williams was noted to be present at the trial, and another playwright, a woman, Mary Hayley Bell, was noted to be present, and eventually, of course, Emlyn Williams came out with a book called *Beyond Belief*.

There does exist in London today a group called Our Society and they meet every few months above a famous restaurant, in a private room. They have dinner and then go over a previous cause célèbre. And you know who these men are? They are the lawyers in the particular case—both prosecution and defense. Now, they're not satisfied with having practiced the trial in open court and disposed of it, they want to go over it again, they're so interested. Of course, the judge isn't present and it is mainly for the benefit of writers, playwrights and all those sort of people who are their guests for the evening as they rehash the case. They have all the exhibits, photographs and everything. And that strikes me as being, well, so far into the subject that how can you go further except to do a murder yourself?

ON THE CHARACTER OF VILLAINS

One of the main essentials in constructing a story is to make sure that your bad man or your villain doesn't behave like one or even look one.

Otherwise, you see, you've taken the line of least resistance, and in reality he can't practice his evil wearing a cap with the word EVIL on it, anymore than a man can be a spy with S-P-Y on the front of his cap. You don't know. It's true of me. A lot of people think I'm a monster. They really do. I've been told that they don't care to be associated with me because of the nature of the work one does. And afterwards I've found women say, "Oh, you're nothing like I thought you were." I'd say, "What did you expect?" They'd say, "Well, we thought you'd be very unpleasant and this and that." It happened more than once. I'm talking not about actresses, but responsible women. And with a complete misconception due to the fact that I deal in crime and that kind of thing, while I'm just the opposite. I'm more scared than they are of things in real life.

Most people don't realize that if you have a man like the Joseph Cotten character [in *Shadow of a Doubt*] who's murdered three or four women for their money or jewelry or what have you, he has to be an attractive man. He's not a murderer in the sense of a fiction murderer where the tendency would be to make him look sinister and you'd be scared of him. Not a bit. He has to be charming, attractive. If he weren't, he'd never get near one of his victims. There was a very famous man in England called Haig, known as the Acid Bath Murderer. He murdered about four people and was a dapper, very presentable-looking little man; he could never have committed these murders without being accepted.

Here [in *Shadow of a Doubt*] Uncle Charlie comes to visit the family and his favorite niece, whose name is Charlotte, even called Charlie by the family, and only by terribly slow degrees does the young girl begin to suspect that beloved Uncle Charlie has something strange about him. Why does he cut pieces from the newspaper? And gradually, and almost imperceptibly, it's brought to a climax where they are so close together that she finally goes to the library and sees the item in the paper that he had cut out and this brings it home to her. Then he makes a plea to her when she challenges him. And he nearly wins her over, and the young man—the young detective—in the story, of course, is the direct antagonist to Uncle Charlie. But she can't betray Uncle Charlie because there's the mother to think of, her family must never, never know. So she has to keep this secret to herself and even forbids the young detective to do anything about it until Uncle Charlie makes two attempts on her life and loses his own on the third attempt, after she has really finally persuaded him that he's got to go.

ON ADAPTATION

There are two schools of thought there. One producer I worked for insisted that a novel be followed meticulously, especially if it was a best-seller, because then the public, having read the scene, would want to see it come to life on the screen. And I felt, myself, that when you consider the vast world audience, a best-seller—I don't care how big it is—doesn't reach anything like the same number of people or meet the same conditions as a film. For example, if you take your, say, Japanese market, it's very possible that the novel hasn't reached a Japanese audience. So my instincts are to go first with the visual and not follow the words of the novel. Follow the story line if you like, but retell it in cinematic form. So that you would read the novel, you get a concept of the story and characters and how you'd start to retell it.

That's what makes me often wonder when I read that X, who has written a novel, has been engaged to write a screenplay of his own novel. Now, that's done again and again, and the reason for it is he can get more money that way in selling his book because he or his agent makes it a condition. Now, in truth you're asking a man to be two things—a screenplay writer with a visual sense and a man who is conscious only of words and descriptions. I mean, a man can take a page to describe, we'll say, a scene of the Hawaiian Islands and what they look like at a certain time of the day and so forth. Where he takes a page to do it, the visualist, if we can coin a new word, sees it immediately. It's a photograph, that's what it is. It's rather like certain styles of reproductive painting. A man spends ages painting this picture—faithfully, accurately—and you say, "Why don't you take a color photograph? It's quicker, and you'll get the same result."

So, one reads a book, and, providing all the story elements are there and the characters are there, it's best then to lay the book aside and start with scene one in cinema terms. The rectangular screen in a movie house has got to be filled with a succession of images. And the public aren't aware of what we call montage or, in other words, the cutting of one image to another. It goes by so rapidly that they [the public] are absorbed by the content on the screen. But such content is created on the screen and not necessarily in a single shot.

For example, devising, in a picture like *Psycho*, the murdering and the stabbing of a girl in a bath—in a shower in a bathroom: this scene is forty-five seconds long, but was made up out of seventy-eight pieces of film going through the projector and coming onto the screen in great rapidity. In fact, in the scene itself, the knife stabbing at the camera never touched the flesh of the woman at any time. You went to her face, you went to her feet, you went to the assailant in quick, rapid shots. But the overall impression given the audience is one of an alarming, devastating murder scene.

I would prefer to write all this down, however tiny and however short the pieces of film are—they should be written down in just the same way a composer writes down those little black dots from which we get beautiful sound. So I usually start with the writer long before dialogue comes into it, and I get on paper a description of what comes on that screen. It is as though you ran a film on the screen and turned off all the sound so you would see the images filling the screen one after the other.

These have to be described. If I'm describing the opening, say, of a film like *Frenzy*, it starts this way: The camera is high above the city of London. In the righthand corner is a heraldic arms device with the word LONDON on it. The camera descends lower and lower until it approaches Tower Bridge and the arms of the roadway have opened. The camera proceeds to go through the opening and is lost in a cloud of smoke from a passing tugboat. When the smoke clears, the camera is now approaching the terrace of what is known as County Hall. As it gets near we see a speaker addressing a group of people. Another angle shows that he is being photographed by press people and he is talking about the pollution of the river and how it has all been cleaned up. We then go to a scene of people leaning over the parapet, turning from the speaker and looking down. From their viewpoint, we see a body floating. There are immediate cries, and from another angle we see the whole listening crowd turn from the speaker and all rush to the parapet to look at this floating body.

Now, you see the way I've described it—I've described what takes place. Of course, interspersed with it later will be the speech of the speaker about pollution and there will be cries of the crowd: "Look, it's a body!" Another voice: "A woman!" Another voice: "She's been strangled! There's a tie." Then another voice: "A necktie murder again! " So these are the things that fill out later. But the early description is literally of the action and the picture.

In a sense, I'm bringing the writer into the direction of the picture, letting him know how I'm going to direct it. So we end up with possibly seventy to a hundred pages of description of the film. I have a very strong visual sense, and while I'm going through this process I am absorbing all the visual side of the film. So what happens? By the time that the script is finished and the dialogue has been added, I know every shot and every angle by heart. So when I'm shooting the picture, I very rarely look at the script because I've now by this time learned the dialogue myself. I have to say I am equivalent to, though maybe not so good as, a conductor conducting an orchestra without a score.

I could almost say I wish I didn't have to go on the stage and shoot that film because from a creative point of view one has gone through that process. That's why, you see, I never look through the camera. People say, "You don't look through the camera?" I say, "Why should I? I'm looking at a screen." When we've been putting this thing down on paper, my mind and my eye are on a motion-picture screen. The only reason one would look through a camera is that, having made a request to the cameraman for a shot, he takes it into his head to do something different. In other words, you're checking up to see whether he's lying or not. And it actually happened to me once. In the first version of a picture called *The Man Who Knew Too Much*, I had a German cameraman and I was a most astonished individual when I went to see the dailies or the rushes—the work of the previous day—and found out he'd used different lenses. Applying his own opinions didn't exactly meet the story requirements. So in a light but halting German, I said a few things.

POV

I'm what they call a purist in terms of cinema, as much as I can be. I'm inclined to go for the subjective. That is, the point of view of an individual, so that visually you do a closeup of him, then you show what he's looking at, then you cut back to the closeup and you see his reaction. The other way is what we call the objective. That's setting the audience to look at the whole action in one. There are a lot of people who believe in that. I use it too. But the picture where pure cinema in the subjective sense was used was *Rear Window*. Here you have a man in one position in one room, looking out. You do a closeup of him—Mr. Stewart—show what he sees. Now you come back to his face and he's reacting. Well, of course, by this process he uncovers a murder situation. This couldn't have been done in any other medium. Certainly not in the theater. It might have been done in a novel, but it would have been a much longer process and without the economy. I did illustrate the power of this kind of treatment when I did the production section for the *Encyclopaedia Britannica*. I said, if you take the man looking, you do his closeup—say it's Mr. Stewart. He looks. And now you cut to what he sees. And you show a woman holding a baby in her arms. Then you cut back to him and he smiles. Now take away the middle piece of film, have his closeup and, instead of cutting to a woman with a baby, cut to a girl in a very risqué bikini. Now you use the same smile, but you've changed him from the benevolent gentleman to a dirty old man only by changing one piece of film. And that is the power of montage.

I haven't done it myself, but I've heard of young directors saying, "I'm going to make the camera be another person," so the camera goes up to the mirror and at the bottom of the screen there's a hand putting on a bow. And you see the face of the man in the mirror. Then the camera moves away and goes all around the room and talks to people, but that's a trick, the camera being a person. You must show the closeup of the person first, then what he sees and how he reacts—that's a subjective treatment. And you can use it in many, many, many ways. I mean, you can do, we'll say, a man falling into the sea. You could do his closeup shooting up and he can be falling. Then you reverse the camera and show what he sees and there's the approaching ocean below. Then back to his face in horror and then you go right into the splash.

It [has always] seemed natural for me to put the audience in the mind of the particular character. You can't do it continually because sometimes the characters get so close together that you'd be looking at a nose. You know, like you go cross-eyed when you are too close to a person. Then you've got to go to the objective. I'll give you an example. In *Frenzy*, when the murder takes place, you see the woman sitting at the desk powdering her nose. She looks up. Now I put the camera where she was sitting and the other man—the murderer—comes in the door, closes the door and wanders around the room. And the camera follows him around, but you intercut that with the girl—the wife in the story-watching him and talking to him. And she's in one position doing that. So the intercut is her head turning and he going until he drops into a chair there. But eventually they do come face to face against the wall. Then I have to go to the objective. I have to detach myself from the woman and look at them both at the same time. Well, she eventually tries to get away, falls on the floor and he throws her into a chair. Now we're back to the subjective again because she in the chair looks up and finds him leering over her. Then you go back to her face again.

DIALOGUE

Obviously, the only thing wrong with the silent film was the fact that people opened their mouths and no sound came out. So when the talking picture came into being, of course, everybody went for talk. And for a time the visual was forgotten. That's why all of a sudden we found that stage plays were being taken from the theater and put into the studio. So dialogue, in a way, took over. The idea —it's almost an impossible thing to achieve—would be to have the dialogue counterpoint to the visual. By that I mean, if you show a girl's face and she's smiling, the dialogue shouldn't be "I am feeling happy," because the words are making the same statement as the girl's face. I achieved [that] once years ago in a film of *Ashenden*—the famous spy of Somerset Maugham. I had the girl, Madeleine Carroll, in a quarrel and tears were streaming down her face. And the man was trying to placate her and she turned to him and she said, "Oh, don't make me laugh!" You see, the words were directly counterpoint to her expression, but unfortunately I think [normally] it would take any writer about three years to work out every line to be in contrast to the visual.

Dialogue carries you along with the scene. But it has to be, in a cinematic film, properly interspersed or overlaid. For example, in *Rear Window* you probably have Stewart looking across through a telescopic lens and making a remark which has some bearing on the activity he's looking at, but you don't see his lips and you don't use his face when he says those words. You lay them over in the scene. Now, I did some other things in *Frenzy* which I've never done before, and this was to use sound dramatically. The absence of it in two cases and making it excessive. For example, when the murderer takes the barmaid up and you know he's going to kill her, I retreat the camera out of the house, across the street and you see the upper windows where the murder is obviously going to take place.

When I say that I'm not interested in content, it's the same as a painter [not] worrying about the apples that he's painting—whether they're sweet or sour. Who cares? It's his style, his manner of painting them—that's where the emotion comes from, same as in sculpture. Any art form is there for the artist to interpret it in his own way and thus create an emotion. Literature can do it by the way the language is used or the words are put together. But sometimes you find that a film is looked at solely for its content without any regard to the style or manner in which the story is told and, after all, that basically is the art of the cinema. And I would like to add that this does not relate to being artistic as such and therefore having an appeal to a very limited, appreciative audience. The whole art of the cinema, it seems to me, is its ability to appeal to a world audience in any language. Therefore, the stress on the pictorial enables you to reach the widest possible audience, whether they be Japanese, Germans, Peruvians, you name it. This always was the power of the cinema.

Now, back in the silent-film days, instead of dialogue, which we couldn't use, we had titles. And the great aim of the silent-picture makers was to be able to tell their story with the minimum of titles. And if [possible] without any at all. So that the whole film from beginning to end was a series of pictorial images. It was achieved in a big picture once only in the history of the cinema, and that was Murnau's *Last Laugh* starring Emil Jannings. That film was about the reverence the Germans had for uniforms and the poor old doorkeeper got too old and was relegated to the men's room. [But] he couldn't go home without the uniform, so he stole it and put it away in a checkroom in a railroad station and wore it home every night. The whole story was done without a single title, without anything. That was the great aim—to reach a complete world audience. I believe that in that film they even invented an imaginary sort of Esperanto language for the advertisements in the street.

THE MACGUFFIN

That really almost is a sidelight on the importance of content. When I made the film *Notorious*, the story was that Ingrid Bergman had to go down, accompanied by Cary Grant, an FBI man, to find out what some Germans were up to in Rio. Among the Germans was an old friend of her father's. Her father had just been sent up for treason. So the question arose, in designing the story for the film, what were the Germans up to down in Rio, what were they doing there? And I thought of the idea they were collecting samples of uranium 235 from which the future atom bomb would be made. So the producer said, "Oh, that's a bit far fetched—what atom bomb?" I said, "Well, both sides are looking for it." We read of the Germans experimenting with heavy water. Of course they were on the atom bomb. I said, "Look, if you don't like uranium 235, let's make it industrial diamonds. But it makes no difference, it's what we call the 'MacGuffin.'" What's that? The MacGuffin is the thing that the spies are after, but the audience *doesn't* care. It could be the plans of a fort, the secret plans of an airplane engine. It's called a MacGuffin because, as the story goes, two men are in an English train and one says across to the other, "Excuse me, sir, what is that strange-looking package above your head?"

"Oh, that's a MacGuffin."

"What's that for?"

"That's for trapping lions in the Scottish highlands."

"But there are no lions in the Scottish highlands."

"Then that's no MacGuffin."

And MacGuffin doesn't matter at all. You have to have it because the spies must be after something. And I reduced it to its minimum in *North by Northwest* when Cary Grant says to the CIA man, "What is this man after?" The heavy, James Mason.

"Oh," says the CIA man, "let's say he's an importer or an exporter."

"What of?"

"Um, government secrets."

And that's all we have to say about it. We didn't have to show anything. But every spy story must have its MacGuffin, whether it's microfilm or whether it's hidden in the heel of the shoe of a woman.

Anyway, this story was sent around to several producers. And the film cost $2,000,000 and grossed $8,000,000 and that was in 1945. These two or three producers who had read the script all turned it down because of the uranium. And I met one of them coming back on the *Queen Elizabeth* after the war and he said to me, "By the way, how did you get on to that atom-bomb thing a year before Hiroshima?" I said, "Well, it's self-evident. I mean, there was something going on." So he said, "Well, when we read the script we thought it was the god-damnedest thing on which to base a picture." I said, "There you are, you lost yourself probably $2,000,000."

ATMOSPHERE IN THE CHASE

In chase films what you do get the opportunity to show is a variety of backgrounds; characters on the run and moving are likely to dodge in a doorway. For example, in *The 39 Steps*, Robert Donat, the hero, is arrested in a police station and he flings himself out through the window into the street and it so happens that the Salvation Army band is going by. So he joins the Salvation Army and marches with them until he reaches an alleyway and he dodges down the alleyway and there's an open door and an elderly lady says, "Ah, at last you're here. Come on, this way." And before he knows where he is, he's on a platform at a political meeting and is forced to make a speech. This is what your chase film should be. You got it in De Sica's film *Bicycle Thief*. There the man searching for his bicycle got into a seance, he got into an old persons' home, he got into a crowd outside a football stadium and a tremendous variety of settings.

People have said to me, "What would you like to make as a picture?" I said I'd like to do twenty-four hours in the city, starting at dawn and ending the following morning. And think of the varieties of backgrounds you'd go through, say, in New York or London. Why, you get yourself in the Stock Exchange, you get yourself a couturiere's, backstage, boxing matches. In the afternoon you get out to Aqueduct, you have racing in it. You have the food markets in the morning. You probably end with the scows going out to the harbor and emptying their rubbish into the sea and polluting everything. You see, in your chase story, your man is on the run, but each stopping-off point becomes a menace to him. As when Cary Grant in *North by Northwest* goes into an auction room. He's trapped. He can't get out. He only gets out one way and that's by bidding in a crazy way. You know, many is the time we've seen a man on the run dodge into a church, and you get that at the end of John Galsworthy's play *Escape*. He's a convict. The whole theme of the play is whether people will hide him or whether they won't. And he gets into a church and hides in a cupboard and the police get there and they say to the parson, "Is there a man here?" And the parson doesn't know what to say. And the guard says, "Parson, Reverend, on your honor, do you have a man in here or not?" And, of course, the parson is saved by the wanted man stepping out. When you devise picaresque films of this nature, you've got to be pretty original each time you stop off or drive your central character into a setting. It could be, you know, into a hospital, into a girls' school. I mean, there are innumerable places he can go. You get that at the end of *Strangers on a Train*. Chasing after a man into a midway on a fairground. The man gets onto a merry-go-round and then there's a fight on the merry-go-round. And you get all the excitement using your artifacts of the midway.

Imagine if part of the escape or the chase got onto a freight train. Now you begin to examine—what does a freight train carry? Cattle? Can you imagine the two poor people—a boy and a girl who are on the run—getting into a van [and being] nearly crushed to death by cattle climbing over their backs and so forth? Or it might be carrying a load of automobiles. So what will they do there? They get up and they make love in an automobile high up while it's being carried by the train. There are tremendous possibilities if you examine all these things. If you take ordinary things, you see, you get into things like the beginning of *Topaz*. You have a whole scene at the Royal Copenhagen works—delicate china which is interesting to look at. And what I do there is to show the process of how they paint the flowers on the china and so forth. And yet there are overtones—unspoken overtones —of the sinister going all through it. You could do it in a bakery. It's the event rather than the setting, the situation, which carries for the audience the contrast [between the] normality of the setting and the situation in which you put it. This is far removed, as you can see, from what I call the creaking-door type of film or what the novelists call the Gothic. You know, you go upstairs and the old latch is undone and—well, you're back to *Frankenstein* then. The nearest I [have come to that, I] would say, is the girl's walk around the house in *Psycho*. Not because the house itself is essentially so Gothic. Actually, it was a very accurate house. There are hundreds of these houses in northern California. We call them California Gingerbread. It's the added fact that somewhere in this Victorian-looking house is a menacing figure with a knife. The audience know it, but they don't know where she's going to pop out. You can do it in a modern house, providing that the audience know that in this innocent-looking house death may appear at any minute.

The California Gingerbread type of house helps the atmosphere—a rather cheesy motel. But what do we have? We have a girl who has stolen $40,000, all of a sudden, out of the blue, attacked in a shower by a woman with a knife. Now, this is such a shock because we have been leading the audience along the lines of $40,000 stolen. But suddenly the twist and the shock is this thing in the shower. From that point on the audience's mind is full of apprehensions, but as the film went on, you got less and less violence on the screen.

There was one quick murder after the shower, but no more in the rest of the picture. But because there were no more, the audience got itself worked up to expect more. To sum it up, you are transferring the menace from the screen into the mind of the audience. And it increased to a point where, with the girl going around the house, it became unbearable to them, until you reach your climax.

SUSPENSE VS. MYSTERY

All suspense, you see, or audience preoccupation is based on knowledge. The word "mystery" often creeps into [descriptions of my movies, but] they're not mysteries. The essential fact is, to get real suspense, you must let the audience have information. Now, let's take the old-fashioned bomb [plot]. You and I are sitting talking, we'll say, about baseball. We're talking for five minutes. Suddenly a bomb goes off and the audience have a ten-second terrible shock. Now. Let's take the same situation. Tell the audience at the beginning that under the table—and show it to them — there's a bomb and it's going to go off in five minutes. Now we talk baseball. What are the audience doing? They're saying, "Don't talk about baseball! There's a bomb under there! Get rid of it!" But they're helpless. They can't jump out of their seats up onto the screen and grab hold of the bomb and throw it out. But one important factor: if you work the audience up to this degree, that bomb must never go off and kill anyone. Otherwise, they will be extremely angry with you.

I made a mistake in an early film [Editor's Note: *Sabotage*] by having a long bomb-suspense thing and I let the bomb go off and kill a little boy. I remember I was at the press show and a very sophisticated press woman came at me with raised fists and said, "How dare you do that? I've got a five-year-old boy at home." And she was furious with me. What must happen is that a foot must touch it and they say, "My God, it's a bomb! Pick it up and throw it out of the window." The moment it's out of the window, off it goes. But we inside are all safe and sound.

Sometimes the audience have no feeling for the victim, but they want [the thief] not to be caught. You see, it's the eleventh commandment—thou shalt not be found out. For example, supposing there's a burglar in a bedroom stealing jewelry from a woman. The woman has gone out, but suddenly she comes back and comes in the front door. What does the audience say? "Quick, burglar—get out, get out. You'll get caught."

In *Frenzy* you have the man in the potato truck. You see, you build up all the suspense—will he get the tie pin out of the girl's hand in time before he's caught? So we show the truck stopped a couple of times, he hides, and eventually he achieves it. But we're rooting for him all the time to get that tie pin back.

WHY DON'T THEY CALL THE POLICE?

Cary Grant on the run in *North by Northwest* is an innocent victim. But in the United Nations he pulls a knife out of a man's back. He holds it and looks at it and everybody in the room points to him. Now, the very thing he ought to do, he can't do—go to the police. Because the police are after him [because of the U.N. incident]. We had that in *The 39 Steps*. Exactly the same situation. So, you see, really, going to the police would end the picture and then it would be a piece of logic which would be very dull. So the story is devised in such a way that he can't go to the police.

[One] situation [like that] would be a spy behind enemy lines—he doesn't know where he can go. I once had a thought that might be an interesting situation—to have a spy, with all papers perfect in every way, parachuted down into Russia. Speaks Russian fluently, everything impeccable. As the door opens for him to parachute out, the little uniformed sergeant with him falls as well, and when the spy lands with the parachute in the Russian countryside, he's got with him a man who cannot speak Russian, wearing a uniform. What is he to do, kill him? So there you have a real dilemma. It's not enough merely to have every hand against him—he's got an encumbrance now. Incidentally, I've never solved that one.

You pigeonhole certain ideas, you know. It's like the one I tried to get into *North by Northwest*: to get into Detroit and have two men walk along an assembly line and the camera goes with them. But in the background is just the frame and you actually see a car go together. And when it gets to the end of the line, all batteries are in, gasoline is in, everything's dried and they drive it off. And one of these two men goes off and opens the door of this newly assembled car and a dead body falls out. And yet we've been watching this thing go together to a detail—but I haven't worked that one out yet. Mount Rushmore was in the pigeonhole for fifteen years before I ever used it [in *North by Northwest*]. The Statue of Liberty[3] is, you know, to me an obvious one. I've often thought to have a scene behind the clock face of Big Ben and that famous bell toll while the men are in there. Then, suddenly, somebody looks up and sees the hands changing the time or something.

I AM AN AMERICAN

I'm actually American-trained because the first job I ever got inside a studio was in London, when Paramount were opening studios in different parts of the world. They opened one in London, I think one in Paris and even one in India. Well, I got a job in the editorial department of the London studio—and they imported everyone from Hollywood. When you went in that door, you might as well just be in Hollywood, because everyone—cameramen, directors, actors and actresses—were all from Hollywood. And being in the editorial department or the script department, that's where I learned to write scripts—from American writers.

I always admired the technical superiority of the American film. As a matter of fact, it was interesting when I made my first film—that was in Munich, Germany, in 1925—the producer came over from London and ran the film. And he came out and he said, "Well, it doesn't look like a Continental film. It looks like an American film." I said, "What did you expect it to look like?" He said, "Well, you know, typical Continental." And I remember the first film I worked on as a writer—not [as] the director, but [as] writer and art director—was reviewed by a leading London paper and the headline was "Best American Film Made in England." And, of course, the influence wasn't the director, it was me designing the sets and writing the script that way, because the director had never been to America.

Basically, the design of [my] early English pictures was almost instinctive. There was less calculation in terms of an audience. It's when I came to America that I became more aware of audiences. And then as one went on, the question came up of (a) avoiding the cliché in my type of material and (b) trying to avoid the repetition of the same situations. And the only way to avoid it is through character: you can have a murder story as a murder story, but by whom? I mean, whom do you choose as a character to participate? And that's where the difference comes.

SHADOW IN A SMALL TOWN

Shadow of a Doubt was one of those rare occasions when a film was to be laid in a small town, so the writer, Thornton Wilder, and I went and stayed in the town, lived in it, got to know the people, got to know the rent of the house where they were living, and came back and wrote the script based on the people and nature and character of the town itself. I always remember, we had a scene with Teresa Wright where she ran across the street and had to speak to a policeman. She ran in front of traffic and the policeman admonished her for it. Of course we had to have an actor for that. So we stood the actor in the middle of the intersection, but the real policeman on the site said, "Look, the traffic's piling up. Tell your actor to let some of the stuff through." He did and then the real policeman says, "All right. Tell him to stop and let some pedestrians across." And he did. A pedestrian—a woman—went up to the policeman and said, "Could you tell me the way to so-and-so?" and she mentioned the street. The actor said, "I'm sorry, I'm a stranger here myself."

The leading character, the heavy, Joseph Cotten, gets killed in front of a train. And we staged his funeral right in the main square of the town at that intersection. It was fascinating to see the whole cortege slowly moving around the main square, then down the side street. We were photographing it with two cameras. And we had a few extras, not many, but all the town's people, who never saw the cameras [because] they were concealed, solemnly took their hats off as the empty coffin went by.

THE BIRDS

What you have in *The Birds* is a kind of overall sketchy theme of everyone taking nature for granted. Everyone took the birds for granted until the birds one day turned on them. The birds had been shot at, eaten, put in cages—they'd suffered everything from the humans and it was time they turned on them. Now there was no repulse. The hero was helpless against them, because they were a collective army. That's why we had an opening which was very lightweight, frivolous, expressing the thought that everybody too easily takes life for granted. The girl's a cocktail-party-going girl with not much upstairs—she's frivolous, well-to-do, and suddenly she gets a dose of nature which pulls her up and everyone else as well. I would say the theme of *The Birds* is don't mess about or tamper with nature. Look, man's fooled around with uranium 235 out of the ground and look where it's brought us. And he's just taken uranium 235 for granted, it's a nothing. But it's plenty. Now, who knows?—it's feasible in the year 3000 or 4000 for all the animals to have taken over. After all, we've had the clearest example of the prehistoric animals who have become extinct. Who knows that man may not end up the same way? He'll be regimented. I mean, brains will be controlled—that's inevitable. Who knows? The brains of the birds may improve. I know that in making *The Birds* we had some extremely clever ravens—answered to their names, pick up cigarettes and matches, do anything we wanted, no problem.

A PSYCHOLOGICAL MACGUFFIN

Marnie is about a fetish. A man wanted to go to bed with a thief. There was a case—horrible case—in England, I think it was about seven or eight years ago, where a one-armed woman sued a woman with one leg for the alienation of her husband's affections. This went before the English lawcourts. And of course, to everyone's astonishment, it turned out that the husband was the real culprit. He had a penchant for maimed women. And the case was thrown out of the courts.

So *Marnie* is about a man who wanted to marry—or marriage came afterward, but he wanted to go to *bed* with a woman whom he knew to be a notorious thief. She tries to uncover the secret [of why she steals compulsively], but I don't think that does much good. I'm sure that even though they went off to get married, she'd probably steal his nightshirt on their wedding night.

There were script problems. It wasn't the opportunity for the comedy I would have liked, because the worst scenes were the girl going to the psychiatrist, [though] they were quite comic in their way.[4]

ON THE FUNCTION OF HUMOR

Irony usually takes the form of a joke. You know, it's like the opening of *Frenzy*. Here's a man talking about the purity of the water, of the Thames River, no pollution, and along comes a body floating. Well, there's a complete irony there, but it's comic irony. At the same time, it's making a plot point: there are necktie murders going on in London.

I think in suspense an audience wants to have a little relief and change of pace and a lark if necessary. But, you see, again in *Frenzy*, you get the wife of the inspector talking over the plot with her cooking and his problems of having to stomach her cooking. But, really, the audience are being nursed along. Petted and worried about so that they laugh while pieces of plot are being thrust into their minds. But we deal with them gently. And in understatement. Understatement.

Let's go back to my early days at school when I feared physical punishment. Lo and behold, I go into the room one day—I know it sounds [as if] I was always going in for punishment. That isn't true. But on one occasion I went in and, of course, there was my favorite priest, my friend. And he shook his head and said, "This isn't nice, is it?" I said, "No, Father." And he took the hand and he let the instrument just drop on it. Very touching, of course. But—oh, all understatement. I'm all for understatement. The stronger the situation, it becomes stronger by the understatement. You see, the world today is full of brutality, but, more than that, [it has kind of] developed into brutality with a smile. It's worse than brutality. You know, it's coming in, pointing a gun at a man and saying, "I'm sorry, but I'm afraid I'm going to have to take your money. I hate doing this because my father always said one shouldn't steal." BANG! He shoots. 'Course that's a horrible situation because he's talking in reasonable terms. Not "Stick 'em up." That's not it. [For example,] the killing of the German in a farmhouse [in *Torn Curtain*]. I wanted to show that without a gun and without a knife it's a very difficult thing to kill. The woman stabbed the man and the blade broke. She couldn't fire the gun because there was a taxi driver outside. She tried hitting his knees with a spade, and eventually, of course, she thought of the gas oven. And having got him on the ground, [there was] this terribly slow process of putting the German's head into the gas oven and holding it there. And one couldn't help think that here we are back at Auschwitz again and the gas ovens. But the main purport of the scene—I remember I was in Paris and I was listening to the BBC and I heard a film man say, "You know, it's only lately I realized what Hitchcock was after. He was trying to show us how difficult it was to kill a man. I thought it was just intended to be a brutal scene." It was awkward and clumsy, but difficult, you see.

HEROINES

I've often been asked why I choose what people seem to call "cool blondes." I think the blonde, really, stems from the tradition of the cinema, whose first heroine was a curly-headed blonde named Mary Pickford. And thereafter she became a symbol of the heroine. I personally object to the blondes who wear their sex round their neck and it hangs in front of them like oversized jewelry. And I've always felt that you should try and discover in the course of your story whether the woman is sexy or not. For example, in the film *To Catch a Thief* I kept cutting to Grace Kelly in profile, very still and not much expression until Cary Grant sees her up to her room. And suddenly, in the doorway, she turns and plunges her lips onto his. Bowls him over completely. The cool blonde does give you somewhat of a surprise if she does turn out to be very sexy. In the main, I would say that the sexiness in women is somewhat geographical. I feel the Scandinavian women are more sexy than the southern European women. I would say that the Englishwoman is more sexy. The southern Europeans, the Italians, the French women, you know, they wear black on Sunday. You mustn't mistake gaieté parisienne for sexy girls doing the can-can. I think if you look at the Swedish-type or the Norwegian-type women in Swedish films they're fairly, I won't say plain, but they're not what you call glamorous girls. And yet they betray on the screen an acute, sharp sense of sex. I sometimes feel that a lot of American women are rather like the southern European women. They talk sex. The magazines advertise sex. And they seem to make a lot of it. And yet, if a man approaches one, it's possible she'll run screaming for Mother.

MAN'S INHUMANITY TO MAN

You're deliberately making things difficult because you demonstrate to an audience that you can be trapped in a crowd and turn to your neighbor and say, "Look, there's a man coming after me!" and nobody in the crowd would believe you. It's the same old thing—people don't want to be getting tangled with others in trouble. We have it in *Frenzy*—here are two people who could give the man an alibi, but not they, they're too human. They want to get out of it, not be involved. And it's the same if you were to rush up to anybody in the street and say, "Quick, quick, where's a policeman? A thief is chasing after me." The people look around and they say, "I'm sorry," and they walk away, they don't want to get involved.

What was the old saw by Robert Burns? "Man's inhumanity to man makes countless thousands mourn." He must have had some reason for saying that. It's a dogfight. I think money has a lot to do with it. It's a dogfight all the time. In my career, I run up against political situations time and time again. I became a director entirely because a particular cameraman had curried favor with the director and the director said he didn't want me on his next picture. It was then I was asked would I like to be a director, which hadn't occurred to me. I was maneuvered deliberately away from my job and I knew who it was and how it was done. It happens in our business all the time. I used to say, "Well, one thing they can't take away from me is my talent." You see, I have a very strong objection to hatred. I feel that hatred is a wasted energy. There's nothing good can come out of it. And I think one of the silliest phrases you can ever hear is to hear somebody say, "I'm going to give him a piece of my mind." Now what good does that do? All you've done is to make an additional enemy. The hardest thing to get anyone to say is, "I'm sorry, it was my mistake." People don't do that. They get mad and they say, "I'm going to get that so-and-so if it's the last thing I do." But the admission of error is a hard thing to come by. And that's why I say I don't hate anybody, I really don't. Maybe if somebody does me wrong, I just turn my back on them. And that may even be crueler, I'm not sure. I'm pretty well a loner. I don't get involved with conflicts. I don't see the point of it. Not even to the point of getting a ticket for parking.

SUMMING UP

Generally speaking, I would say that first of all, possibly from the age of fifteen, I was a devotee of film. I mean, I didn't read fan magazines at the age of fifteen or sixteen, I read trade papers. So I used to be aware of the making of films and was determined to get into them eventually. I didn't want to get in as a director. It didn't occur to me that I would be a director of films. I just wanted to be a part of it. And the earliest days I was in the editorial department and then did assistant-director work on the stage on "crowd days," as they called them then. This, coupled with one's reading habits, which veered toward the adventurous. I don't mean Robert Louis Stevenson, but—say, Sherlock Holmes and then, of course, John Buchan, who wrote *The 39 Steps*, *Greenmantle* and many famous English [spy] books. They were very elegant, and of course they were very, very descriptively written. And the hero was inevitably the adventurer—preferably, the gentleman adventurer. I think Buchan's work was a tremendous influence on me. Then, in another direction there was a famous woman writer, Mrs. Belloc-Lowndes. It was her story *The Lodger* which became my first English-made picture.

I remember there was a period when I was learning to write scripts—I fought terribly hard, [but] I could not understand how the various cuts went together. It seemed almost like a blank wall to me. Then one day, all of a sudden, I discovered it. And then I learned cutting. And out of that, of course, learned the pure cinema.

Having started to write, I became involved with the German film industry, which in its day was the greatest—even greater, from an artistic standpoint, than Hollywood. I mean, they were making films like *Siegfried* and the *Ring* operas and all of [Emil] Jannings' films. And I became tremendously influenced by them.

My style was influenced [by] the German—angles of photography, the visual ideas. And it was the visual ideas that began to come to one very, very instinctively. There was no sound in those days. And in the film *The Lodger*, which was about Jack the Ripper, I even show him going out at night, shot from above a big staircase with a continuing handrail. And all you saw was a white hand going down. This, I would say, is almost oblique. And I suppose it's part of one's mentality that one is driven toward the oblique. Not to do the obvious. To avoid the cliché. And gradually—I suppose it's the religious training—the general theme became the triumph of good over evil. And that maintains itself even to this day, actually.

And so it goes on, and so the next film, obviously, will have to be a crime film, not necessarily a murder film. It will have to have humor. But, most of all, it's got to have some fresh background. And where that will be I don't know. It may be in the kitchen of a hotel, it may be on the assembly line in Seattle where Boeing are building 747s. Think how nice it would be: the interior would be the young lady and her lover seated in two unfinished seats, with aluminum walls and an empty background, making love.

NOTES

    1. Hitchcock means a prep school, not a university.

    2. In which MacDonald Carey, as a policeman who has tried to warn Teresa Wright that her uncle, played by Joseph Cotten, may be a psychopathic murderer, attempts to explain to her that the world is more dangerous than she believes.

    3. Used as the setting for the climax of the chase in *Saboteur*.

    4. These scenes did not survive the final cut and were never shown to the public.

Plot Formations

ROBIN WOOD

One of the clearest ways to demonstrate, simultaneously, the validity of the auteur theory and the necessary qualifications to it, is to examine the relationship between Hitchcock's British and American films, a relationship of both rupture and continuity. When one passes from the British films to *Rebecca*, one feels at once in—on certain levels—a different cinematic world: the film, quite simply, *looks* different. The reasons for this are obvious enough: the availability of a higher budget; the dominating presence of Selznick (a rival auteur), his preoccupation with prestige, expensiveness, "finish," but also his own authorial inclinations and obsessions; the availability not only of Hollywood technicians with their highly developed and sophisticated professionalism, but of "the Hollywood way of doing things." My sense of the tangible difference is impressionistic: I have not gone into the laborious statistics of shot counts, shot lengths, number of times the camera moves, types of camera movement, ratio of close-ups to long shots, etc., regarding statistics with a certain suspicion. My impression is, then, of far greater technical fluency or fluidity (which is not to be taken as necessarily an evaluative judgment), and of greater (or more pervasive) depth to the images. The lean economy and wry humor of the British films have gone, replaced by Hollywood's luxury and Selznick's melodramatic romanticism. One caveat is instantly necessary: this cannot be taken, without heavy qualification, as a straight Britain/Hollywood opposition. Selznick's presence is clearly crucial: the shooting/editing practices of many of Hitchcock's later masterpieces are actually closer to the austerity of the British films than to the luxuriance of *Rebecca* (*The Paradine Case*, to which Selznick can again lay some authorial claim, can be taken as confirmatory evidence). Hitchcock was able, after *Rebecca*, to make movies in Hollywood that are "British" not only in setting but in "look" (*Suspicion*).

And the stylistic discontinuity of *Rebecca* on one level is counterpointed by its stylistic continuity on another: Hitchcock was able to develop his interest in point-of-view editing and spectator-identification techniques. Most strikingly, that Hitchcock "signature" so familiar from the later films—the forward point-of-view tracking shot—appears here for, I believe, the first time (a perception originally of Michael Walker's which I have found no evidence to refute). This must be seen, I think, as a logical

Hitchcock's Films Revisited, Robin Wood, 1989. Copyright © Columbia University Press, New York. Reprinted with permission of the publisher.

continuation and refinement of Hitchcock's earlier techniques, rather than as a phenomenon somehow dependent upon the move to America. The point-of-view montage techniques that reach their ultimate mastery and elaboration in films like *Rear Window*, *Vertigo*, and *Psycho*, are already highly developed in the British period.

It is clear that Hitchcock approached the plunge into American culture with caution. The first "American" films are either set in England (*Rebecca*, *Suspicion*) or are picaresque adventure films (*Foreign Correspondent*, *Saboteur*) in which the Americanness of the leading characters is more incidental than essential: the fact that *Saboteur* can be seen as a loose remake of *The 39 Steps* confirms this. (One may note here that no less than seven of the films of the American period are set in England—in whole or in part—plus one shot in England and set in Australia). In the midst of the first five Hollywood films is *Mr. and Mrs. Smith*: here, direct contact with American culture is mediated by the presence of a genre (screwball comedy) with already highly developed and clearly defined conventions. It is only with *Shadow of a Doubt* and *Lifeboat* (the sixth and seventh Hollywood films) that Hitchcock begins to grapple with the realities and mythologies (material, cultural, spiritual, ideological) of "America." I hope I shall not be taken as suggesting that these films lack generic mediation, that American life and values are somehow present in them as unqualified "reality"; but it seems clear that here Hitchcock confronts American capitalism in a way that the insulated stylization of screwball comedy enabled him to evade.

Again, the discontinuity on one level is countered by the continuity on another. If all the major elements of Hitchcock's mature style are already present in the British work, the same is true of the films' basic plot formations. It is here—in the continual recurrence and variation of a number of simple embryonic structures, separately and in combination—that the essential unity of the oeuvre is most evident. I list here what seem to me the basic formations (without claiming that the list is exhaustive or that it accounts for all the films), giving what appears to be the work in which the formation is first clearly established (a British film in every case), followed by a list of its major successors, British and American.

1. THE STORY ABOUT THE FALSELY ACCUSED MAN. *The Lodger*, *The 39 Steps*, *Young and Innocent*, *Suspicion*, *Saboteur*, *Spellbound*, *Strangers on a Train*, *To Catch a Thief*, *The Wrong Man*, *North by Northwest*, *Frenzy*.

2. THE STORY ABOUT THE GUILTY WOMAN. *Blackmail*, *Sabotage*, *Rebecca*, *Notorious*, *The Paradine Case*, *Under Capricorn*, *Stage Fright*, *Vertigo*, *Psycho*, *The Birds* (arguably), *Marnie*.

3. THE STORY ABOUT A PSYCHOPATH. *The Lodger*, *Murder!* *Shadow of a Doubt*, *Rope*, *Strangers on a Train*, *Psycho*, *Frenzy*.

4. THE STORY ABOUT ESPIONAGE/POLITICAL INTRIGUE. *The Man Who Knew Too Much* (1934), *The 39 Steps*, *The Secret Agent*, *Sabotage*, *The Lady Vanishes*, *Foreign Correspondent*, *Notorious*, *The Man Who Knew Too Much* (1956), *North by Northwest*, *Torn Curtain*, *Topaz*; also *The Long Night*, the film Hitchcock was planning when he died, and of which a draft screenplay has been published.

5. THE STORY ABOUT A MARRIAGE. *Rich and Strange*, *Sabotage*, *Rebecca*, *Mr. and Mrs. Smith*, *Suspicion*, *Under Capricorn*, *The Man Who Knew Too Much* (1956—which I see as being about a marriage in a sense in which the British version is not), *Marnie*; to which I would add *Rear Window* and *Frenzy*, neither centered exactly on a marriage, but in both of which "marriage" is a pervasive preoccupation. *Family Plot* also has its relevance here.

The "falsely accused man" films typically take the form of what Andrew Britton has termed the "double chase" plot structure: the hero, pursued by the police, pursues the real villain(s). He is always innocent of the crime of which he is accused but (perhaps ambiguously) guilty of something else: at the least, egoism and irresponsibility (*North by Northwest*), at the most of a *desire* that the crime be committed (*Strangers on a Train*). Somewhere in between lies the attribution of *sexual* guilt, a concept that has undergone such transformation during our century that a proper understanding of (at least) some of the earlier films has become problematic: today's audiences may have difficulty in grasping that, say, Richard Hannay (in *The 39 Steps*) is to be regarded as "guilty" because he anticipated a night of "illicit" sex with a woman who (after all) picked *him* up, not the other way around, but the apprehension is crucial to a reading of the film's narrative progress.

The falsely accused man films move unanimously toward the protagonist's rehabilitation/restoration to society (often, as in *Strangers on a Train*, disturbingly, as he remains essentially unregenerate). One can make a general (not absolute) distinction here between the British films and the American: in the latter the implicit critique of the hero tends to be carried further, and his redemption (when he is felt to *be* redeemed) accordingly requires a more radical transformation. Unlike Thornhill in *North by Northwest*, the male protagonists of *The 39 Steps* and *Young and Innocent* do not have to undergo any major evolution (such as learning to defy patriarchal authority in order to express their identification with and commitment to a woman). On the whole, the British films fit into the patriarchal order more comfortably, with less sense of constraint and dissonance (which is not to say that such qualities are absent). A comparison of the two versions of *The Man Who Knew Too Much* confirms this.

The "guilty woman," on the contrary, is *always* guilty: whether we know this from the outset (*Blackmail*, *Marnie*) or learn it subsequently

(*The Paradine Case*, *Vertigo*), she *did* commit the crime of which she is (initially or later) accused.[1] This sexist imbalance (which tells us more about our culture in general than about Hitchcock in particular) is partly rectified by the sympathy the films extend to their transgressive women: if Rebecca *should* have been the heroine of the film that bears her name, Mrs. Paradine is certainly the heroine of *The Paradine Case*, and the final effect of *Vertigo* is that of a denunciation of male egoism, presumption, and intransigence. Far more than the falsely accused man films, the guilty woman films belong predominantly to the American period. Mrs. Verloc (*Sabotage*) is not by any means a fully characteristic example, her guilt being dubious, her crime more a matter of intention than execution, the feelings that give rise to it morally justified even from the most conventional standpoint. That leaves, among the British works, the extraordinary *Blackmail*, in many respects the most strikingly anticipatory film of the entire British period. *Blackmail*, one might say, is Hitchcock's *Stagecoach*: the (relatively) early major work in which all the tensions and contradictions that structure the later films are clearly articulated, manifesting themselves as uncontainable within a coherent traditional value system or a "satisfying" resolution. A glance at the list of titles will suggest—justifiably I think—that the guilty woman category represents the richest vein in the Hitchcock mine, the area of greatest disturbance and tension, from which his most profoundly troubling and subversive films have been worked.

If the falsely accused man's destiny is to be restored (perhaps with some improvement) to the social order, the case of the guilty woman is inevitably more problematic, the resolution depending on the degree of her guilt and having more to do, perhaps, with the constraints of the Motion Picture Code than with Hitchcock's or the spectator's sympathies or moral judgment. Those guilty of, or complicit in, murder (Mrs. Paradine, the Judy Barton of *Vertigo*) must die; others can be restored to "normality" (a normality that Hitchcock's work in general discredits) only after more or less severe punishment and suffering; others still suffer fates that even the most conventionally moral and judgmental viewer must see as disproportionate (Marion Crane in *Psycho*, Melanie Daniels in *The Birds*). In no single case, I think, does the film invite us to view the punishment with complacence or satisfaction: typically, we are left with a sense of unresolved dissonance that relates, at bottom, to the fundamental strains produced by our culture's organization of sexuality and gender.

Obviously, the falsely accused man films and the guilty woman films exist in an intricately dialectic relationship of complementarity/opposition, a relationship that is surely the lynchpin of the entire Hitchcock oeuvre. One can examine it further by considering the role of women in the falsely accused man films and of men in the guilty women films. In the former, the woman characteristically occupies a subordinate position; she is initially antagonistic to the hero (accepting automatically the social assumption

of his guilt), then learns (usually by intuition) to be assured of his innocence, to trust and support him. *The 39 Steps*, *Young and Innocent* and
Saboteur are the purest instances, but many other films work variations
on this pattern. *Spellbound* is complicated by the fact that Dr. Peterson
falls in love with Ballantyne at first sight, and by the more determining fact
that Ingrid Bergman has star precedence over Gregory Peck; *Strangers on
a Train* is complicated by the fact that Ruth Roman is already (if unofficially) engaged to Farley Granger before she suspects him of murdering his
inconvenient wife; *North by Northwest* is complicated by the fact that Eva
Marie Saint knows that Cary Grant is innocent before she meets him, as
well as by the fact that she is herself a "guilty woman"; *The Wrong Man* is
complicated by the fact that the protagonist's wife, far from being support-
ive, goes insane under the stress.

The role of the male in the guilty woman films is subject to even greater
variation, in which the one constant appears to be that the man is never
cleanly exonerated or endorsed. There are two major functions, the split
depending on the question of whether the woman can be "saved" (the
notion of salvation becoming here itself somewhat problematic, since it
depends in its turn on her relationship to the patriarchal order which the
films in general tend to undermine or discredit):

a) If the woman, because of the degree of her guilt, has to die, the man
   is effectively responsible for her death. There is no Hitchcock film in
   which he literally despatches her himself (the death of Juanita in
   Topaz might be considered an exception), although the logic of
   Rebecca is clearly that he *did*, and we know that the change from
   the novel was dictated by the Motion Picture Code, not anyone's
   actual desire. In *The Paradine Case*, Mrs. Paradine's desperate climactic confession is directly provoked by her defense barrister's
   intransigence in insisting on her innocence (because he is madly in
   love with her); in *Vertigo*, we have little doubt that Scottie would
   rather have a dead Judy than a live one, if she really isn't (or can't be
   transformed into) Madeleine.

b) If the woman's guilt is not such as to put her beyond the pale of
   the law, the hero's function is to guide her back, suitably chas-
   tized for her transgressions, within the bounds of patriarchal
   "normality." This is of course, put like that, a commonplace
   enough version of the "happy ending"; except that in Hitchcock's
   films it typically acquires disturbing and dissonant undertones.
   The hero's "love" for the woman, his desire to save her, is characterized above all as a desire for power over her, and his saving of
   her develops connotations of an alternative form of entrapment:
   Marnie's "I don't want to go to prison, Mark, I'd rather stay with
   you" conveys the effect precisely, not only of the end of *Marnie*,
   but of that of *Blackmail*. *Under Capricorn* provides a fascinating

variation and partial exception: its happy ending, one of the most unambiguous in all of Hitchcock, is achieved because the woman's "savior" *loses* her.

It remains to note a few exceptions to the general rules of these two categories. Uncle Charlie in *Shadow of a Doubt* is a *rightly* accused man, and so (it transpires) is the Jonathan of *Stage Fright*; the Ivor Novello of *The Lodger* and the Cary Grant of *Suspicion* would have been too if Hitchcock had been allowed to shoot the endings he claims he wanted. Conversely, Grace Kelly in *Dial M for Murder* is, like the falsely accused men, innocent of the crime of murder but guilty of a sexual "crime," adultery. Marlene Dietrich in *Stage Fright* is not directly guilty of the murder of her husband, but guilty of setting up Jonathan to commit it for her.

The "psychopath story" sometimes combines with the falsely accused man story: *The Lodger, Strangers on a Train, Frenzy*. It should be clear that I am thinking here in quite superficial terms of those films in which the character's psychopathic nature is made explicit and in which he is the "villain" (if often the character toward whom the energies of the film seem drawn as to a magnet);[2] I am not thinking of the blatant psychopathology of many of Hitchcock's ostensible heroes (*Rebecca, Notorious, Vertigo*). As with the guilty woman films, the psychopath is often the center of fascination, at the hero's expense—though never, like some of the guilty women, a primary identification figure. He also functions at times as the hero's "double" in the celebrated "exchange of guilt" theme traced throughout Hitchcock's work by Rohmer and Chabrol: *Strangers on a Train* and *Frenzy* are the two most developed examples.

The "espionage story," though it recurs fairly frequently, is the least essential to the overall structure of meaning in the Hitchcock oeuvre— often closer to a MacGuffin than a plot formation. But from the films listed in this category one can extract a coherent group in which espionage/political intrigue is a central concern and develops a particular thematic resonance: *The Secret Agent, Notorious, North by Northwest, Torn Curtain, Topaz*. Two factors distinguish this group (occurring either separately or in combination): the sense of the inevitable corruption and contamination of political intrigue, expressed especially in the souring or poisoning of human relationships (the pervasive, unifying theme of the apparently diffuse *Topaz*); and the victimization of women within the domain of masculinist politics. In *Notorious, North by Northwest*, and *Topaz*, the struggle for power between two opposing patriarchal authority structures (nominally the Good Law and the Bad Law, but both are discredited by the film) crystallizes itself as the struggle to possess, manipulate, or dominate a woman. The ultimate, emblematic expression of this is the death of Juanita in *Topaz*, provoked by her French lover, carried out by her Cuban lover.

If "stories about a marriage" are relatively rare, their implications are far more pervasive. From *Rich and Strange* through to *Frenzy*, the attitude to marriage is remarkably (given the very high value placed on that institution within patriarchal ideology in general and the Motion Picture Code in particular) bleak and skeptical. This may account for the perfunctory, strictly "conventional" nature of so many Hitchcock happy endings: the expected construction or reconstruction of the heterosexual Couple is presented without much evidence of engagement or conviction (e.g, *Shadow of a Doubt*, *Stage Fright*, *The Paradine Case*, *Strangers on a Train*) or with overt skepticism (*Rear Window*). The films centered on a marriage are scarcely more encouraging. Leaving aside the unresolvably problematic *Suspicion*, consider the following:

Rich and Strange. The couple try to escape from the boredom and staleness of their marriage by seeking adventure, then, finding adventure even worse, sink back into boredom and staleness with a sigh of relief.

Sabotage. Mrs. Verloc has married her unappealing and self-preoccupied husband to provide security for her younger brother; discovering that Verloc has been responsible for the boy's death, she "accidentally murders" him.

Rebecca. Maxim de Winter marries the (unnamed) heroine because he sees her as a helpless child, his "little girl," whom he can mold and dominate; in the course of the film she grows up, and romance abruptly evaporates.

Rear Window. The Thorwald marriage—wherein the husband murders and dismembers his wife—is presented consistently in relation to the central projected marriage between Jefferies and Lisa, carrying the tensions in their relationship to their logical culmination.

Marnie. Mark forces Marnie into marriage, ostensibly to save her from the clutches of "some other sexual blackmailer," in reality to dominate and tame her by curing her neurosis. The film is reticent about what will happen after she is cured (compare *Rebecca*).

Frenzy. The film's central structural opposition is that between the Blaneys' marriage and the Oxfords' marriage, the former disordered, violent, and broken, the latter ordered and permanent, built upon a willed mutual forbearance ironically counterpointed by pervasive signs that the husband and wife unconsciously detest each other. In *Frenzy*, marriage is treated as purely a social institution, devoid of emotional validation; significantly, the ending is striking for the absence of any attempt to construct a new heterosexual couple.

There are two marriage films in which the couple's union carries somewhat more positive connotations. But *The Man Who Knew Too Much*

(1956 version) in fact stresses the tension between husband and wife far more strongly and convincingly than their solidarity, and the ending offers no guarantee that those tensions have been permanently resolved. *Under Capricorn* is another matter: for all the authority of the mise-en-scène, the film belongs as much to the woman-centered melodrama (and to Ingrid Bergman) as it does to Hitchcock. But even here there is an anomaly that slightly disturbs the resolution. The narrative logic demands, here, the restitution and celebration of the marriage, yet Hitchcock denies us the satisfaction of its logical culmination, a convincingly realized scene of marital reconciliation.

This leaves *Mr. and Mrs. Smith*. Even the most dedicated auteurist is unlikely to claim it as among Hitchcock's successful, fully realized works, but in the present context it takes on an interest out of proportion to its achievement. An almost painfully unfunny screwball comedy, the film's peculiar character—its thin and crabbed distinctiveness—develops out of a direct conflict between auteur and genre. The obvious and very telling comparison is with *The Awful Truth*, McCarey's genius being as compatible with the genre as Hitchcock's is alien to it. The two films share a number of structural features, the parallels being close enough to suggest a direct connection: both open with the dissolution of a marriage and end with its reaffirmation; most of the intervening narrative movement is activated by the couple's experiments with alternative partners. Both films contain a scene in a nightclub where the husband feels humiliated when his wife sees him in the company of an "inappropriate" other woman, and both culminate in a movement away from the city for a denouement in a country lodge where the obstacles to reunion are dismantled. In *The Awful Truth* we don't doubt for a moment that the couple will and should be reconciled, not only because this is demanded by the generic conventions but because, under McCarey's direction, Cary Grant and Irene Dunne communicate a constant and incorrigible affection for and delight in each other. Even the scene of Grant's ultimate humiliation—when Dunne, masquerading as his fictitious, irrepressibly vulgar sister, invades a society gathering in the home of his snooty new fiancée—is colored by the glances of reluctant admiration he can't help casting at her. The inner movement of the film—like that of all the finest examples of the genre—is a progress toward liberation (however qualified), especially liberation from restrictive social and gender roles and norms.

Nothing of this transpires in *Mr. and Mrs. Smith*. Here the final reconciliation seems motivated entirely by the exigencies of the genre. Robert Montgomery seems to want Carole Lombard back solely because her leaving him is an affront to his male ego. There is no sense at the end that the marriage has been radically transformed or that "male presumption" has been "chastised" (Andrew Britton's felicitous formula for *The Awful Truth*) into anything new or positive. We are, as in *Rich and Strange*, back to square one, to a marriage characterized by loveless bickerings and artificially contrived reconciliations.

Hitchcock's films cannot of course produce an alternative to marriage as our culture knows it. What they *do* provide is a thoroughgoing and radical analysis of the difficulties placed on successful heterosexual union by the social structures and sexual organization of patriarchal capitalism.

NOTES

1. The figure of the guilty woman occurs already—if not very interestingly—in *Easy Virtue*, but the film's plot structure scarcely anticipates that of the later guilty women movies, and it seems reasonable to claim *Blackmail* as the film that established the pattern.

2. One may well question whether "psychopath" is an appropriate term for the Handel Fane of *Murder!*, which I included in my list; but the whole point about Fane is his deviance from social/sexual norms, and in terms of his *function* he belongs with the psychopaths.

Games Hitchcock Plays

THOMAS LEITCH

Ten years after his death, Alfred Hitchcock's genius for self-advertising ensures his continuing status as one of the best known of all film directors. Audiences all over the world know what he looks like because they have seen images of him in most of his films and television shows. Hitchcock's introductions to "Alfred Hitchcock Presents" and "The Alfred Hitchcock Hour" made his persona as familiar to audiences as many star performers of fifties television. These introductions were so popular that they were later eerily resurrected for posthumous episodes of "The New Alfred Hitchcock Presents". Hitchcock poses in each introduction as impresario who stands outside the frame of the story, free to comment ironically on the characters and events within the story, the conventions of commercial television. ("And now for something *really* horrible" is a favorite lead-in to a commercial), and his own frequently ridiculous figure, tricked out as an elephantine archer or an overgrown baby.

This elaborately ironic pose is maintained in the trailers to *Psycho* and *The Birds*, in which Hitchcock the impresario gives a talk about the subject of his new film, taking the audience on a facetious tour of the Bates house and motel or discussing his forthcoming lecture on our friends the birds. But in each case the trailer ends with an unexpected segue to a shot from the film itself. Hitchcock draws back the shower curtain to reveal a closeup of Janet Leigh screaming or looks off-camera right to a matched shot of Tippi Hedren crying, "They're coming!" Each segue is a joke that blurs the distinction between the world of the story and the world outside, a distinction the trailer had begun by insisting on. The trailer to *Frenzy* confuses this distinction further by cutting Hitchcock's remarks to the audience into the continuity of several scenes of the movie. Retrieving what he tells us is his necktie from around the neck of a strangled woman, Hitchcock looks at the camera and asks, "How do you like my tie?" looks right and says, "How do you like it?" then cuts to a shot of Barbara Leigh-Hunt saying, "My God! The tie!" The trailer emphasizes the film's ghoulish humor by treating murder as a joke and the director as a naif who has wandered into his own movie.

But the most problematic of Hitchcock's public images are his celebrated cameo appearances—his brief unbilled roles—in virtually all his films. Even more perversely than Hitchcock's trailers or television introductions,

Reprinted from *Find the Director and Other Hitchcock Games* (Athens: University of Georgia Press, 1991), 1–30. Copyright © The University of Georgia Press.

the cameos pose serious difficulties for leading models of narrative by playing with the distinction between the world of the film (the diegesis, the world contained within the   cinematic discourse, the world of the characters and their problems) and the world outside (the world of the filmmaker and the audience, who see the film as an artful fiction and so are able to adopt myriad perspectives on the diegetic world unavailable to the characters). Any audience that recognizes Hitchcock aboard Uncle Charlie's train in *Shadow of a Doubt* holding the world's best bridge hand or sitting in a Copenhagen hotel lobby in *Torn Curtain* distastefully raising a diapered baby from his knee will be reminded that the movie they are watching is only a movie, but this realization will not break the movie's spell; if it did, the audience would not be able to enjoy the rest of the movie. On the contrary, spotting Hitchcock's cameo provides an additional source of pleasure for sharp-eyed audiences, and both director and audience are called on to exercise considerable ingenuity in devising and recognizing these cameos. Hitchcock's best-known cameo, his appearance in *Lifeboat* in before-and-after newspaper photos for a weight-loss product called Reduco, suggests the nature of the relationship the cameos establish between the director and his audience. Hitchcock told François Truffaut that he had great difficulty in coming up with a way he could appear in a one-set film with so few characters but that he finally hit on the newspaper ad as a solution which would not only provide for his appearance but would also memorialize his recent weight loss.[1] Evidently by 1943 Hitchcock considered himself honor-bound to appear in every one of his feature films, even though his appearance might be hard to find. And the audience was expected by now not only to be familiar with Hitchcock's profile but to be interested in its changing shape as a personal revelation, as if the film were a mass-produced Christmas card on which the cameo were a scribbled personal message.

Hitchcock sometimes appears in costume in his cameos, but he never plays a character; the whole point of each cameo is that this is no ordinary character but rather someone whose mode of existence is different from that of every other character in the movie. Truffaut's remark that his first appearance as part of a crowd in *The Lodger* helps to "fill the screen" aptly implies that the passersby Hitchcock affects in his films never have any function in the story, never interact significantly with the principals (Hitchcock appearing in *Stage Fright* looking askance at Eve Gill telling herself that she is Doris Tinsdale is delivering a judgment, not making any impression on her), and never even speak.[2] The sole purpose of such apparitions—they cannot truly be called characters, for Hitchcock makes no pretense of playing a role shaped by the requirements of the diegesis— is to be recognized. The exception that proves the rule is Hitchcock's cameo in *Rope*, in which he appears briefly in the background in the costume and attitude of Mr. Kentley. Mr. Kentley is a character, but Hitchcock is not playing this character, for he does nothing in the role but walk away from the camera for a few seconds. Hitchcock is merely impersonating Mr. Kentley, a character played by Sir Cedric Hardwicke; if he is acting at all, he is playing Hardwicke playing Mr. Kentley.[3]

Specifying the mode of existence of Hitchcock's cameos poses a stumbling block for dominant modes of narrative theory. Communications models of narrative, in which stories are messages sent by their authors to their receivers, are inadequate to describe the situation of a film director using his own image as a means to communication, both because the image cannot be decoded according to a communications model—"Look, there's the director!" is not a message communicated by the diegesis but a perception that requires the audience to assume a perspective outside the frame of the diegesis—and because, as Edward Branigan notes, the author of a text cannot simply appear within a text as the author. Branigan, following Roland Barthes, observes that "the artwork provides no context within which to locate the author," who "is located in the text only as a *subcode* of the code of narration and not as someone who speaks, expresses the codes."[4]

But Branigan's own empiricist model of narration, although far more sophisticated than the communications model he is criticizing, does not adequately describe Hitchcock's cameos either because it does not make the kinds of distinctions that give the cameos a witty power unlike that of other directors' appearances on film. When Branigan argues that "Hitchcock appearing in his own film is not the director made manifest but a figure trapped as an object of a film process," he is overlooking the decisive ways in which Hitchcock's appearances are different not only from the appearances of such director-stars as Chaplin, Keaton, and Olivier, whose films are typically organized around their performances, but from the appearances of other directors like Renoir, Welles, Huston, and Truffaut, who take dramatic roles in their own, or other directors', films.[5] Characters in fictional films, whether or not they are played by the director, are functions of the discourse: their significance is established through the ways in which they participate in the diegesis (the characters they play, their bearing on the plot, their interrelations with other characters having a cognate diegetic significance). But the significance of Hitchcock's cameos is essentially that they make an image of the director available for recognition. (Hence new audiences' inveterate questions about where Hitchcock appears in *Rear Window* or *Dial M for Murder*.) It is possible to speculate, as Maurice Yacowar has done, about the thematic significance of the cameos, individually or as a group, but simply recognizing Hitchcock can provide a characteristic pleasure even for an audience who makes no attempt to connect his appearance to the characters or story in a particular film or to a pattern of cameos in his other films.[6] Unlike the fictional characters played by other directors, Hitchcock through his cameos manages to appear in his films without being constrained in at all the same ways by the requirements of their diegesis.

Although Hitchcock's introductions to his television program establish a clear distinction between the world of the audience and the world of the story, his cameos have the opposite effect, because they introduce a nondiegetic figure into the story without stepping unambiguously outside the frame of the diegesis. Nor is this figure some historical personage like Napoleon as played by Charles Boyer in *Conquest* or Benny Goodman appearing with his band in *The Gang's All Here* but the storyteller himself, the creator rather than a performer. In this regard it is quite unlike the figure of Somerset Maugham as played by Herbert Marshall in *The Moon and Sixpence* and *The Razor's Edge* or those of the other storytellers whose narrative activity Branigan analyzes in his discussion of cinematic point of view because it is only secondarily a mimetic figure, and never directly a figure for perception; that is, the audience is never encouraged to adopt the cameo as a guide for its own perceptions, a surrogate storyteller or audience. Instead, the joke behind the cameos—that the storyteller is presenting himself neither as the storyteller nor as a fully articulated character but as a figure on the margin of the fictional world—depends on a kind of double awareness Branigan's theory does not ascribe to the audience.

In other words, it is the audience's desire for pleasure (the pleasure of recognizing the director hidden in the discourse), not its desire for justifying particular narrative devices (cut-in close-ups or voice-over commentary that can be assigned to a narrator), that gives the cameos their point, since they constitute a device whose point is that it can be recuperated only as a device (to recognize the cameo is automatically to note its potentially disruptive force). The resulting effect cannot be explained by theories of narrative which depend on establishing a dualism between *histoire*, or story (the events of a narrative apart from any given representational form—for instance, the Cinderella story), and *discours*, or discourse (a particular narration of a given story—for instance, Charles Perrault's or Walt Disney's *Cinderella*). Even dualistic theories organized around the problem of pleasure (what makes this shot worth watching?) rather than Branigan's problem of narrative motivation (how can this shot be logically justified?) cannot account for the effect of the cameos. Consider the influential argument of Christian Metz that most audiences think of the movies they watch as stories, natural sequences of events that the camera just happened to capture; even though they know all along that what they are watching is just a movie, they react with anger or fear or exultation as if it were an unmediated story.[7] Sometimes, however, a movie will remind the audience that it is not a story by dropping its naturalizing devices and emphasizing the artifices that make it a discourse. At such times the audience has the exhilarating or disconcerting feeling of falling out of the story or otherwise having its attention drawn to a diegetic frame whose existence the audience usually chooses to ignore. Hitchcock's cameos have the effect of reminding the audience of the filmmaker's power and his film's status as an artifact, an artful discourse rather than a transparent story.

But Metz's account, like Branigan's, is inadequate to the effects Hitchcock's cameos actually produce. The audience's two kinds of awareness of *Lifeboat* as story and as discourse should, according to Metz, be perpetually at war with each other as the audience struggled to find some stable point of view from which to follow and interpret images on the screen; in particular, Hitchcock's cameos would operate as a distracting interruption, like the network logo during a late-night television screening that reminds the audience that this is only a movie. But audiences who recognize Hitchcock at all are not really distracted, even pleasurably, from the story because their experience of the film as story and discourse is not nearly so sharply split; in watching a Hitchcock film, they do not shuttle neatly back and forth between two kinds of awareness.

The problematic status of Hitchcock's cameos also challenges other psychoanalytically based theories of pleasure. Psychoanalytic theories using analogies between the movie screen and the dream screen of early childhood to argue that movies inscribe their audiences into a particular position by requiring them to adopt certain attitudes in order to follow and enjoy their stories fail to account for the fact that the cameos do not inscribe passive, unconscious audiences through cultural constraints but rather engage audiences on a conscious, contractual, elective basis by providing a distinctive pleasure for audiences who recognize Hitchcock's sly appearances and allowing audiences who do not do so all the other pleasures associated with Hitchcock's movies.[8] The example of *Lifeboat*, whose cameo so taxed the director's ingenuity, suggests that the cameos are better considered as a contract equally binding on director and audience than as a means of inscribing either into the discourse on the basis of unconscious motives. If Gaylyn Studlar is correct in arguing that "cinema is not a sadistic institution but preeminently a contractual one based on the promise of certain pleasures," Hitchcock's cameos can serve as a paradigm for cinematic pleasure.[9]

A much more promising model for the relationship Hitchcock's cameos establish with their audience is the constructivist theory developed by David Bordwell. Agreeing with Studlar that it is unnecessary and misleading to theorize an audience inscribed by the cinematic discourse—"I see no reason to claim for the unconscious any activities which can be explained on other grounds," he remarks—Bordwell describes the audience for fictional films as actively engaged in a process of constructing a story, an activity directed by operational cues. "A film," argues Bordwell, ". . . does not 'position' anybody." Despite the advantages of this constructive model over psychoanalytic models of inscription, however, it cannot account for the quirky effect of Hitchcock's cameos because Bordwell is at such pains to

banish the storyteller from his narrative theory, which "presupposes a per-
ceiver, but not any sender, of a message," that he breaks the tie between
the represented Hitchcock—the fat Cockney onscreen—and the putative
storyteller, denying the very source of the cameos' power.[10]

If none of these theories of cinematic narrative adequately explains the
effects of the cameos, is there a superior alternative model? Branigan
observes that "narration has been analyzed . . . as a simple unrolling, a logical progression, a violation, a set of oppositions, a set of alternatives, a
control on connotation, a logic of reading, a reconstruction of unconscious mechanisms, and as a literal telling."[11] This list omits another
model that is still more promising: the conception of narration as a game
between a storyteller and an audience. Like Metz's analysis of cinematic
syntax and Branigan's of point of view, the analysis of narrative as a game
is based on an analogy with language, but this analogy, based on the later
work of Wittgenstein, emphasizes the point of cinema's rules rather than
the ways in which they facilitate understanding.[12] In short, it treats films as
objects of pleasure rather than as objects of knowledge, and considers
their rules as defined by their purpose in promoting the goals of the players—filmmakers and their audiences—whatever role understanding plays
in those goals.

Although formal game theory, first developed as a mathematical model
for analyzing social strategies (generating predictive or prescriptive rules
concerning the most efficient ways to submit a bid, cast a vote, or deploy a
nuclear arsenal), has rarely been applied to the analysis of narrative and
never, as far as I have found, to narrative cinema, theorists like Johan
Huizinga and Roger Caillois have long recognized the affinities between
storytelling and other games whose rules are designed to promote pleasure. Considering Hitchcock's cameos as moves in a game of hide-and-
seek—or, more accurately, find the director—not only explains their narrative status more precisely but illuminates their special role in
Hitchcock's films, revealing their exemplary status as patterns for the ways
the director's films operate and the kinds of pleasure they are designed to
provide.

Games provide an obvious model for the relations Hitchcock's films
establish between the filmmaker and the audience because games serve so
often within the stories of the films themselves as models of the diegesis,
from the chess game between the Lodger and Daisy (a game punctuated
by his playful remark, "I'll get you yet," and his picking up a poker while
she bends over to pick up a fallen piece) to the game of blindman's buff at
Cathy Brenner's birthday party, a game interrupted by the first mass attack
of the birds. In between, Hitchcock's heroes and heroines play tennis (in
Easy Virtue and *Strangers on a Train*), shoot skeet (in the 1934 *The Man
Who Knew Too Much*), dress up in masquerade (in *Blackmail*, *The 39
Steps*, *Rebecca*, *Stage Fright*, *To Catch a Thief*), and even play another

game of blindman's buff (in *Young and Innocent*). Probably the most sustained use of a particular game to provide the controlling metaphor for the characters' behavior is Hitchcock's boxing film, *The Ring*, one of the few films in which he takes screen credit for the scenario.

More generally, games provide a frame which contains, defines, or sharpens the suspense evoked by a genuinely threatening situation in many films which present attempts to deal with serious problems as a variously successful game, from Gilbert's and Iris's idyll in the baggage car in *The Lady Vanishes* to Blanche Tyler's enthusiastic performances as a medium in *Family Plot*. The fact that most of these games—Ted Spencer's attempt to pass off his spying on the conspirators as a lark in *Sabotage*, Huntley Haverstock's escape from his hotel room to Carol Fisher's room in *Foreign Correspondent*, Alicia Huberman's theft of the key to her husband's wine cellar in *Notorious*, Michael Armstrong's tensely ritualized attempt to lose his pursuing watchdog in the museum in *Torn Curtain*— are considerably darker reveals the intimate connection between games and Hitchcock's brand of suspense, which typically quibbles on the diegetic distinction between playing and pretending to play a game—a figure for the characters' activity that has considerable relevance to the audience's activity as well.

Finally, Hitchcock has directed a number of films which seem, despite the absence of particular recognizable diegetic games like hide-and-seek and blindman's buff, to be developed in an unbroken skein of games. The nonsensical continuity of *Number Seventeen* makes a great deal of sense if the film is considered as a series of games (among the characters, and between the director and the audience) which are actually variations of a single game (invoking and exploding the conventions of the thriller for a cast of characters who never take these conventions entirely seriously themselves). One way to distinguish between the two versions of *The Man Who Knew Too Much* is to note the much greater dependence of the first version on ludic metaphors; the film might be described as dramatizing the liberation of the Lawrence family through learning to play better. The pattern is reversed in *Secret Agent*, which shows the disillusioning consequences of treating international intrigue as a game. Among Hitchcock's later films, *Strangers on a Train* is most clearly organized around the metaphor of a game—the resonances of Guy's status as a tennis player are economically indicated by the adventures of his cigarette lighter, with its crossed tennis racquets over the inscription "A. to G."— but *Rope* and *North by Northwest* are equally dominated by ludic patterns. "And now let the fun begin!" exults Brandon as the guests for his post-strangulation party begin to arrive; and Philip Vandamm greets Roger Thornhill's attempts to establish his own identity with the weary disclaimer—"Games? Must we?"—which establishes the ludic tone of the film from the beginning.

The point of listing all these incidences of games within Hitchcock's films is not to argue that games have a unique importance in Hitchcock's work. Games are common in commercial cinema, and it is hard to imagine Hollywood genres like the musical and the romantic comedy existing without them. Furthermore, games have a much greater diegetic importance in the work of a director like Howard Hawks, who uses games and play as a radical metaphor for all human action, than in Hitchcock's films. The importance of games for Hitchcock is not their significance within the diegesis but their role as a figure for the relation between the storyteller and his audience, a relation which not surprisingly is often imaged within the diegesis as a game. The games the characters play are most significant as a metaphor for the games Hitchcock plays. . . .

Like other games, Hitchcock's films posit a world defined by rules governing the behavior of its players. These rules do not constrain the players except by prior consent (e.g., Hitchcock's self-imposed decision to film *Rope* entirely in long takes). To the extent that they inscribe or position the audience, they do so on a contractual basis, with the implied stipulation that observing them will increase the audience's pleasure and the director's success. Within these contractual boundaries, Hitchcock's games have three leading functions: to beguile audiences by domesticating or making light of potentially threatening situations, to administer salubrious shocks to audiences by outraging their sense of propriety or exposing them to exhilarating dangers, and to encourage them to fall into misidentifications and misinterpretations which have a specifically moral and thematic force. The first of these functions can be illustrated by *The 39 Steps*, *Strangers on a Train*, and *To Catch a Thief*; the second by *Rope*; and the third by *Psycho*.

The most general function of Hitchcock's games is by definition to amuse the audience, and the simplest effect of Hitchcock's most characteristic set-pieces is to encourage the audience to adopt a perspective more amusing and amused than that of the characters immersed in an action they take much more seriously. Descriptions of Hitchcock's mise-en-scène as a place in which threats are everywhere, nothing is necessarily what it seems to be, every friend is a potential enemy, and mystery lurks around every corner overlook a fundamental aspect of the films' appeal, for the Hitchcock world as seen by its characters (and aptly described by such a menacing formula) is very different from the Hitchcock world seen by the audience. To speak most generally, the audience sees that it is at the movies, the only place where every gesture has a meaning, where stylistic consistency is the basis of knowledge and pleasure, where the visual and auditory field becomes a world much more salient than the world outside. This world is far from being Hitchcock's exclusive domain: movies as different as *Gone With the Wind* and *Casablanca* and *On the Town* depend for their effects on invoking a world more amusing, more close-textured, more salient than the audience's own. This is essentially the world of the movies, a place which promises to be both more interesting and more coherent, more deserving of the name world, than the world outside the frame.[13]

Movie audiences are constantly supplying temporal, causal, and thematic connections the movie leaves implicit, as when a film cuts from a shot of the hero and heroine embracing by moonlight to a close-up of bacon and eggs cooking in a skillet to the accompaniment of offscreen whistling. Audiences work to supply such connections and to impute an implicit value to what they see and hear because otherwise movies would be literally pointless. The payoff of Hollywood movies, the reason so many audiences are motivated to play the games they offer, is the consequent ability to enter a world and follow a story more expressive, more dramatic, more stylish, more continuously interesting than their own. Hitchcock's ludic storytelling often has a more specific point, for audiences are not only required to supply the missing connections or the implicit point in order to follow the story but are repeatedly rewarded with a witty recognition of their astuteness, as in the famous moment in *The 39 Steps* when Hitchcock cuts from a shot of Richard Hannay boarding a train to Scotland to escape the investigation of a murder in his flat to a close-up of an old woman opening a door, seeing the shadow of a corpse, and turning toward the camera to scream, only to have the sound of the scream covered by the sound of a train whistle as the film cuts again to a shot of a train emerging from a tunnel. In return for the assumptions audiences make about the identity of the woman and her relation to the train, they are rewarded with an exhilarating sense of intimacy with the film's world as a place where such moments are common—and where it would not be surprising to see the director standing in a crowd. The episode assumes not only a certain degree of attention—many audiences will miss its significance—but an attention focused on the specifically discursive aspects of the film ("now what's *that* doing there?"). Hitchcock never affects the transparent camera style of Chaplin or Hawks. Such a style, which is designed to be seen through, to draw attention to the performers rather than the director, tends to establish the screen as a window rather than a painting, conflating the film's world with the audience's world.[14] But the Hitchcock world is always the world according to Hitchcock; it cannot be entered and enjoyed without some awareness of the rules that make it worth entering.

In Hitchcock's films as in games like tennis or Monopoly, the audience's pleasure is governed by rules which mark off a world which its members always know is not their own, but which is neither a self-enclosed alternative world nor an artificial world trying to pass itself off as real. A great deal of the audience's pleasure in Hitchcock's films is provided by moments like the director's cameos that ought, according to the traditional model of narrative, to disturb its sense of the film's coherence.

Instead, however, these moments intensify the audience's pleasure in the film by establishing a unifying style that confirms a belief that this world is a world, not just a spool of images or a series of events strung together.

Even an audience that is watching Hitchcock's films just for the story is encouraged to take note of their discursive features and is constantly rewarded for doing so. This discursive awareness is hardly unique to Hitchcock's audience; the audience for films in any Hollywood genre could not enjoy *Rambo* or *Lethal Weapon* as an exercise in escapism if it were not well aware of the formulaic nature of the generic convention; otherwise the audience would feel unpleasurably threatened instead of protected by the nature of the predictable generic conventions.[15] Largely because the promise of commercial films depends so largely on the audience's cultivating a double awareness of cinematic images at once representational and formulaic, audiences typically develop the ability to take pleasure in the film's play with the line between story and discourse without thinking self-consciously about the director's technique or about the problems posed for narrative theory. When Guy goes to a tennis club in *Strangers on a Train* to get some practice for an upcoming tournament and to get his mind off his wife's murder by the ingratiating psychotic Bruno, Hitchcock cuts from a shot of Guy on the court to a long shot of the grandstand, with every spectator's head ticktocking in unison to follow the ball except for one, Bruno's, which stares straight ahead. This shot does not tell audiences anything they do not already know about the action and characters, since it has already been established that Bruno is obsessively attached to Guy and follows him everywhere. But it carries an additional potential to amuse them because of its audacity and witty economy, using their knowledge of the conventions of visual representation (the odd figure is the one to look at), tennis (to follow a game, you need to keep shifting your eyes back and forth), and Hollywood movies (would any audience outside the movies move their heads in such metronomic unison?) to draw them further into the story instead of keeping them at a distance.

Set-pieces like this one can draw audiences further into the story by making them more intimate with the world of the film. An audience who recognizes Bruno in the stands is invited to be delightedly appreciative of Hitchcock's artifice; the shot would fail with an audience whose reaction was "Look, there's Bruno again" or "Bruno sure is interested in Guy." But the shot is not supposed to make the audience focus on the storyteller either. Like Hitchcock's cameos, it plays on the customary distinction between story and discourse to create a no-man's-land not adequately described by communication, psychoanalytic, or mimetic theories of narrative. The audience's self-conscious appreciation of this shot—it can hardly be appreciated unselfconsciously—does not necessarily make its members more aware of Hitchcock the storyteller, but it does make them more aware of the narrative style that makes the film distinctive and amusing.

Hitchcock's stylized view of the cat-and-mouse game Bruno is playing with Guy gives the moment a different effect on the audience than it has on Guy (even though the view is presumably available to him as well, neither he nor any other character seems to notice the joke), but the two games—the characters' games with each other, and the director's game with the audience—are closely related. In general, Hitchcock uses diegetic games between his characters as figures for his own relation to his audience. Even the discovery of the body in Hannay's flat, whose wit depends on a conjunction of sound and image unavailable to any character, is prepared by Hannay's earlier and unexpectedly droll escape from his building in the guise of a milkman. But the relation between the games within Hitchcock's films and the games offered by those films, so straightforward in these examples, can be considerably more complex. *To Catch a Thief* offers a remarkable succession of games—the police officers' opening pursuit of retired cat burglar John Robie, his tense standoff with the staff at Bertani's, his pursuit first by Danielle Foussard and later by Francie Stevens, his masquerades as Oregon lumberman Conrad Burns and as Francie's black servant at the climactic costume ball, his final flight from Francie—which are in terms of the film's diegesis almost entirely inconsequential. The police finally catch Robie only to let him go; Bertani and Foussard are only pretending to be hostile to him, since they have planned the robberies he is suspected of themselves; Danielle flirts with him knowing very well that he is not the cat burglar, since she is; Francie is not fooled by his disguise, nor is it really necessary, since the insurance agent Hugheson could easily have arranged a meeting between them; even Robie's final flight is only a move in a game, since he asks Francie to leave only to take her hand in a gesture of commitment. But all these games, which mean so little to the characters, mean a great deal to audiences, for they tell them how to watch the movie, establishing the basis for a playful relationship between Hitchcock and his audiences that allows them to take this story of theft, suspicion, paranoia, betrayal, and sexual jealousy as a divertissement, a witty and romantic trifle whose suspense is defined precisely as the ritualistic suspense of light comedy.

These games I have been discussing in *The 39 Steps*, *Strangers on a Train*, and *To Catch a Thief* all have the effect of lightening the films' tone by creating a perspective that defuses the threatening potential of a dangerous situation. But games can serve more equivocal functions as well. In *Rope*, as in *To Catch a Thief*, the characters' games provide a figure for the director's games, but this figure takes on a much darker tone, since Brandon's cat-and-mouse game with the guests who do not know their dinner is being served from a chest containing the body of absent guest

David Kentley—a game whose force will redound on Brandon when he becomes the mouse to Rupert Cadell's cat—is, like Hitchcock's game with his audience, essentially a sadistically playful tease. The sardonic sense of humor that makes Brandon such a good game player—he is the only character who repeatedly makes deliberate jokes about David's murder—has an underpinning of barely controlled hostility revealed by one exchange. When Kenneth doesn't want to bring Janet's drink to her in the bedroom because "you'd like David to come in and find us together," Brandon genially replies, "Oh, no, that would be too much of a shock." In killing David for a lark, Brandon has not only carried out the ultimate practical joke but has provided himself with a basis for a series of running dialogue jokes at the expense of his guests. He typifies the image of Hitchcock as a manipulative practical joker whose primary relationship to his audience is condescending and adversarial.[16] The game Hitchcock is playing in *Rope* is less condescending than the game Brandon is playing, since Hitchcock's audiences at least know they are playing a game; but the audacity of many of Hitchcock's images—the moment when the camera first pans to reveal the buffet table, or when it reveals Brandon dropping the murder weapon into a drawer in between swings of the kitchen door—seems intended to shock audiences into amusement rather than beguiling them.

Hitchcock plays an even more punitive game in the opening of *The Wrong Man*, based on the story of Manny Balestrero's false arrest for robbery. When Manny, having decided to pay his wife's dentist bills by borrowing on his life insurance, goes to his insurance company, Hitchcock frames him in a medium close-up from the teller's point of view showing him reaching with an all-too-familiar gesture into his inside overcoat pocket just as Bernard Herrmann's music swells ominously. Is Manny going to pull a gun and rob the office? Of course he doesn't; he just takes out his insurance policy, whose cash value he wants to determine. But the gesture has troubled the teller, who will proceed to identify Manny as the man who recently held up the office, and for a crucial second it troubles the audience as well. Hitchcock is teasing viewers by misdirecting them—one of his favorite moves—and the tease here implicates the audience, as it usually does in Hitchcock's films, in a moment of judgment that resonates through the film. For the rest of the film Hitchcock makes it impossible for audiences to feel superior to Manny's persecutors by punishing them for that moment when they thought he might be a thief.

The combination within game-playing of cooperation (agreement on rules and goals within the game, mutual desire to have the game succeed) and competition is closely connected to the thematic paradoxes of the suspense thriller Hitchcock chose as his genre. Consider for example the central importance in virtually all Hitchcock's films of the idea of home. Homes have many thematic associations Hitchcock routinely trades on: the safety of a place of shelter or refuge, the stability and security of long-

standing assumptions, the basis for self-definition through family relationships and a genetic sense of identity. At the same time, home is a ludic
topos in Hitchcock's work, a place like home in games of baseball or
Parcheesi, a final goal the pleasurable lack of which makes play possible
(so that arrival home is merely the signal for putting a new piece in play or
starting the game over again). Hitchcock's heroes and heroines are nearly
always strongly attracted to ideals of home, but their plots subvert these
ideals by pulling them out of their safe homes, betraying the promise of
home as a haven, even undermining the notion that a secure identity can
be based on one's ties to one's home.

Home is thus a goal both desired and deferred as the end of narrative,
and audiences' ambivalence toward this goal—they want the principals to
arrive home safely, but not just yet—opens the space for a profoundly con-
tradictory attitude toward home and its associations which develops in
Hitchcock's work beginning, not surprisingly, with his departure from
England to America in 1939. Hitchcock thereafter frequently invites audiences to endorse domestic values his films undermine comically (*Rear
Window* and *To Catch a Thief*), melodramatically (*Rebecca, Suspicion,
Shadow of a Doubt, Under Capricorn*), or ironically (*Rope* and *Psycho*).
This ambivalence toward home and domestic values is at the heart of the
games Hitchcock plays in his American films.

The audience's willingness to defer the principals' desired arrival home
for the sake of their entertaining adventures along the way points to
another essential paradox of Hitchcock's films. Thrillers entertain audiences by making them apprehensive, uncertain, or frightened. How can
anyone enjoy a film that puts sympathetic characters in danger? A purely
rational answer would begin with the observation that audiences' enjoyment of thrillers depends on their appetite for vicarious experiences that
would be anything but appetizing in their own lives; they find them amusing in movies because of the assurances offered by the conventions of all
stories (this is happening to someone else, not themselves), the more particular conventions of Hollywood movies (the story will proceed to an
ending that settles the principal problems raised by the plot, reassuringly
definitive hints will be given about the characters' future lives, everything
on the image track and sound track will turn out to be worth their attention), and the specialized conventions of suspense films (the conflict
between heroes and villains will always have some significant point, there
is always a reason or pattern behind every threat, the ending will resolve
the mystery). These conventions reassure audiences who understand
them, and audiences who do not—small children, for example—do not
usually enjoy suspense films.[17]

Once the reassuring conventions of the thriller have been established in
a given film, audiences can endure a good deal of suspense, mystification,
and anxiety with pleasure because they know that these feelings are only

temporary and necessary to intensify their pleasure in the resolution; they know the world of the film is a place where many unpleasant things are possible but trust that their vicarious suffering will be worthwhile. The result is that their suffering does not feel like real suffering but like a teasing game, a necessary prelude to the pleasures they expect eventually and therefore a pleasure itself. In other words, the pleasure audiences take in thrillers, as in many other narrative genres, is essentially projective and anticipatory, a pleasure defined and guaranteed by the promise of what is to come. Audiences who feel sufficiently reassured by a thriller's generic conventions can enjoy what would otherwise seem like perversely violent, sensational, or shocking stories.

But this rational argument for audiences' self-interest is incomplete, since Hitchcock's audiences often pay an unexpectedly heavy price for their thrills. Since thrillers from *Dead of Night* to *A Nightmare on Elm Street* scare audiences by violating a reassuring convention of earlier thrillers (in both these cases, the suggestion that whatever you saw can't hurt you because it's only a dream), the history of the suspense genre is largely a history of successively broken taboos. A remarkable feature of Hitchcock's films is that they not only violate conventions established by other suspense films but systematically challenge their own conventions, the rules of Hitchcock's game, in what often turns out to be the basis of a new game. Sometimes these challenges merely confirm the audience's sense of the Hitchcock world as a place where unexpected things happen to the audience as well as the characters. The apparent death of Richard Hannay halfway through *The 39 Steps*, though it startles first-time audiences of the film, is not really unpleasant to audiences who assume that there's been some sort of mistake and that it'll soon be cleared up—as it is when Hannay reappears alive a minute later. But often Hitchcock goes further, threatening the rules that make his world a world audiences enjoy spending time in. When the apparent death of Marion Crane less than halfway through *Psycho* turns out to be the real thing, the audience needs to find a new way to enjoy the film, since the terms it seemed to project (a crime story about a woman who steals forty thousand dollars and runs away to her boyfriend, raising questions about what he'll say and how she'll get punished—since, given the conventions of Hollywood filmmaking in 1960, she *has* to get punished) become inadequate once the apparent heroine is dead. Marion's death does not make *Psycho* any more difficult to follow, but it does make it more difficult for first-time viewers to enjoy. In order to enjoy the film, they need to find a new frame of reference that will make her death worthwhile. The long sequence following Marion's murder offers one such frame—the film is really about Norman and the mystery of the Bates Motel—which uninitiated audiences eagerly adopt, since it is less painful to give up their identification with Marion than to persist in mourning her and give up the possibility of pleasure for the rest of the film.

If suspense films depend on the paradox of pleasure-in-fear but resolve it by their use of reassuring generic conventions which make the audience's fear pleasurable, Hitchcock adds the complication of always threatening to undermine those conventions, even those he has established himself. Hitchcock's stylistic games are different from the games of other directors like Lubitsch not only because the thematic material they ritualize—the audience's fears and forbidden desires—is potentially more dangerous, but because the contractual rules that allow audiences to enjoy their fears are themselves more unstable. Critics have often noted the way these rules are broken in *Psycho* and other late films, but in fact they are always in danger of being broken, even when they are actually reaffirmed. Once the bomb goes off on a crowded bus in *Sabotage* in 1936, audiences can never be sure for the rest of Hitchcock's career that things will turn out all right for their identification figures, and each happy ending is purchased with sharpened anxiety. Nor is Hitchcock's challenge to his audiences limited to tricking them into identifications that turn out to be equivocal. Subverting the audiences' identifications is only one aspect of a much more general pattern in Hitchcock's work: a tendency to undermine the narrative conventions that make his stories worth watching.

Hitchcock's challenge to narrative conventions, like his fondness for encouraging equivocal identifications, depends on the fact that audiences' ability to perceive any series of filmed images as parts of a story inevitably carries strong moral concomitants. Perceiving Bruno as the solitary spectator who is watching Guy places them in Guy's position of being spied on; realizing that Hannay's char has discovered the body in his flat both intensifies their sense of his danger and confirms the film's tensely comic tone, insulating them from the worst consequences of that danger; laughing at Brandon's jokes about murder increases their uneasy complicity with him. Audiences' involvement in any film melodrama depends on the moral attitudes they adopt toward its characters and situations. In Hitchcock's films this involvement is always potentially equivocal even at its most straightforward. After establishing in the opening scene of *Sabotage* that someone has caused a blackout in London by pouring sand into an electrical generator, Hitchcock cuts from the question "But who?" to a close-up of Oscar Homolka striding purposefully toward the camera over the menacing title music. Although there is no evidence apart from the conventions of film melodrama to assume that this man is the saboteur, most audiences do assume it, adopting a specifically moral attitude toward Verloc, Homolka's character, in order to resolve the film's images into an intelligible narrative sequence. Eventually their suspicions are confirmed. After returning home and washing sand off his hands, pretending to his wife that he has been napping all afternoon, and expressing private satisfaction with the blackout and annoyance when it ends, Verloc goes to a clandestine meeting where he takes responsibility for the incident. But for the first fifteen minutes of the film, audiences have the pleasure of inferring Verloc's guilt for themselves, coupled with the moral responsibility of condemning him.

In *Sabotage* this responsibility provides an additional source of pleasure. Since Verloc is as guilty—and as unattractive—as he seems to be, taking sides against him confirms all audiences' comfortable moral assumptions. But Hitchcock often uses similar narrative conventions to manipulate audiences into more equivocal moral judgments, as when he imputes the guilt of the Lodger or of Richard Blaney in *Frenzy* or the innocence of Norman Bates. In such cases audiences' pleasure at following the story is complicated by their having taken the wrong side.

Hitchcock's films are fun to watch largely because they abound in such casually witty moments as the shot of Bruno in the grandstand or the blending of the char lady's scream with the train whistle.[18] But the example of *The Wrong Man* suggests that this fun is often more equivocal than it appears; Hitchcock's narrative imputations typically involve audiences more deeply in his story by forcing them to resolve an obscure or ambiguous situation in order to follow the story. His choice of the thriller, with its emphasis on crime or espionage, as his preferred genre means that the audience's interpretation is never neutral, for it entails not only sympathy but apprehension, moral judgment, and the possibility of dangerous mistakes, as when audiences trust or condemn the wrong person, or when they identify closely with someone who turns out to be a victim or a criminal. Every story presents more and less sympathetic characters, but in thrillers these characters are innocent and guilty in a technical sense essential to Hitchcock's deceptively two-dimensional moral labels of good guys and bad guys. Throughout Hitchcock's films, every gesture offers an obvious interpretation, but every interpretation is suspect. Under these circumstances, interpretation itself becomes a game which pits wary audiences against the resourceful filmmaker, so that, as in the games of beguilement and outrage, audiences find intensified pleasure simply in following the story.

The fact that so many audiences enjoy Hitchcock's films shows the extent to which Hitchcock's world, like the world of Astaire and Rogers musicals or *Friday the 13th*, establishes rules which make it entertaining after all, but these rules could not be inferred from any single film because Hitchcock repeatedly changes them. In *Sabotage* the first man the camera follows after a crime has been revealed turns out to be the criminal, but in *Frenzy* he turns out to be innocent. *Psycho* begins as if it were going to tell Marion's story, but after her death audiences must recast it as the mystery of the Bates Motel in order to justify their involvement in it. Of course, the process of recasting the story after being deceived provides a new source of pleasure which can in turn be formulated and mastered. In other words, the hallmark of the audience's experience of Hitchcock's world is that its members are made to want to be challenged—to have called into question their expectations about what will happen next and how they should react to it and who is the guilty party and how it will all turn out—so that mastering the challenge becomes an additional source of pleasure, and the challenge itself, like Hitchcock's cameos, finally confirms their sense of each film as part of the Hitchcock world. Although Hitchcock consistently exploits the contractual basis of narrative conventions, the way they establish rules that will make the audience's experience of his films worthwhile, he repeatedly violates the terms of the narrative contract, redefining the terms under which his films are to be followed, understood, and enjoyed. This repeated and pleasurable challenge and redefinition of the narrative contract form the most distinctive feature of Hitchcock's films.

NOTES

1. François Truffaut, *Hitchcock*, rev. ed. (New York: Simon and Schuster, 1984), pp. 158–59.

2. Truffaut, *Hitchcock*, p. 158.

3. Commentators do not agree where Hitchcock is to be found in *Rope*. Truffaut spots him crossing the street after the main title (p. 158), and Maurice Yacowar, *Hitchcock's British Films* (Hamden, Conn.: Archon, 1977) thinks he is present only in the "discussion" of *Notorious* (p. 277).

4. Edward Branigan, *Point of View in the Cinema* (Berlin: Mouton, 1984), pp. 40, 41.

5. Ibid., p. 40.

6. See Yacowar, *Hitchcock's British Films*, pp. 270–78.

7. See Christian Metz, *The Imaginary Signifier: Psychoanalysis and the Cinema*, trans. Celia Britton et al. (Bloomington: Indiana University Press, 1977), pp. 94–95.

8. The bibliography of psychoanalytic (especially Lacanian) approaches to cinema could go on for many pages. The two most influential treatments remain Metz, *Imaginary Signifier*, and Laura Mulvey, "Visual Pleasure and Narrative Cinema," *Screen* 16, no. 3 (Autumn 1975): 6–18.

9. Gaylyn Studlar, *In the Realm of Pleasure: Von Sternberg, Dietrich, and the Masochistic Aesthetic* (Urbana: University of Illinois Press, 1988), p. 182.

10. David Bordwell, *Narration in the Fiction Film* (Madison: University of Wisconsin Press, 1985), pp. 30, 29, 62. Bordwell's model of film viewing is based most explicitly on the work of Helmholtz and the literary theory of the Russian Formalists, but it is closely related to the reader-response criticism of Wolfgang Iser. See Iser, "The Reading Process: A Phenomenological Approach," in *The Implied Reader: Patterns of Communication in Prose Fiction from Bunyan to Becket* (Baltimore: John Hopkins University Press, 1974), pp. 274–94, and *The Act of Reading: A Theory of Aesthetic Response* (Baltimore: John Hopkins University Press, 1978), especially pp. 180–231.

11. Branigan, *Point of View in the Cinema*, p. 174.

12. Wittgenstein's best-known statement of this analogy is in *Philosophical Investigations*, 3d ed., translated by G.E.M. Anscombe (New York: Macmillan, 1958), section 492: "To invent a language could mean to invent an instrument for a particular purpose on the basis of the laws of nature (or consistently with them); but it also has another sense,

analogous to that in which we speak of the invention of a game" (p. 137e). For the importance of the "point" of a game, see section 564 (p.150e).

13. For more on the world movies create, see Leo Braudy, *The World in a Frame: What We See in Films* (Garden City: Doubleday, 1976); and Stanley Cavell, *The World Viewed: Reflections on the Ontology of Film*, enlarged ed. (Cambridge: Harvard University Press, 1979).

14. See Braudy, *World in a Frame*, p. 48, for this distinction.

15. John G. Cawelti has argued that it is indeed a vital function of generic conventions to allow audiences to expose themselves to material that would otherwise be too threatening. See Calwelti, *Adventure, Mystery, and Romance: Formula Stories as Art and Popular Culture* (Chicago: University of Chicago Press, 1976), pp. 17–19.

16. A representative assessment of Hitchcock as a sadistic manipulator, "a poker-faced tease who likes to pinch our nipples," is David Thomson, "The Big Hitch," *Film Comment* 15, no. 2 (March/April 1979): 26–29. See Donald Spoto, *The Dark Side of Genius: The Life of Alfred Hitchcock* (Boston: Little, Brown, 1983), for many examples of Hitchcock's non-cinematic practical jokes on friends and colleagues.

17. Contemporary theories of narrative have often approached the issue of cinematic pleasure in very different terms. Compare for example Roland Barthes's distinction between *plaisir* (rational, calculated pleasure) and *jouissance* (orgasmic bliss) in *The Pleasure of the Text* (1973), trans. Richard Miller (New York: Hill and Wang, 1975), and the psychoanalytic theory of pleasure adopted by Teresa de Lauretis in *Alice Doesn't: Feminism, Semiotics, Cinema* (Bloomington: Indiana University Press, 1984).

18. Hitchcock must have been fond of this auditory pun, for he had already used a similar pun for the discovery of the artist's body in *Blackmail* and would use another one at the corresponding moment in *Young and Innocent*.

CLOSE-UPS

Rape vs. Mans/laughter: *Blackmail*

TANIA MODLESKI

The issue of sexual violence must be central to any feminist analysis of the films of Alfred Hitchcock. In film studies, Hitchcock is often viewed as the archetypal misogynist, who invites his audience to indulge their most sadistic fantasies against the female. Some critics have even argued that Hitchcock's work is prototypical of the extremely violent assaults on women that make up so much of our entertainment today. Thus, Linda Williams has claimed that *Psycho* is the forerunner of the slasher films of the 1970s and 1980s (films like *Halloween* and *Friday the Thirteenth* and their numerous sequels), however superior it may be in aesthetic value to these later films.[1] As might be expected, such films are usually thought to appeal largely to males; women, it is claimed, can enjoy such films only by assuming the position of "masochists."[2] Rape and violence, it would appear, effectively silence and subdue not only the woman *in* the films—the one who would threaten patriarchal law and order through the force of her anarchic desires—but also the women watching the films: female spectators and female critics.

Recent criticism has explored the relation between interpretation in the arts and interpretation in legal discourse. Not surprisingly, analyses like Ronald Dworkin's "Law as Interpretation," while insisting that interpretation is necessarily political, ignore the significance of gender and thereby perpetuate the myth that the legal system is, in Catharine MacKinnon's words, "point-of-viewless" and "universal," that it can incorporate and adjudicate women's experience as fully as it does men's.[3] Women like MacKinnon who wish to expose the partiality of the legal system have done so by focusing on the issue of rape in order to show how interpretation always locates the meaning of the act in the man's point of view. "Under conditions of sex inequality, with perspective bound up with situation, whether a contested interaction is rape comes down to whose meaning wins."[4] I suggest that the question of whose meaning wins is equally pertinent to interpretation in literary and film criticism and that to insist on the very different meaning a given text may have for women is in fact an act of survival of the kind Adrienne Rich believes is always at stake in feminist revisions.[5]

Blackmail (1929) is the story of a shopkeeper's daughter, Alice White, one of the first in a long line of tormented blonde heroines that Hitchcock

Reprinted from *The Women Who Knew Too Much: Hitchcock and Feminist Theory* (NY: Routledge, 1988), 17–30.

featured throughout his career. Our introduction to this character is postponed, however, until the end of the film's lengthy, entirely silent, opening sequence, which shows the capture, interrogation, and booking of a criminal. Following this sequence, shot in quasidocumentary style, the film's detective hero, Frank Webber (John Longden), meets his fiancée, Alice White (Anny Ondra), in the outer rooms of Scotland Yard. Alice is petulant because Frank has kept her waiting for half an hour, but she perks up when a heavy, mustachioed detective whispers something in her ear. She exits laughing, pointedly excluding Frank from the joke, although he valiantly tries to share in the mirth. At the cafe they go to for their date, Alice deliberately picks a quarrel with Frank so that she can keep an assignation she has made with another man, an artist named Crewe (Cyril Ritchard), who at the end of the evening persuades the hesitant Alice to come up to his studio. Their conversation outside the building is punctuated by close-ups of a mysterious man listening intently to hear what they are saying. The man calls to the artist, who explains to Alice that the interloper is a "sponger." Once inside the building, Crewe stops in the foyer and—so much for passionate seduction scenes—checks his mail, queries his landlady about a disturbing note he has received, and finally ascends the staircase with Alice, the camera emphasizing this movement by recording it in a single impressive crane shot from the side of the stairwell. *Blackmail* is one of the first of many Hitchcock films associating a room at the top of the stairs with sexuality and with danger and violence to a woman. There ensues a very curious scene that ends with the artist assaulting Alice, dragging her screaming and struggling to his bed where she finally stabs him to death—an event that occurs offscreen, behind the bed curtains. We simply see her hand reach out and grab a knife conveniently placed near some bread on a night table; then there is an ominous silence, and the artist's lifeless arm falls outside the curtains. Alice sneaks home after an agonized night of wandering the streets and manages to get into bed just before her mother comes up to wake her.

Meanwhile Scotland Yard enters the case, and Frank finds Alice's glove during a search of the studio. When he visits her father's shop, where the family also lives, and takes Alice into the phone booth to talk, the two are surprised by the stranger who was lurking about the studio the night before—a Mr. Tracy (Donald Calthrop). Tracy has found Alice's other glove, and he begins to blackmail the pair, installing himself comfortably at the breakfast table with her puzzled parents. But when Frank learns that Tracy was observed by the artist's landlady the night before and is now Scotland Yard's chief suspect, he gleefully begins to taunt and threaten Tracy despite Alice's protests. There ensues a frantic chase that eventually winds up on the domed roof of the British Museum, where Tracy plunges through a skylight while on the verge of identifying Alice as the killer. The chase is intercut with closeup shots of Alice paralyzed with guilt and fear, and it ends as Alice decides to write a note to Frank declaring her intention to confess, since she cannot bear the thought of an innocent man's suffering for something she has done. When she gets into the office of the Chief Inspector, however, she finds Frank there and before she can disclose the truth, the phone rings, and the inspector instructs Frank to handle the matter. Frank removes her from the office and acknowledges awareness of what she has done; on their way out they encounter the mustachioed detective who ushered Alice in and who laughingly asks Frank, "Well, did she tell you who did it? You want to look out or she'll be losing your job, my boy." The men laugh heartily at the thought of "lady detectives" on the police force, of women usurping male roles and possessing masculine knowledge, and the camera tracks in on Alice visually caught between them, trying to force herself to laugh along. Then, as she catches sight of something out of the frame, her expression sobers, and the final shot of the film shows us what she sees: a picture of a laughing, pointing jester, painted by the murdered artist, that recedes from a closeup view as a detective carries it down the hall.[6]

Even so cursory a summary suggests the extent to which the film, through a classically Hitchcockian "parallel reversal," may be viewed as a "set-up" of the woman, who begins the film by flirtatiously laughing at another man's joke to provoke her lover and ends by standing between two detectives who share a joke at her expense. Here the woman literally and figuratively occupies precisely that place that Freud assigned to women in the structure of the obscene joke: the place of the object between two male subjects.[7] It might be argued that one of the main projects of the film is to wrest power from the woman, in particular the power of laughter, and to give the men the last laugh, thereby defusing the threat of woman's infidelity, her refusal to treat with proper seriousness patriarchal law and authority. Alice's private joke with the second detective is, after all, occasioned by her expecting "the entire machinery of Scotland Yard to be held up to please her," as Frank sarcastically observes. In other words, she unreasonably demands that the law conform to her, instead of accepting the reverse.

It is scarcely accidental that contemporary feminist theory has stressed the subversive potential of woman's laughter, as for example, Hélène Cixous does in "Castration or Decapitation?" where she recounts the parable of the warrior Sun Tse. Instructed by the king to train the king's wives in the arts of war, Sun Tse found that "instead of learning the code very quickly, the ladies started laughing and chattering and paying no attention to the lesson." So he threatened them with decapitation, whereupon they stopped laughing and learned their lessons very well. "Women," concludes Cixous, "have no choice other than to be decapitated, and in any case, the moral is that if they don't actually lose their heads by the sword, *they only keep them on condition that they lose them*—lose them, that is, to complete silence, turned into automatons."[8] If castration is, as Laura Mulvey has persuasively argued, always at stake for the male in classical narrative cinema, then decapitation is at stake for the female—in the cinema as elsewhere. In the scene in the studio, Alice tries to paint a picture on the artist's canvas, and she draws the head of a woman. The artist takes her hand, guiding it to "complete the masterpiece," and draws a nude female body, which Alice then signs, authorizing, as it were, man's view of woman and thereby consenting to the silencing of her own possibly different ideas about herself. Maurice Yacowar writes of this episode, "That routine is a comic miniature of the scene in the studio, the girl having gone to his room for some playful headwork, conversation, but (artists being what they are) finding the body soon forced into play."[9] Thus does the critic, with his little oxymoronic witticism about rape, add his voice to the chorus of male laughter that ends the film.

The nude is only one of two important pictures in *Blackmail*. The second is the jester. In the artist's studio Alice at first laughs at the picture and even points back at it, but after she has stabbed Crewe it seems to accuse her, and she lashes out and tears it. Later, when Frank discovers Alice's glove in the studio, he immediately confronts the jester, who appears to be mocking Frank's cuckoldry. At the end, a realignment has clearly taken place, and the sound of male laughter, Frank's included, accompanies the image of the laughing jester pointing at an Alice who can no longer even smile. According to Yacowar, "the clown is the spirit of corrective comedy, recalling the shrewd, manic wisdom of the jester in *King Lear*. . . . The painting, like its dapper, elegant artist, works as a test of the people it meets. It is the very spirit of irony, seeming innocent but a tricky test of its viewer's moral alertness."[10] Every jester, I suppose, is bound to recall *King Lear*, but in any case, what the Spirit of this jester comically "corrects" is a world in which the female is temporarily in control. If Yacowar is right to see a self-reflexive element in the painting, to see, that is, the artist in the film as a representative of Hitchcock the artist, then by extension, the filmmaker's work of art, *Blackmail*, would be like the painting in the final shot, a cruel but not unusual joke on woman, a joke which the critic retells in his own style.

Commentators have most often praised *Blackmail* for its innovative and creative use of sound. In particular, they have pointed to the breakfast table scene, in which Alice, having stabbed a man to death just hours before, listens to a chattering neighbor deplore the killer's choice of a knife for the murder weapon; the voice becomes a mumble, with only the often repeated word "knife" clearly audible; then with the camera fixed on a closeup of Alice, her father's voice comes on the soundtrack asking her to "cut us a bit of bread." As the voluble neighbor drones on, another closeup shows Alice's hand reaching out hesitantly to pick up the utensil, which she sends flying when the word "knife" suddenly screams out at her. Generally critics of the film content themselves with celebrating the cleverness of such manipulations of sound without discussing its narrative function; they simply admire the way Hitchcock "so masterfully controls [this element] by turning the cinematic screws."[11] And even when they do consider the matter further, they tend to discuss Hitchcock's concern with "the limits and the problems of human communication."[12] What is remarkable to me, however, is that this first British sound film specifically foregrounds the problems of *woman's* speaking.

To begin with, we can cite a historical accident, one that nevertheless profoundly affects the way we experience the film. Since Anny Ondra, the Czech actress who plays Alice, had much too pronounced an accent for the daughter of a British shopkeeper, Hitchcock had another woman, Joan Barry, stand near the camera and say the lines that Ondra mimed. In a way, the film is uncannily prophetic, anticipating all those sound films for decades to come in which women are more spoken than speaking, hysterics reduced to communicating in "body language," to use Yacowar's telling phrase.[13] As Ondra clearly hesitates before each line, listening for her cue, and then accompanies the lines with slightly exaggerated gestures, she does indeed resemble Cixous's "automatons"—a word, moreover, that captures the marionette-like nature of Alice's movements after the murder when she emerges from the bed dazed and "out of herself," holding the knife in what Deborah Linderman notes is a "phallic position."[14] She has, after all, usurped the male prerogative of aggression against the opposite sex.

Further, as we have seen, the film apparently works to reduce Alice to a silent object between two male subjects—and this objectification occurs not just at the end. The film repeatedly places Alice in a triangular relationship with two men: Frank and the artist; the artist and the film's spectator; Frank and the blackmailer; and Frank and the laughing detective. One of the most famous shots occurs in the artist's studio and involves a "split screen" effect: Alice changes clothes on one side of the artist's screen while on the other side Crewe sings and plays the piano with his back to Alice, whose undressing is thus presented pornographically for the sole delectation of the film spectator. As Deborah Linderman observes, woman is here positioned at the point of a triangle "completed by two male sightlines," which subsequently collapse into "a single point of identification" between the male viewer and Crewe. For Linderman, this scene provides evidence for Raymond Bellour's thesis that "in classical cinema the spectator is *always* male."[15]

Alice appears at the point of another triangle later when Frank is gloating over the turned tables in his dealing with the blackmailer. She is seated, quaking, in the foreground of the image, and the blackmailer and Frank stand talking on either side of her in the background. Frank maintains that though Tracy will try to blame the murder on Alice, "our word's as good as, or perhaps a bit better than, that of a jailbird." At one point during the scene the camera cuts to a medium closeup of the blackmailer who says, "When the surprise comes, it won't be for me." There is a pan to Alice, and he continues, "It's my word against hers." Unable to bear it any longer, Alice gets up and goes round to Frank's side, with the camera following, and says, "Frank, you . . . you can't do this"; he tells her to be quiet, and she walks around behind the two men where she is again caught between them as the camera pans back and forth. When Tracy asks, "Why can't you let her speak?" Frank replies, "You mind your own business. And in any case she'll speak at the right moment." Tracy begins to plead and even tries to return the blackmail money, but Frank ignores it. As the camera follows the blackmailer's hand pulling the money back in front of Alice's body, the shot neatly captures her role as object of exchange between males. When Frank continues to disregard Tracy's pleas, Tracy falls back on his previous formula, "All right, then, it's still my word against hers."

But what might Alice say about her situation if she could speak about it? What language adequately describes the episode in the artist's studio? What, in short, *is* the woman's "word" against which the blackmailer pits his own? Lindsay Anderson describes the incident leading to the murder as a seduction;[16] Donald Spoto calls it an act of "violent love" on the part of the artist: "his passion overcomes him and he attempts to make violent love to her."[17] John Russell Taylor characterizes it as "a fairly violent pass."[18] Hitchcock himself uses the word "rape" on one occasion and "seduction" on another, suggesting that for him, as for many men, there's not much difference between the two.[19] Eric Rohmer and Claude Chabrol also speak of rape, but only to introduce a doubt. They write, "He apparently tries to rape her," and they go on to suggest that she gets what she deserves: "To defend her virtue, which one would have thought to be less precious to her, she stabs him with a breadknife."[20] Raymond Durgnat actually subjects Alice to a mock trial; after appearing to consider both sides of the issue, he concludes, "Hitchcock would not have been allowed to show incontrovertible evidence of rape even if he had wanted to so there's room for doubt even on the issue of whether Alice is right in thinking she's being raped rather than merely forcibly embraced."[21] "Forcible embrace" or "violent love": the oxymorons seem to proliferate when rape is the issue. In the court over which he presides Durgnat effectively eradicates the very category of rape (at least as far as the film world is concerned) by ruling that a condition of its legal existence must be the kind of "incontrovertible evidence" that it is illegal to show. Another Alice finds herself in Wonderland. In any case, it is impossible to imagine what would constitute adequate proof for the male critic, since it is a question here of *attempted* rape. The film, after all, does have the artist begin to pull Alice across the room while she screams to be let go, then we see the shadows of their figures projected on the wall as he pushes her into his bed, where the struggle continues until shortly after Alice seizes the knife. Interestingly, since the episode is not presented directly to the spectator's view, it is a question here of accepting the veracity of the woman's words, her expression of protest and fear. As frequently occurs in real life, critics in the main refuse to accept the woman's negative, claiming that Alice unconsciously wishes to be ravished.[22]

Like Frank denying Alice the right to speak, then, the critics seem intent on silencing an interpretation of the film that would adopt the woman's point of view. For the film is indeed susceptible to this kind of interpretation, which, moreover, would not necessarily require reading entirely "against the grain." The very fact that critics resort to such tortuous language and logic to discredit a reading of the film that as yet nobody has proffered suggests that *they* may be the ones who are going against the grain in trying to acquit the artist and convict the woman. John Russell Taylor, who adopts the guise of prosecuting attorney, remarks, "After all, the victim had only taken her up to his apartment (willingly enough on her part) and made a fairly violent pass at her—it would be difficult even to maintain that she killed him while resisting rape. So she would seem to be guilty of at least an unpremeditated panic killing, worse than manslaughter."[23] Like prosecutors in real life, the critics consider the woman's willingness to go with the man sufficient justification for any liberty, however violent, he chooses to take. The question becomes: to what extent does the film share this point of view and make us condemn the woman for her sexual availability? Here it is important to stress that while Alice is nervously flirtatious, she is hardly the one-dimensional vamp of so many films of the period. As a matter of fact, the scene in the artist's studio strikes me as remarkable for its subtle nuances and complexities. First, as even Yacowar unwittingly concedes, Alice is clearly much more interested in "headwork," conversation, with that exotic species of being, the artist, who flatters the shopkeeper's daughter with his attentions. Second, she is persuaded to don the revealing costume by the lure of participating in the artistic process, since Crewe has promised to let her model for him. After she emerges from behind the screen in this outfit, she prances gaily around the room, more like a child playing dress-up than a woman of doubtful virtue.

And if we turn to consider the artist's role, Cyril Ritchard's performance does little to suggest the passionate nature critics continually project onto his character: from the moment Crewe checks his mail in the foyer to the time he sings the jaunty tune, "Miss Up-to-Date," at the piano, while Alice strips behind a screen, his behavior is thoroughly nonchalant. His abrupt violence is all the more startling and disturbing for the contrast it makes to his earlier casual air. Critics have taken the lyrics of the song, which suggest that modern woman has abandoned old-fashioned morality, as further proof of Alice's guilt. But the artist's declaration, "That's a song about you, my dear," clearly points to an alternate reading of the scene. For the artist continually works to *construct* the woman as sexual and hence as responsible for her attack: in the song he sings, in the painting he "helps" her finish, in his gesture of pulling the straps of her costume down from her shoulder—in all these acts, the artist reveals that the sexual woman is a product of male desire and male artistic practice.[24]

The point is, then, that the same scene can elicit very different responses depending on its viewers' experience and values. It is possible for a male critic to celebrate the tendency of art to "force" woman's "body into play," while a feminist critic might see a self-reflexive element here and be led to deplore the way art so easily becomes the alibi for sexual violence against women. Since the scene is presented more or less "objectively"— or, if anything, slightly emphasizes Alice's reactions—a feminist interpretation is available to the female spectator without her necessarily having to adopt the position of "resisting viewer" (to paraphrase Judith Fetterley).[25]

In such an interpretation, moreover, the issue of guilt that critics continually invoke in discussions of Hitchcock films gets inflected very differently. Rohmer and Chabrol write, "*Blackmail* . . . prefigures other aspects of films to come . . . especially, the famous notion of the 'transfer' of guilt, which we see expressed here for the first time in the parallel editing showing on the one hand the blackmailer's desperate flight from the police and on the other, an admirable series of close-ups of the true murderess prostrate in remorse and prayer."[26] Now, of course, whether or not the "transfer" occurs depends on whether or not the woman is guilty in the first place; and the purpose of my analysis has been to challenge the assumption of her guilt by activating a word that is never uttered in the film—and that male critics continually strike from the record—in order to argue that Alice is the victim of an attempted rape (and thus acts in self-defense).

Certainly, however, Alice experiences a great deal of guilt, which is acutely rendered not only in the sequences referred to by Rohmer and Chabrol but in the shots detailing her night of wandering the London streets following the murder. As she walks aimlessly about in a state of shock, shots of passersby are superimposed over her image, lending the objective world around her a ghostly air; the arm of a traffic cop metamorphoses into the arm of the murdered man; a neon sign depicting a gin bottle is transformed into a knife moving up and down. The sign reads "White for Purity" (White is, of course, Alice's surname), and many critics take it to be an ironic commentary on Alice's so-called "panic killing" of a man to defend a purity "which one would have thought to be less precious to her."[27] The scene ends as Alice suddenly comes upon a tramp sprawled in the street with his arm outstretched in the manner of the dead man. Her scream merges into the scream of the landlady who, in the next shot to which Hitchcock abruptly cuts, has just discovered the murdered man.[28] The entire sequence works to draw us deeply into Alice's subjectivity, to make us identify with her anguish and fear (and this empathy is encouraged through and beyond the famous breakfast table scene discussed earlier). An ironic—hence distanced—reading of the "White for Purity" sign thus goes against the grain of the sequence, which suggests rather the extent to which Alice feels sullied and dirtied by her experience. That the experience of sexual violence induces guilt in woman is understandable when we reflect on how patriarchy would convict her not only of murder, but, preeminently, of sexuality as well (we recall Taylor's condemnation of Alice simply for accompanying the artist). Given such attitudes on the part of men, women's guilt over the latter "crime" may easily be as great as over the former—a state of affairs that the film captures by the image of Alice sneaking up to bed in the morning just as she would have if she had been enjoying a love tryst rather than tormentedly walking the streets after having stabbed a man to death. Woman's sexual guilt, a major preoccupation in Hitchcock's films, is obviously not "transferable" to men, and until such sexual asymmetry is recognized the real complexity of the theme of guilt in the films cannot be fully grasped.

The point I wish to stress here is that while on the surface *Blackmail* seems to offer an exemplary instance of Hitchcock's misogyny, his need to convict and punish women for their sexuality, the film, like so many of his other works, actually allows for a critique of the structure it exploits and for a sympathetic view of the heroine trapped within that structure. This means that the female spectator need not occupy either of the two viewing places typically assigned her in feminist film theory: the place of the female masochist, identifying with the passive female character, or the place of the "transvestite," identifying with the active male hero. In an important and influential essay, "Film and the Masquerade: Theorising the Female Spectator," Mary Ann Doane discusses these positions in the light of psychoanalytic theories of femininity. Interestingly for our purposes (since we have been considering *Blackmail* an elaborate joke on woman), Doane offers a visual "joke" as an analogy for the situation of the female spectator at the cinema. Her example is a 1948 photograph by Robert Doisneau, "*Un regard oblique*," in which a man and a woman (the woman centered in the frame) stand before a picture of which we see only the back. The woman is looking intently at the picture, but the man to her left is glancing across to the other side of the frame which reveals the picture of a female nude. Doane remarks, "[N]ot only is the object of [the woman's] look concealed from the spectator, her gaze is encased by the two poles defining the masculine axis of vision. . . . On the other hand, the object of the male gaze is fully present, *there* for the spectator. The fetishistic representation of the nude female body, fully in view, insures a masculinisation of the spectatorial position. The woman's look is literally outside the triangle which traces a complicity between the man, the nude, and the spectator."[29]

Doane proceeds to analyze this photographic joke in the light of Freud's discussion of obscene jokes, which, in contrast to "smut," require the female as object of desire to be absent, while a third party, a man, comes to take the place of the woman and "becomes the person to whom the smut is addressed" (p. 30). Although in *Blackmail*, the question is not consistently one of "smut" or obscenity,[30] nevertheless, there are striking similarities to the situation described by Freud, as Alice, the original addressee of the joke, finds her place ultimately usurped by a man who laughs at a joke told at her expense. It might be tempting to see in *Blackmail* what Doane sees in the Doisneau photograph: a little parable of the female spectator, inevitably excluded from the terms of the film's address. Doane argues that because women cannot "fetishize" and therefore cannot adopt the "distance so necessary for an adequate reading of the image, . . . Doisneau's photograph is not readable by the female spectator—it can give her pleasure only in masochism. In order to 'get' the joke, she must . . . assume the position of transvestite" (p. 87). But are these indeed the only options available to the female spectator?

There seems to me in Doane's formulation a major confusion between the notion of "getting," or reading, a joke and the idea of receiving pleasure from it. While it may be true that in order to derive pleasure from the joke, a woman must be masochistic (we will return to this issue), surely a woman (*as* woman) may at least "get" the joke even if she doesn't appreciate it, just as, say, a Black may comprehend a racist joke without adopting the guise of a white person or assuming the position of masochist. It even seems reasonable to suppose that the oppressed person may see more deeply into the joke than the oppressor is often able or willing to do, as well as into many other situations in which he or she is ridiculed, attacked, or persecuted (we might speculate that Freud's Judaism contributed to his analysis of tendentious jokes). Surely Doane herself in her analysis, or "reading," of the joke is speaking neither as a masochist nor as a man (a transvestite) but as a woman who deeply understands the experience of women's oppression under patriarchy—and not only understands it, but quite rightly resents it. Thus there is at least one response to the joke other than the pleasure of the masochist or the immediate enjoyment of the male spectator, and that response seems to me crucial in theorizing the female spectator: I am referring to the anger that is provoked in the object of a hostile or obscene joke at the moment of "getting" it, even if that anger remains unconscious or is quickly suppressed. In my opinion, feminist film theory has yet to explore and work through this anger, which for women continues to be, as it has been historically, the most unacceptable of all emotions.

As for Doane's denial of pleasure to the female spectator, women are undoubtedly prevented from indulging in the same unreflecting laughter enjoyed by male spectators, but this deprivation is of course hardly a loss and, in any case, other pleasures remain possible. First of all pleasure is involved in analysis itself, in understanding how the joke works even when it works against women. In the context of a study like Doane's, the joke may actually become a source of feminist humor or make a feminist point by itself. Shoshana Felman has shown how a change in modes of address may transform the objects of laughter into subjects. At a feminist conference Felman repeated Freud's witty exclusion of women from his examination of femininity, and in doing so she elicited laughter from her largely female audience, thereby demonstrating the power of recontextualization.[31] Similarly, I think of my study here as a contribution to the development of female subjectivity in that it analyzes in the context of a feminist inquiry the works of the filmmaker whom some would call the greatest practical joker as well as the greatest misogynist.

Secondly, one can find pleasure in acknowledging and working through one's anger, especially when that anger has long been denied or repressed. This is a pleasure Hitchcock's films repeatedly make available to women. It has long been noted that the director is obsessed with exploring the psyches of tormented and victimized women. While most critics attribute this interest to a sadistic delight in seeing his leading ladies suffer,[32] and while I am even willing to concede this point, I would nevertheless insist that the obsession often takes the form of a particularly lucid exposé of the predicaments and contradictions of women's existence under patriarchy. We have already touched upon the ways *Blackmail* may be read—"got" or interpreted—by women. It shows, for example, the dilemma of women continually charged with sexual guilt even when they are the victims of male violence. And it shows women reduced to objects in men's relations with each other.[33] A recurring, almost archetypal shot in Hitchcock's films focuses on the heroine trapped between a figure of the law and one of lawlessness—in *Blackmail*, between Frank, the lover/detective, and Tracy, the blackmailer. This placement and the woman's discomfort indicate that *both* men are threatening to her, that she is caught within a structure that needs her to ensure "human communication" (men's dealings with other men, as Lévi-Strauss has theorized them), but at the price of negating her own language and experience. Hitchcock's films have the merit of revealing woman's status as radically outside the law: on the one hand, she is not like the blackmailer, a criminal who can be readily named and identified as such, despite Rohmer and Chabrol's suggestion of the psychic interchangeability of the two. On the other hand, patriarchal law can hardly consider her innocent, nor can it possibly offer her real justice, since its categories precisely exclude her experience—an exclusion to which the critics we have quoted amply bear witness as they strain the limits of patriarchal discourse in order to subdue the truth of this experience.

It is a commonplace in discussions of Hitchcock's films that even though the director may be considered a stern moralist, he nevertheless continually exhibits a profound distrust and fear of the forces of the law. This attitude potentially places him in a sympathetic relation to his outlaw heroines. Obviously it is not necessary to assume conscious intention on the director's part; as a matter of fact, there is virtually decisive evidence that Hitchcock was oblivious to the interest and sympathy he created for his heroine. In a discussion of the art of film direction, for instance, Hitchcock gave the following précis of *Blackmail*'s plot:

> Imagine an example of a standard plot—let us say a conflict between love and duty. This idea was the origin of my first talkie, *Blackmail*. The hazy pattern one saw beforehand was duty—love—love vs. duty. . . . I had first to put on the screen an episode expressing duty. . . . I showed the arrest of a criminal by Scotland Yard detectives and tried to make it as concrete and detailed as I could. You even saw the detectives take the man to the lavatory to wash his hands—nothing exciting, just the routine of duty. Then the young detective says he's going out that evening with his girl: They are middle-class people. The love theme doesn't run smoothly; there is a quarrel and the girl goes off by herself, just because the young man has kept her waiting a few minutes. So your story starts; the girl falls in with the villain—he tries to seduce her and she kills him. Now you've got your problem prepared. Next morning, as soon as the detective is put onto the murder case, you have your conflict—love versus duty. The audience know that he will be trying to track down his own girl, who has done the murder, so you sustain their interest: They wonder what will happen next.[34]

Aside from the inaccuracies of plot, this description, repeated by some critics, distorts the film's psychological and emotional interests, which are centered in Alice, not the detective. In fact, the film is so strongly invested in the heroine and her conflicts that Frank becomes almost a secondary character, or, perhaps more accurately, a symbolic embodiment *of* these conflicts. In her room after the murder, Alice looks up at the wall and sees a photograph of Frank in his policeman's uniform staring down at her: the shot vividly and poignantly conveys the conflict between love and pride, on the one hand, and shame, guilt, and especially fear, on the other. The conflict continues to be the focus of the film's interest—for example, at the breakfast table, shortly after the knife episode, when the camera lingers on a closeup of Alice and, in the words of John Longden, "the ring of the shop-door bell [is] lengthened and magnified like a note of doom."[35] Interestingly, Longden incorrectly remembers this as the moment when the blackmailer enters the shop, but the fact that it is Frank who slowly and inexorably enters the frame while Alice stands behind the counter waiting for her fate to be sealed, that it is Frank who, as her future husband and the representative of law and justice, signals the heroine's doom, makes the scene much more ironic.

Indeed, throughout the film, Hitchcock continually points an accusatory finger at the law in general and Frank in particular, indicating both their lack of human compassion and their complicity in the criminality to which they are theoretically opposed. The dissolve in the opening sequence from the criminal's face in closeup to a gigantic finger print is one such instance of Hitchcock's sarcastic treatment of the police, as is the later cut from the chief inspector wringing his hands to the blackmailer performing the same gesture at the Whites' breakfast table. In the context of such round condemnations of the penal system, Hitchcock's decision to cut away from Alice during the rape scene to a high-angle shot of the policeman below, walking his beat in total oblivion (a shot that repeats an earlier one taken from Alice's point of view), suggests a sympathy for and possible identification with the imperiled woman. Finally, Frank himself becomes strongly implicated in the film's critique of the law. Immediately upon discovering that Scotland Yard is after Tracy for the murder of the artist, Frank begins to taunt, threaten, and abuse the suspect, knowing full well, as he later admits, that Alice, not Tracy, has killed Crewe. Frank, then, is morally responsible for the death of a man innocent of the crime for which he is unofficially executed.

The ironies in *Blackmail* are, finally, much more subtle and prolific than those Hitchcock originally intended. He wanted to end the film with Alice being apprehended, and Frank, in the washroom as he was in the beginning, being asked by a fellow detective, "Are you going out with your girl tonight?" to which he would respond, "No, not tonight." Again, the actual film displaces Frank as the center of interest to focus on Alice and her predicament—a predicament that renders ironic both the film's title and its "happy" ending, and does so, moreover, from the woman's point of view. It hints, as *Marnie* will do years later and much more strongly, that the bond linking the man and the woman is his knowledge of her guilty secret (guilty, that is, in patriarchal terms), that the union is founded on the man's ability to blackmail the woman sexually.[36]

As for the last shot, which seems to point the finger directly at Alice, as the jester is carried down the hall (the nude portrait on the reverse side) thus suggesting the collusion of the director and audience with the male characters, my interpretation of the film has been meant to elicit other possible readings of this ending. In particular, we note that the film withholds the reverse shot which would confirm the sense that it is Alice at whom the joke is aimed. Without the reverse shot, it is as if the spectator himself becomes the final butt of the film's humor: perhaps that very male spectator to whom all classical cinema is supposedly addressed, he who thinks himself secure in his masculine identity, at one with the other male figures in the film. My concern has been, in part, to show the extent to which the film undermines patriarchal law and creates sympathy for and an identification with the female outlaw. It is precisely the possibility of such an identification that is the source of so much desire and so much dread in so many Hitchcock films to come.

NOTES

1. See Linda Williams, "When the Woman Looks," *Re-vision: Essays in Feminist Film Criticism*, ed. Mary Ann Doane, Patricia Mellencamp, and Linda Williams, The American Film Institute Monograph series. Vol.3 (Frederick, MD: University Publications of America, 1984), p. 96.

2. This, as we shall see, is part of Mary Ann Doane's argument in "Film and the Masquerade: Theorising the Female Spectator," *Screen* 23, nos. 3–4 (September–October 1982): 80. Doane is drawing on Laura Mulvey's discussion, "Afterthoughts on 'Visual Pleasure and Narrative Cinema,' Inspired by *Duel in the Sun*," *Framework* 15/16/17 (Summer 1981): 13.

3. Ronald Dworkin, "Law as Interpretation," in *The Politics of Interpretation*, ed. W.J.T. Mitchell (Chicago: University of Chicago Press, 1983), pp. 249–70. Catharine MacKinnon, "Feminism, Marxism, Method, and the State: Toward Feminist Jurisprudence," *Signs* 8, no. 4 (Summer 1983): 639.

4. MacKinnon, "Feminism, Marxism, Method," p. 652.

5. Adrienne Rich, "When We Dead Awaken: Writing as Re-vision," in *On Lies, Secrets, and Silence: Selected Prose 1966–1978* (New York: Norton, 1979), p. 35. "Re-vision—the act of looking back, of seeing with fresh eyes, of entering an old text from a new critical direction—is for women more than a chapter in cultural history: it is an act of survival. "

6. Hitchcock shot this film twice—once as a silent film and then again as a sound film. For an interesting discussion of the slight differences in the two texts, see Charles Barr, "*Blackmail*: Silent and Sound " *Sight and Sound* 52. no. 5 (1983): 189[-}93.

7. Sigmund Freud, *Jokes and Their Relation to the Unconscious*, trans. James Strachey (New York: Norton, 1960), p. 99.

8. Hélène Cixous, "Castration or Decapitation?" trans. Annette Kuhn, *Signs* 7, no. 1 (Autumn 1981): 42–43. See also Judith Mayne's discussion of Demeter's laughter as an "emblem of what the rethinking of spectacle might entail" for feminist film theory. "The Limits of Spectacle," *Wide Angle* 6, no. 3 (1984): 15.

9. Maurice Yacowar, *Hitchcock's British Films* (Hamden, CT: Archon, 1977), p. 110.

10. Yacowar, *Hitchcock's British Films*, p. 111.

11. Donald Spoto, *The Dark Side of Genius: The Life of Alfred Hitchcock* (New York: Ballantine, 1983), p. 133.

12. Yacowar, *Hitchcock's British Films*, p. 103. Beverle Houston and Marsha Kinder also pursue this line in their analysis of the film. See their *Close-Up* (New York: Harcourt Brace Jovanovich, 1972), pp. 52–58.

13. Yacowar, *Hitchcock's British Films*, p. 108.

14. Deborah Linderman, "The Screen in Hitchcock's *Blackmail*," *Wide Angle* 4, no. 1 (1980): 26.

15. Linderman, "The Screen," p. 25.

16. Lindsay Anderson, "Alfred Hitchcock," in *Focus on Hitchcock*, ed. Albert J. LaValley (Englewood Cliffs: Prentice-Hall, 1972), p. 50.

17. Donald Spoto, *The Art of Alfred Hitchcock* (New York: Doubleday, 1976), p. 19.

18. John Russell Taylor, *Hitch* (London: Faber and Faber, 1978), p. 100.

19. François Truffaut, *Hitchcock* (New York: Simon and Schuster, 1983), p. 63; and Alfred Hitchcock, "Direction," in *Focus on Hitchcock*, p. 33.

Hitchcock listens in on Alice (Anny Ondra) in *Blackmail*

Photo Collection of Ronald Gottesman

Scottie (James Stewart) rescues Madeleine Elster/Judy Barton (Kim Novak) in *Vertigo*

Photo Collection of Ronald Gottesman

Curious Couples

Dev (Cary Grant) regards Alicia (Ingrid Bergman) suspiciously in *Notorious*: " . . . Alicia is defined as the object of the gaze, Dev encoded as the source of the look" (Michael Renov)

Photo Collection of Ronald Gottesman

Jeff (James Stewart) directs his male gaze at Lisa (Grace Kelly) in *Rear Window*

Photo Collection of Ronald Gottesman

Alice (Anny Ondra) framed by Frank, her detective/lover (John Longden) and Tracy, the blackmailer (Donald Calthrop), in *Blackmail*: " . . . the film apparently works to reduce Alice to a silent object between two male subjects" (Tania Modleski)

Photo Collection of Ronald Gottesman

Ann (Edna Wonacott) framed by the disinterested detective Saunders (Wallace Ford) and her sister's detective/lover Jack (MacDonald Carey) in *Shadow of a Doubt*

Photo Collection of Ronald Gottesman

Terror in Unexpected Places

Roger (Cary Grant) in the cornfield in *North by Northwest*

Photo Collection of Ronald Gottesman

Norman Bates (Anthony Perkins) in Cabin One in *Psycho*

Photo Collection of Ronald Gottesman

20. Eric Rohmer and Claude Chabrol, *Hitchcock: The First Forty-Four Films* (New York: Ungar, 1979), p. 20.

21. Raymond Durgnat, *The Strange Case of Alfred Hitchcock, Or the Plain Man's Hitchcock* (Cambridge: MIT Press, 1974), p. 88. While Durgnat's analysis purports to explore the moral ambiguity of the film and while he even concludes that Alice experiences too much guilt relative to the other characters, nevertheless such remarks as the one I have quoted indicate his confusion about the issue of rape that he treats in such a high-handed manner. And like Hitchcock, he too appears to use the words "rape" and "seduction" interchangeably.

22. See, for example, Elizabeth Weis, *The Silent Scream: Alfred Hitchcock's Sound Track* (East Brunswick, N.J.: Fairleigh Dickinson University Press, 1982), pp. 28–59. Weis's discussion of the film is heavily influenced by male critics and is even more emphatic than many of them in its insistence that the woman is subconsciously inviting her own rape.

23. Taylor, *Hitch*, p. 100.

24. See Kaja Silverman's analysis of *Histoire d'O* for an extensive demonstration of how a text works to construct the sexualized woman. "*Histoire d'O*: The Construction of a Female Subject," *Pleasure and Danger: Exploring Female Sexuality*, ed. Carole S. Vance (London: Routledge & Kegan Paul, 1984), pp. 320–49.

25. I am referring, of course, to Judith Fetterley's book, *The Resisting Reader: A Feminist Approach to American Fiction* (Bloomington: Indiana University Press, 1978). Daniel Cottom forcefully makes the point about interpretation that I am stressing: "No way of reading is wrong in itself; it can only be declared wrong under specific political conditions, which therefore must be treated as the subject of sociohistorical differences within any literary [or film] theory that would not blindly identify itself with an imaginary law." "The Enchantment of Interpretation," *Critical Inquiry* 11, no. 4 (June 1985): 580. Interestingly, Cottom focuses in his essay on the interpretation of jokes. He cites the following example: "Why do women have vaginas? So men will talk to them," and points out that this joke may be "brutally sexist, cynically feminist, or something else entirely," depending on the context in which it is told (p. 576). A joke in Yvonne Rainer's film, *The Man Who Envied Women*, illustrates this point. The joke, told by one woman to another as they sit in a restaurant, is as follows: "A man is a human being with a pair of testes attached, whereas a woman is a vagina with a human being attached." In the context of Rainer's film, what might in other situations be locker-room humor becomes "cynically feminist," as are many of the other jokes in the film.

26. Rohmer and Chabrol, *Hitchcock: The First Forty-Four Films*, p. 23.

27. See also Spoto, *The Art of Alfred Hitchcock*, p. 20: "This White girl is certainly for purity. She even kills for it!"

28. Given this merger of the voices of Alice and the landlady, it is interesting to consider that it is the landlady—another woman—who is unwittingly responsible for Alice's ultimate escape from patriarchal "justice."

29. Doane, "Film and the Masquerade," p. 85. Hereafter cited in the text.

30. In any case, Samuel Weber has pointed out that the distinction between obscene jokes and aggressive jokes cannot be strictly maintained. *The Legend of Freud* (Minneapolis: University of Minnesota Press, 1982), p. 103.

31. Freud wrote, "Throughout history people have knocked their heads against the riddle of the nature of femininity. . . . Nor will *you* have escaped worrying over this problem—those of you who are men; to those of you who are women this will not apply—you are yourselves the problem." Quoted in Shoshana Felman, "Rereading Femininity," *Yale French Studies*, no. 62 (1981): 19.

32. Spoto's biography, *The Dark Side of Genius*, dwells on this obsession in fascinated and obsessive detail.

33. For a discussion of interpretive triangles in literary theory, see Mary Jacobus, "Is There a Woman in This Text?" *New Literary History* 14, no 1 (Autumn 1982): 117–42; and

for a discussion of triangles in literature, see Eve Kosofsky Sedgwick, *Between Men: English Literature and Male Homosocial Desire* (New York: Columbia University Press, 1985). An interesting analysis of Samuel Richardson's *Clarissa* in terms of the issues of rape and the silencing of women may be found in Terry Castle, *Clarissa's Ciphers: Meaning and Disruption in Richardson's Clarissa* (Ithaca: Cornell University Press, 1982).

34. Hitchcock, "Direction," pp. 32–33.

35. Quoted in Spoto, *The Dark Side of Genius*, p. 133.

36. Alexander Welsh considers this possibility in his analysis of the film in *George Eliot and Blackmail* (Cambridge: Harvard University Press, 1985).

Keeping Your Amateur Standing:
Audience Participation and Good Citizenship in Hitchcock's Political Films

INA RAE HARK

In *Foreign Correspondent* (1940) reporter Johnny Jones scornfully remarks to Carol Fisher about the Universal Peace Party, headed by her father, Stephen Fisher, "What is it that makes him or you think that an organization like this made up of well-meaning amateurs can buck up against those tough military boys of Europe?" Stung, Carol later departs from the text of her speech at the Party's banquet to inquire, "I should like to ask anyone who has called us well-meaning amateurs to stand up by his chair and tell us why a well-meaning amateur is any less reliable than a well-meaning professional at a moment like this." The film situates these remarks in a context of profound irony, since it subsequently emerges that, unknown to Carol, the Universal Peace Party is a front for an espionage organization run by decidedly ill-meaning professionals. Though they are misapplied, Carol's sentiments are nevertheless validated when the amateur foreign correspondent Jones, a simple reporter with "a fresh unused mind," thwarts the spies' efforts to obtain information vital to Germany in the imminent hostilities of the second World War.

Although *Foreign Correspondent* is the first Hitchcock film to articulate it in explicit terms, this ideology of the amateur had operated in the director's political thrillers from their inception. The contrast between amateur and professional had been a key element in the British spy thrillers of the teens and twenties, including those novels by "Sapper" and John Buchan that inspired Hitchcock's first two spy films, *The Man Who Knew Too Much* (1934) and *The 39 Steps* (1935)[1]; but in working the contrast out over his career, Hitchcock transformed it into his own model of the political relationship between citizen and government in a democracy. Repeated sequences in the political films portray an audience, in which the amateur sits, and a performance or lecture that the professional enemies of democracy control or manipulate. A detailed analysis of such sequences in *The Man Who Knew Too Much* and *The 39 Steps* will constitute a major portion of this essay; other cases occur in the *Foreign Correspondent* banquet; Mrs. Sutton's charity ball in *Saboteur* (1942); the auction in *North by Northwest* (1959); and the ballet in *Torn Curtain* (1966). These recurrent

Reprinted from *Cinema Journal* 29, 2 (Winter 1990), 8–22. Copyright © University of Illinois Press.

sequences work out a linkage between good citizenship and a particular kind of audience participation, as contrasted with the passive behavior of silent or easily led spectators, who represent a populace ripe for totalitarian subjugation.

Deriving this figure of the good citizen-amateur as inscribed in Hitchcock's films requires a positioning of this figure within the intersecting cultural and textual codes, and the historical moment, of its first production. That moment encompasses the years 1934 through 1938 in England, during which five of the six films Hitchcock directed were spy thrillers, with all but one (*The Lady Vanishes*, 1938) produced for Gaumont British by Michael Balcon and Ivor Montagu and scripted (partially or totally) by Charles Bennett. The five films derived from the major strains of the British espionage novel of the early twentieth century: Sapper (*The Man Who Knew Too Much* began as a scenario called *Bulldog Drummond's Baby*); Buchan (*The 39 Steps*); Somerset Maugham's "Ashenden" stories (*The Secret Agent*, 1936); Joseph Conrad's *The Secret Agent* (*Sabotage*, 1936); and the Graham Greene-Eric Ambler "innocent abroad" model (*The Lady Vanishes*). After Fritz Lang's *Spione* was released in 1927, the thriller had become a popular cinematic as well as literary genre. The films of Conrad Veidt, according to Patricia Ferrara, brought the genre "most notably" into the English cinema. Ferrara goes on to observe that "Hitchcock's renewed Gaumont period, and the increasingly negative reception of Hitchcock's more downbeat B.I.P. films from 1930 to 1933, were also influential in pushing Hitchcock into light spy thrillers. Once he began making them, the public and critical enthusiasm for his output kept him working in the genre."[2]

Since Hitchcock had planned to film at least the first two projects before rejoining Balcon's production company, it is hard to say how much Balcon's involvement from the beginning of the series really shaped the films or their political ideology. At the very least, he gave Hitchcock the opportunity to explore politics and encouraged him to continue in this vein when the first two films became such stunning international successes. But to separate Hitchcock's contributions from those of Balcon, Montagu, or Bennett, to the construction of the protagonist in these spy thrillers is impossible, and probably irrelevant. Suffice it to say that out of their collaboration emerged this figure of the citizen-amateur, a figure that would persist in other Hitchcock films long after the director left his collaborators and England behind.

In a broader cultural sense, the citizen-amateur of Hitchcock's films was produced by the operations on the popular literary thriller of personal, political, and historical factors. Hitchcock's admiration for and familiarity with literary thrillers is well-documented. His original idea for *The Man Who Knew Too Much* stemmed from a wish to create a kidnapping plot as an original story into which to insert the Bulldog Drummond character, who had already received four screen treatments, including a big-budget 1929 American version from Samuel Goldwyn, starring Ronald Colman. John Russell Taylor reports that the filming of *The 39 Steps* enabled Hitchcock to realize "a long-standing ambition, since Buchan was one of his favourite writers and he had already toyed with the idea of filming an even more elaborate Buchan subject, *Greenmantle*."[3] In this taste, Hitchcock revealed himself typical of his class and gender, for as Michael Denning reports, "The early thriller of Wallace, Buchan, and Sapper was the basic reading stock of working-class and lower-middle-class men and boys."[4] Furthermore, Hitchcock related his boyhood experience of reading thrillers to the formation of his political attitudes. In a 1973 interview with Joyce Haber, Hitchcock remarked: "I remember reading John Buchan's '39 Steps' in my teens. Maybe that instilled fear in me—fear of policemen."[5]

By 1934, when Hitchcock was shooting his first political film, Britons had ample reasons to be more conscious than usual of international politics in fact rather than fiction, and their confidence in the ability of their governmental institutions to deal effectively with external threats had undergone stringent testing. The ramifications of the worldwide Depression had precipitated the financial crisis of 1931 and the subsequent formation of the coalition National Government. Despite the furor caused by Ramsay MacDonald's apparent betrayal of his Labour constituents, the National Government did stave off the economic catastrophe whose threat had brought it into being. The electorate would decisively return the government to power in the general elections of 1935.

Overshadowing the consequences of the Depression in the mid-thirties, however, were fears of another war. Patrick Kyba notes that "disillusionment with war and fear of its weaponry led many in Britain to seek a new method of preserving the peace. They turned from traditional diplomacy to the world forum and looked to Geneva rather than the Foreign Office to prevent the outbreak of another war."[6] English public opinion at the beginning of the decade strongly opposed rearmament. Many hoped that the Geneva Disarmament Conference, which met from 2 February 1932, until 8 June 1934, would serve as a principal instrument in bringing about a lasting peace. These same persons had criticized the National Government for impeding the Conference's aims by not committing itself to unilateral disarmament. Yet when Germany left the conference on 14 October 1933, and openly accelerated its already substantial clandestine rearmament, sentiments shifted. The Government began a modest rearmament program, concentrated on the Air Force, because "the fear of aerial bombardment in inter-war Britain was unprecedented and unique."[7] In November 1933 the Committee on Imperial Defence had "instructed its supply officers to plan for a hypothetical war within five years."[8] By 1935 Mussolini's invasion of Abyssinia had further demonstrated that if British parliamentary democracy might not suffice to keep the world free from war, the international pacifism of the League of Nations held out little better hope for achieving that goal.

The international situation during that inter-war period that William McElwee has dubbed "Britain's locust years"[9] created a climate of uncertainty that gave the ideology of the literary thriller continuing and widening appeal in British popular culture. Yet the thriller itself was changing in the thirties, and Hitchcock's adaptations of the older Sapper and Buchan traditions reflect this change. The protagonists, as Denning observes, were transformed from "the enthusiastic and willing amateur that [Buchan's] Hannay is" to "an incompetent and inexperienced amateur in a world of professionals" similar to the central figures of the thrillers that Eric Ambler began writing in the late thirties; he notes that "the entangled innocent is a favorite character of Hitchcock's film thrillers, particularly *The Lady Vanishes* (1938)."[10] (Ambler in fact became a close friend of Hitchcock's when he married the director's valued production associate Joan Harrison; Hitchcock wrote the introduction to a 1943 anthology of Ambler's fiction, *Intrigue*.)

The Hitchcockian amateur thus synthesizes the Buchan and Ambler models. He is nevertheless a figure distinct from either. The "heroic amateur" or "clubland hero" such as Bulldog Drummond or Richard Hannay— the descriptive tags are Denning's and Richard Usborne's—is amateur in the sense that the English gentleman is always amateur. His are the ethics of the public school, the playing field, and the colonial administrator. He works as an independent contractor who can help out the official espionage network at need. Drummond has his own semi-professional, spy-catching organization. Although Buchan's Hannay, like Hitchcock's, is initially enmeshed innocently in the intrigue and has to pursue the spies in order to clear his name, he achieves that goal halfway through *The 39 Steps*; his subsequent adventures in that and the other Hannay novels find him a more detached associate of Walter Bullivant of the Foreign Office.

The majority of Hitchcock's amateurs, on the other hand, become involved in intrigue only because it touches them personally. And once the amateurs have extricated themselves from the web of plot and counterplot, they get out of the business. This distinguishes the novel and film versions of Richard Hannay; a similar distinction results from the writing out of Drummond from the final version of *The Man Who Knew Too Much*. As John Russell Taylor notes, "*The Man Who Knew Too Much*, of course, was the final form of *Bulldog Drummond's Baby*, reworked so that all reference to the Sapper character was removed; the hero, though basically the same gentlemanly type, was even more of an amateur at this kind of intrigue."[11] Those Hitchcock spy films in which the protagonists more closely resemble the semi-professional clubland hero usually present their victories as much more morally ambiguous than those of Richard Hannay or the Lawrences (see, for example, *The Secret Agent*, *Notorious*, *Torn Curtain*, *Topaz*).

Therefore the "pure" amateurs in the first two thrillers function neither as needed adjuncts to the professionals nor as helpless victims whom the professionals must bail out. They are simply people whose opposition, usually aroused by chance, prevents the enemy professionals from damaging the security of the state. Hitchcock's protagonists frequently find their own freedoms and welfare threatened, while the guardians of democracy are either unable to help or have unwittingly joined the ranks of democracy's enemies. Philip Dynia sums up the situation well: "In Hitchcock's more obviously political films, the state fails miserably to protect ordinary individuals suddenly involved in utterly irrational and potentially fatal machinations. Hitchcock's heroes must rely on their own strengths if they are to be vindicated, let alone survive."[12]

What kind of counter-politics, if any, evolves in these films? Critical opinion remains divided. Ferrara, for example, believes that Hitchcock's political films always refuse to take sides on the issues and that the director "was dead right about the esthetic propriety of leaving politics in the background and avoiding confrontation."[13] Conversely, Sam Simone sees Hitchcock as a political activist on behalf of democracy, going so far as to interpret the Statue of Liberty in *Saboteur* as "Hitchcock becom[ing] Mr. Liberty carrying the torch."[14] Biography lends support to Ferrara's position in that Hitchcock resolutely refused to involve himself with politics in his public life. Taylor frequently comments on Hitchcock's "resolutely nonpolitical" stance: "He carefully avoided getting involved in anything connected with politics—he even refused, much to the left-wing Ivor Montagu's disappointment, to become president of the screen technicians union, the A.C.T.T., when in 1936 they decided to put their house in order and become a force to reckon with in the industry, and wanted someone of Hitch's eminence to lend his support in a prominent way."[15] Nevertheless the film texts do generate certain political attitudes that vindicate Simone's position, if not the extreme rhetoric with which he states it.

First, the films do advocate what I would term the "promised results" that democratic governments profess to ensure for their citizens: freedom of expression, protection of individual rights from authoritarian suppression, the creature comforts produced by the workings of bourgeois capitalism. Hitchcock does not transmit any of the implicit fascism that permeates the Sapper and Buchan novels. He does, however, as Philip Dynia indicates, lack faith totally in institutionalized and bureaucratized democratic government as an instrument for generating these promised results. For Hitchcock, democracy as an institution cannot guarantee its benefits to the individual unless the individual actively works to retain them. Yet, conversely, achieving the goals of individual survival often results in the preservation of the democratic society. The Hitchcock heroes, while extricating themselves from the web of political intrigue through their own amateur efforts, accomplish a simultaneous defeat of those seeking to undermine the state. John M. Smith has aptly designated the resultant political philosophy as one of "conservative individualism."[16]

Yet the individual does not succeed alone. The majority of other ordinary citizens can tell innocent from guilty, patriots from fifth columnists, if only the amateur protagonist makes them aware of the options. They frequently then help him to elude capture and defeat democracy's enemies. While the Capraesque, populist rhetoric about the regular folks uniting to help each other destroy the totalitarian threat, which Barry Kane spouts in *Saboteur*, seems stylistically out of key for a Hitchcock film, it is ideologically appropriate. It precisely describes, for instance, the plot of the director's only non-espionage political film, *Lifeboat*. His British and American films alike ridicule representative democracy—elected politicians are as useless as bureaucrats—but endorse participatory democracy. The analogy with audience participation therefore follows logically.

The Hitchcock political film employs spectatorship as one metaphor by which to delineate the perils for citizens who are content to sit quietly in the audience while the spectacle of world affairs unfolds before them. By their position as spectators, citizens may discern dangers to which active government professionals are blind. Because the government acts but does not see, spectators who see must eventually act. Events invariably force them to engage in audience participation if they are not to forfeit their own safety or that of their loved ones.

I will examine the beginnings of this phenomenon, as depicted in *The Man Who Knew Too Much* (1934) and in its successor, *The 39 Steps* (1935), by focusing on the portrayal of audiences within the films who attend formal performances depicted onscreen. Both films climax with sequences in which an amateur's disruptive interjection from the audience foils the aims of armed enemy agents whom the British police and Foreign Office professionals, on guard in the house, fail to discern. In both shooting sequences a shout mingles with a gunshot, and this interaction occurs several other times throughout the films. The actions that constitute these sequences demonstrate the extent to which the polite forms of complacent democratic societies suppress the free expression of ideas that democracy ostensibly encourages; the shout is both a warning of the dangers of such strictures *and* an illustration of the necessity of violating them if democracy is to endure. The behavior that circumstances demand of the filmed spectators is implicitly a model for that of the spectators watching the film in acting out their own roles as citizens.

Hitchcock's films have been a *locus classicus* for discussions of film spectatorship. Stephen Heath begins his essay on narrative space with an example from *Suspicion*.[17] Kaja Silverman refers to *Psycho* in her discus sion of suture in *The Subject of Semiotics*.[18] Laura Mulvey's seminal essay on "Visual Pleasure and Narrative Cinema" uses *Vertigo* as a test case.[19] William Rothman's booklength study of the director focuses on the "murderous gaze" posited in Hitchcock's *oeuvre*. These and countless other analyses demonstrate that the Hitchcockian cinema concerns itself excessively with positioning the viewing subject as complicitous with the narration and reducing the subject's power to break that identification even as the speaking subject becomes more and more venal.

This positioning of the film's viewer as guilty, voyeuristic spectator corresponds to the positioning of the acquiescent audience member within the film as bad citizen. The parallel also implies a correlation between the totalitarian manipulators of audiences within the films and the filmmaker as manipulator of the film's audience. This parallel is not, I believe, coincidental. Although Hitchcock in the shout sequences avoids using audiences viewing films[20] in favor of those viewing live performances under the direction of some authority figure (symphony conductor, master of ceremonies, clergyman), this does not diminish the implications for the film's spectators. The shift simply foregrounds for the viewers their subjection to the cinematic apparatus as controller of the narration. Because Hitchcock could so easily bend his audiences to his cinematic will, he had considerable concern about the ease with which dictators could trick free citizens out of their democratic rights. Taylor reports that Peter Viertel, the screenwriter for *Saboteur*, had the native-born fascist Tobin refer to the American people as "the moron masses" because that was "a pet term of Hitch's to describe his audience."[21] Just as *Saboteur*'s protagonist works to arouse those masses to protect themselves from totalitarian domination, so the political films challenge citizens to break suture and disrupt those performances designed to lull them into complacent reliance upon authority.[22]

In *The Man Who Knew Too Much*, complacency about international relations is mirrored by the complacency, bordering on bored resentment, expressed by Bob and Jill Lawrence about their stable family life. Their banter expresses a desire to rid themselves of the presence of their adolescent daughter, Betty. Chief among Betty's annoying traits is that she is a disruptive spectator. The film begins as she darts from the audience at a downhill skiing competition to rescue a dog, thus toppling Louis Bernard and literally throwing the Lawrences, the "good" spies, and the "bad" spies together. Next, her excited chatter about being allowed to stay up late draws repeated shushings from the audience at the shooting match between her mother and Ramon. Although it is the chief spy Abbott's musical watch that actually spoils Jill's aim, she blames her loss on her daughter's distractiveness. "Let that be a lesson to you; never have children," Jill complains, only half jokingly. The parents' subconscious wish is barely articulated before it is granted: because the family has stumbled into the political entanglements that are the profession of these seemingly amateur sportsmen, Betty is kidnapped. To regain her, which is to recommit themselves to the idea of having a child and being a family, Bob and Jill must in fact follow their daughter's lead by becoming ill-behaved spectators and learning to resist the pressures of the grown-up world to remain silent no matter how fraudulent—or dangerous—a performance is going on before them.

Throughout the film, indications that the enemies of freedom depend upon silencing or covering up the voices of ordinary citizens are everywhere. The doors leading into the dentist's office and the spies' hideout are soundproofed. Our first glimpse of Betty after she is kidnapped shows Ramon's hand covering her mouth. (Abbott later praises her as "quiet as a little mouse.") The point of the kidnapping itself is of course to keep the Lawrences quiet. Conversely, the spies are preoccupied with disguising the socially disruptive sound of gunfire that their plots entail with the socially-sanctioned sound of music. This procedure occurs not only in the Albert Hall assassination attempt but in the ballroom when Louis is killed and when the organist plays at the Tabernacle of the Sun to drown out the sound of chairs crashing as Bob struggles to escape; they cannot shoot him because even the organ music will not sufficiently mask a gunshot. As Elizabeth Weis remarks of the Albert Hall sequence, "The choice between screaming and remaining silent is related to one of the film's major concerns: the contrast between silence and oral expression that differentiates the spies from the heroes of the film.[23]

The crucial question the film raises as its plot unfolds is, then, whether the Lawrences will finally stand up, speak out, and be heard. Even though the kidnapping shatters the Lawrences' complacency about their domestic equilibrium, it does not immediately convince them that threats to the family of nations should concern the citizen as much as threats to the family at home. They tell the Foreign Office representative Gibson that the life of their child must supersede the safety of "some foreign statesman we never heard of." Gibson's analogy to Sarajevo fails to move them, as does his parting shot, "If there is any trouble, I hope you'll remember that you're to blame." Eventually the Lawrences will break their silence in time to save the statesman, Ropa, but for their own reasons, not Gibson's. After all, his professional agents, no less than the "enemy's," operate by constraining ordinary citizens to silence. If the kidnappers' note reads "Say nothing or you will never see your child again," Louis's dying admonition to Jill had been "Don't breathe a word of this to anyone." It is only after Bob and Jill have each sat as informed spectators at events where both audience and performance have been coopted to the assassins' ends that they acquire their daughter's instinct to speak out against such evil,[24] and deliver the shout that will frustrate it.

Bob's initiation occurs during the worship service at the Tabernacle of the Sun. He and his sidekick Clive enter in the middle of the service, and the moving camera emphasizes their separation from the other spectators as well as the disruptiveness of their intrusion into the unity of the hymn-singing congregants. Their efforts to communicate under cover of this singing further mark them as ill-behaved spectators. Raymond Durgnat observes that "the sleuthing hero and his pal do all the things our childish irreverence dreamed of during those long and dingy services."[25] But the female spy's ascension to the dais to invite the newcomers to undergo "a very simple process of control" confirms that this ritual performance lacks legitimate spiritual authority; the "childish" instinct to misbehave in this church stems from a more significant kind of spectatorship than that of the blindly obedient congregants. Although this totalitarian ritual—Clive is called up onto the platform to have his mind made "white and blank"— masquerades as audience participation, it, like the dentist's earlier attempt to anesthetize Bob, is, in fact, a *reductio ad absurdum* of the polite silence required of spectators at the performance of any socially sanctioned activity. It implies that such quiescent politeness by their citizens well suits the plans of political professionals of all nations. Abbott reinforces this implication when he sends the political assassin on his way to the Albert Hall with the mocking admonition, "It's impolite to be late for a concert."

Even the spectacle of Clive hypnotized does not initially shake Bob from his passive spectator's role. It is only when he learns that Betty is also in the Tabernacle that he unleashes his shout by tossing the now empty chairs at his captors. Before they can regain control, Clive has escaped with the knowledge that the assassination will take place at the Albert Hall. Following Bob's instructions, he imparts this knowledge both to a professional, the bobby on the corner, and to an amateur, Jill. The policeman, acting as one professional to another, takes the word of the spy-as-clergyman over that of the bumbling dilettante and hauls Clive off to jail for "disorderly behavior in a sacred edifice." Jill leaves to join still another audience and eventually deliver the decisive shout and shot of the film.

It is fitting that it is Jill, not Bob, who fully develops as the spectator-participant, for Bob is essentially a reactive rather than an active character. Inserted reaction-shot closeups of him pervade the film. He can improvise actions when danger threatens, but detached amusement is his metier. Throughout the St. Moritz sequences he occupies positions in the audience while Jill and Louis perform in sporting events or on the dance floor. After his capture, he serves primarily to illustrate the conduct of the stiff-upper-lip Englishman under pressure. In contrast to her husband, Jill's greater habituation to initiative and performance has better prepared her to realize the role of Hitchcockian good citizen.

The wordless sequence at the Albert Hall concert juxtaposes the ostensible performance—shots of musicians, conductor, choral singers—before the assembled crowd to the real drama within the audience between Ropa and his potential assassin Ramon; Jill is the sole in-house spectator aware of this latter drama. The camera frequently becomes her eyes as she turns from killer to victim and back again with ever-increasing urgency. While such shots invite the film's audience to share her perceptions, that audience's perceptions already exceed hers because it knows that the clash of the cymbals will cue the assassin's fire. The editing of the Albert Hall sequence also makes the film's audience aware of a third drama to which only it is privy as spectator—the drama of whether Jill will risk the lives of her husband and child by breaking her silence to prevent the assassination.

The dozen times the film cuts back to a closeup of Jill after it has shown the objects of her gaze make us aware of her as object of our gaze. This in turn makes us reevaluate the implications of what we see through her eyes. On the one hand, we see her considering alternatives. The child's brooch she clasps in her hand competes with her view of the police stationed at the exits and so prevents her revealing to the authorities the deadly nature of the view she knows to be concealed behind the curtain of Ramon's box. Perhaps she hopes by the force of her gaze to so link Ropa, Ramon, and the police that each will realize the role of the other in the assassination drama without requiring Jill's overt participation. But the sequence equally suggests that Jill's is the only presence mediating the fatal contact between Ropa and Ramon, so that if she does not act, she will appear more an accessory than a neutral spectator to the murder. The contradictions are so violent that, momentarily, Jill's gaze fails: the frame blurs, but immediately the gray haze is transformed into a background that accentuates the sharp focus of a gun barrel invading the frame. The spectator's gaze alone cannot substitute for her participation, nor can her relinquishment of spectatorship absolve her of the consequences of gazing without acting.

While the film thus endorses audience participation in the face of all prohibitions, it provides no clue as to how the individual comes to recognize the necessity for participation. We are shown clearly, in closeup, Jill's preliminary decision not to act, as her view of the brooch causes her resolutely to settle in her seat, staring straight ahead, merging her gaze with that of the spectators around her and trying to impersonate their composure. But our participation in her subjectivity, as well as our simultaneous ability to fix her with our gaze, is rescinded in the seconds that lead up to her scream. Quick cuts from Ropa to the gun readying its aim are followed by a long shot as Jill rises, and shout and shot combine. The moment of realization—or is it just the culmination of frustration?—remains unseen.

Whatever its motivation, Jill's breaking of silence frees her to go to the authorities and put them on Ramon's trail back to the Tabernacle. Yet her having done the professionals' job for them by saving Ropa still does not enable the professionals to save Jill's daughter. The police actions in the ensuing siege comprise one bungle after another. They cannot reach the upper floor of the building where Bob and Betty are being held because they cannot break through the heavy steel door. Then, when Betty appears on the roof, pursued by Ramon, the police sharpshooter will not fire for fear of hitting the child. So Jill as spectator must participate once again, seizing the rifle and winning her rematch by shooting Ramon and toppling him from the roof. Just as Jill's shout had freed her, her shot mobilizes the onlookers to burst noisily through the police lines to rush the building. The next shot reveals that the police have now penetrated into the upper floors. We never see how they get through the steel door, but the editing suggests that the transformation of the crowd from passive spectators to active citizens enabled their entrance.

The onlookers in this scene of *The Man Who Knew Too Much*, like the Tabernacle worshippers, constitute a working-class audience whose behavior is less circumscribed by codes of polite silence than that in the upper-class circles in which the Lawrences habitually move. In the music hall sequence that begins *The 39 Steps*, the protagonist, Richard Hannay, is immediately marked out as a gentleman among a similarly working-class crowd by his coat, tie, and manner of speaking. It is to the difficulties inherent in galvanizing and redirecting the speech of this "lower" class of spectators that addresses itself.

William Rothman's excellent discussion of this film emphasizes that it is "a fantasy or allegory about the condition of spectatorship,"[26] but despite its very marked parallels with *The Man Who Knew Too Much*, *The 39 Steps*'s exploration of spectatorship and audience participation complements rather than reproduces that of its predecessor. Although the opening music hall and concluding Palladium sequences are fairly analogous in narrative purpose to the St. Moritz and Albert Hall performances, the spectatorial codes of the respective audiences differ widely. When a timid fellow in the audience tries vainly to ascertain from the music hall's living encyclopedia the cause of pip in poultry, his wife chides him, "don't make yourself so common." Her reservations about spectators becoming spectacles do not seem to govern the rest of the crowd, however. Mr. Memory must cope with a crying baby, hecklers who ridicule both him and his questioners, and eventually a fight at the bar that turns the audience into a mob. The audience at the provincial Scottish political rally later in the film is better-dressed and better-behaved, but still verbally vociferous and unruly, ready to shout down a bombastic orator with, "We've had enough of you."

The problem here is not to prompt silent citizens to speak out but to endow the crowd's random, conflicting utterances with purposiveness. At the same time, that purpose must not require the subordination of the spectator's individual voice to that of an illegitimate authority. Although Mr. Memory's interchanges with his audience appear to be more democratic than the one-sided relationship between performers and audience at the Albert Hall, they really are not. Memory does not invite a genuine dialogue with his audience, nor even add to their store of information. The questioner must already know the correct answer in order to validate Memory's response. Nor can questions of any significance beyond factual verisimilitude fit into the show. When a woman shouts out "Where's my old man been since Saturday night?" Memory dismissively asks for "a serious question, please," as if the recitation of statistics about boxing and horse-racing championships were more serious than the location of a missing husband. Thus, the participation Memory invites is as hollow a reflection of free speech as that demanded by the spurious priestess at the Tabernacle of the Sun.

Richard Hannay moves in the course of the film from being one of Memory's accessories in furthering his tautological pseudo-communication, with its ritual "Am I right, sir?"/"Quite right" exchange, to initiating the one genuine exchange of information ever to be included in the act. With his shout from the audience at the Palladium, which compels Memory to divulge his connection to the spy organization, the rootless Hannay replaces the meaningless miles between Winnipeg and Montreal that were the subject of his first question to Memory with the far more significant thirty-nine steps and earns for himself the status of good citizen of the Hitchcock world. The film portrays his gradual education in political spectatorship through the changing cinematic representations of performer—audience interactions from the Music Hall, to the Assembly Hall, to the Palladium.[27] This education culminates in Hannay's voice becoming the voice that publicly exposes the danger to the democratic state, a theft of secret airplane engine plans, no doubt meant to suggest the frenzied efforts, then culminating in England, to develop the Hurricane and Spitfire fighters.

Editing, camera angles, and point of view immediately reveal the unequal partnership between performer and spectators at the music hall. Several shots take the audience's eye view of Memory, showing him to be a distant figure glimpsed over the backs of a number of people's heads and situated above their eye level. Even closer shots that contain only Memory or his stage partner are taken from a low angle. When the camera shows closeups of audience members' faces, however, frequent panning and cutting, and a lack of shot/reverse shot complementarity, mark these views as independent and not linked to Memory's gaze. The exchanges of speech are not reciprocal. He attempts to control and direct their speech (and even their panic, by having the orchestra play over the sounds of the riot); they may either consent or rebel. What the spectators may not do is instigate any independent speech act that advances their own interests rather than Memory's. Hannay, by twice offering the question about the distance from Winnipeg to Montreal, reveals himself eager to accept Memory's manipulation of his voice.

Hannay's performance at the political rally teaches him that a legitimate desire to speak to the best interests of an audience can unify them and win their unforced support for a speaker. Although Hannay's words sound like typical political rhetoric, they actually correspond precisely to his emotions about his own situation as a falsely accused citizen pursued by malevolent professionals. His sincerity, his lack of separation between public and private selves, his amateur standing as it were, win over the audience that had responded with hostility to the previous speakers, a hectoring demagogue and a nervous minor party official who spoke too quietly to be understood. Here the camera chronicles a growing sense of communication and connection between speaker and spectators.[28]

From the moment the direct gazes of all the others on the dais reveal to Hannay that they believe him to be the featured speaker of the rally, he engages in an equal exchange of gazes with his audience (intercut with his observation of the unsettling arrivals of Pamela and the Professor's agents). The shot/reverse shot alternation sutures the respective views of speaker and spectators without including both in one frame, where placement would inevitably lead to subordination of one to the other, or weakening the power of the gaze by including the gazer, back to the camera, within his field of vision, as in the music hall sequence.

When Hannay concludes his preliminary remarks and takes on Memory's role as fielder of questions from the audience,[29] the camera begins at a medium distance slightly elevated above him. As his responses to the crowd grow more confident and more stirring, the distance becomes closer and the angle lower with each succeeding edit. Likewise, his views of the spectators grow closer, and within the frame we see their previous apathy stirred to active approbation. This performance also concludes with the spectators rising from their seats, but now the mob is united in its purpose of joining physically with the performer on the platform rather than succumbing to internal conflicts and the necessity to flee the auditorium, as it had in the music hall.

This lesson on how the balance of power between speaker and spectator can fluctuate serves Hannay in good stead for his confrontation with legitimate and illegitimate professional authority at the Palladium. The camera tells us that the spectator's time has come at last. Shots of the audience, within which Hannay and Pamela are singled out through closeup, the backstage area, and the entrances and exits patrolled by the police far outnumber those of the stage. Performers and audience do not share the frame. Mr. Memory's introduction occurs offscreen while the camera focuses on Hannay's realization, via a sweeping gaze through opera glasses, of the link between Memory and the Professor, who is present but concealed in a curtained box as was Ramon at the Albert Hall.

When the police are about to remove Hannay from his newly empowered spectatorial milieu, he delivers his shout, demanding to know the identity of the thirty-nine steps. Just as Jill's centrality to the camera vanished at the instant she screamed, so Hannay becomes a barely visible component of the larger audience when he shouts out his question. The frame at that moment is dominated by the back of Memory's figure at the bottom center. He has thus been reduced to the position that several of his questioners had to occupy at the music hall.[30] The film then cuts to a tight, tilted closeup of Memory's face as Hannay's voice repeats the question, a repetition that signifies not a plea for Memory's attention, as it had in the music hall, but an insistence that Memory not break his contract with his audience. And Memory, compelled to play his audience's game at last, gives him the answer.

The sequence proceeds to its typical conclusion as the Professor shoots Memory, leaps onto the stage, and is shot in turn. As in the other two performances depicted in *The 39 Steps*, and as at the conclusion of *The Man Who Knew Too Much*, the crowd ends up on its feet, and it is only after the citizens' liberation from the social codes of spectatorship that the professional guardians of democracy can eliminate the external threat to the welfare of the state.

As Hitchcock moved from the immediate political dangers that culminated in the second World War to the more ambivalent conflicts of the Cold War, he became less convinced that such amateur endeavors and audience participation have any far-reaching or lasting international benefits. In the 1956 version of *The Man Who Knew Too Much*, the Foreign Office man, far from telling the distraught parents that their failure to speak may have disastrous global consequences, complains because the contentious factions in the threatened statesman's country don't just kill each other at home and leave the British out of things.

At the same time, however, the need for the individual citizen to protect him or herself because the professionals will not grows even more pressing. And audience participation, in this more limited context, remains a central metaphor. In fact its political significance emerges explicitly only in the very late *Torn Curtain*.[31] The film's protagonists, Michael Armstrong and Sarah Sherman, trapped in the audience at a performance of *Francesca da Rimini* while the police have blocked the doors and are combing the aisles in pursuit, escape when Michael, inspired by synthetic flames on stage, shouts "Fire," causing a panic that prevents the East German police from reaching them. To shout "Fire" in a crowded theater is of course the standard example of the abuse of free speech. But for

Hitchcock, to shout "Fire" from the audience, to violate the decorum of democracy, may be the only way that individual citizens can assure that democratic freedoms remain theirs in actuality as well as in theory.

NOTES

1. See John Cawelti and Bruce Rosenberg, *The Spy Story* (Chicago: University of Chicago Press, 1987), 43; and Michael Denning, *Cover Stories: Narrative and Ideology in the British Spy Thriller* (London: Routledge, 1987), 12.

2. Patricia Ferrara, "The Discontented Bourgeois: Bourgeois Morality and the Interplay of Light and Dark Strains in Hitchcock's Films," *New Orleans Review* 14, no. 4 (1987): 79

3. John Russell Taylor, *Hitch: The Life and Times of Alfred Hitchcock* (New York: Pantheon, 1978), 126.

4. Denning, *Cover Stories*, 24.

5. Joyce Haber, "Hitchcock Still Fighting Hard to Avoid the Conventional," *Los Angeles Times Calendar* (4 Feb. 1973): 11.

6. Patrick Kyba, *Covenants Without the Sword: Public Opinion and British Defence Policy 1931–35* (Waterloo, Ont.: Wilfred Laurier University Press, 1983), 11.

7. Uri Bialer, *The Shadow of the Bomber: The Fear of Air Attack and British Politics 1932–1939* (London: Royal Historical Society, 1980), 2.

8. Kyba, *Covenants Without the Sword*, 76.

9. William McElwee, *Britain's Locust Years 1918–1940* (London: Faber, 1962).

10. Denning, *Cover Stories*, 67–68.

11. Taylor, *Hitch*, 124.

12. Philip Dynia, "Alfred Hitchcock and the Ghost of Thomas Hobbes," *Cinema Journal* 15, no. 2 (1976): 39.

13. Ferrara, "Discontented Bourgeois," 87.

14. Sam Simone, *Hitchcock as Activist: Politics and the War Films* (Ann Arbor: UMI Research Press, 1985), 82.

15. Taylor, *Hitch*, 72; 132.

16. John M. Smith, "Conservative Individualism: A Selection of English Hitchcock," *Screen* 13, no. 3 (1972): 51.

17. Stephen Heath, *Questions of Cinema*, (Bloomington: Indiana University Press, 1981), 19ff.

18. Kaja Silverman, *The Subject of Semiotics*, (New York: Oxford University Press, 1983), 207–14.

19. Laura Mulvey, "Visual Pleasure and Narrative Cinema," *Screen* 16, no. 3 (1975): 6–18.

20. The Radio City Music Hall scene in *Saboteur* might be classified as a shout sequence, but movie viewers in Hitchcock films generally illustrate subjective psychological states rather than sociopolitical relationships (see, for example, *Sabotage*, *Rebecca*).

21. Taylor, *Hitch*, 181. The actual phrase in the film is "moron millions." Either the scenario modified Hitchcock's expression, Viertel has misremembered the line, or Taylor has misquoted Viertel.

22. The challenge occurs in the nonpolitical films as well. See, for instance, Maurice Yacowar's assertion: "And as characterizes the ironic artist, his work is less a matter of statement than a series of tests for his audience, a challenge to its independence from his sleight of hand and trickery of tone." Maurice Yacowar, *Hitchcock's British Films*, (Hamden, CT: Archon, 1977), 13.

23. Elizabeth Weis, *The Silent Scream* (Rutherford, N.J.: Fairleigh Dickinson University

Press, 1982), 80. Although Weis emphasizes the moral, rather than the political implications of this contrast between silence and speaking out, our analyses of *The Man Who Knew Too Much* necessarily overlap in several particulars.

24. Betty displays an immediate and vocal revulsion for both Abbott and Ramon when her parents still see them as amiable fellow vacationers.

25. Raymond Durgnat, *The Strange Case of Alfred Hitchcock* (London: Faber, 1974), 123.

26. William Rothman, *Hitchcock: The Murderous Gaze*, (Cambridge, MA: Harvard University Press, 1982), 117.

27. These sequences are marked out as parallel not only by their diegetic similarities but by each being introduced by a shot of a sign that names the building.

28. There is no doubt that the assembly hall sequence mocks the ideal of participatory democracy to some extent (see Rothman, *Murderous Gaze*, 127; Weis, *Silent Scream*, 160), but I see it as a mockery of professional politicians rather than a wholesale denial of the possibility that democracy can work through citizen involvement (see also Yacowar, *Hitchcock's British Films*, 188–89; Ferrara "Discontented Bourgeois," 82–83).

29. See Rothman, *Murderous Gaze*, 127.

30. At the music hall, Memory had occupied a similar position in the frame when he acknowledged Hannay's question and welcomed him as a Canadian to England. Directly following that shot was the sequence in which the crowd became a mob, so in both instances the linking of Hannay and Memory in the frame prefigures Memory's loss of control over his audience. At the Palladium, however, Memory is subject to Hannay's voice rather than the other way around.

31. *Torn Curtain* articulates the amateur-professional dichotomy overtly once more. Michael's CIA contact, the "farmer," complains, "Why can't you leave this intelligence work to us professionals?" In the later context, however, the very notion of professionalism is unstable. Michael, while an amateur spy, is a professional physicist, and the object of this particular espionage operation is a scientific secret. So he reminds the farmer, "It takes a scientist to pick a scientist's brain."

From Identification to Ideology: The Male System of *Notorious*

MICHAEL RENOV

Over the past decade or so, the French semiotician and literary critic Raymond Bellour has undertaken a series of studies of the classical American cinema in an effort to determine the constitutive, systematized elements of its construction. Bellour's close textual examinations of *Marnie*, *The Birds*, *The Big Sleep* and *North by Northwest*, in concert with the work of other critic/theoreticians (notably, Christian Metz, Thierry Kuntzel and Stephen Heath) have emphasized the effects of symmetry and homogeneity in the Hollywood product, achieved through a textual mastery and systematic structuring of breaks, excesses and enigmas. The critical methods employed in these analyses are rigorous and exhaustive—clearly influenced by *S/Z*, Roland Barthes' seminal analysis of a Balzac novella which painstakingly demonstrates the overdetermined character of each effect of meaning through a play of codes or textual voices.[1]

But it is Bellour's work which is of particular interest for this essay, for he has centered his analyses on the works of Alfred Hitchcock in the belief that these films focus upon, yet continually displace, the highly conventionalized formal and thematic movements of classical American cinema[2] (that problematic term attached to the mainstream Hollywood films of the Thirties, Forties and Fifties). For if indeed the effects of homogeneity and balancing within a narrative system are achieved via the organization of breaks and recuperations, it is the Hitchcock film which tests the limits of such a schema through the continuous manipulation of the most disruptive elements of classical cinema (the radical closeup, the montage sequence, the zoom and especially the point-of-view shot). In addition, the Hitchcockian oeuvre is obsessively concerned with the fundamental drives which fuel the cinematic machine, namely the desires to see and to know. Hitchcock's *Notorious* (1946), the object of the present analysis, is a text which develops a complex system of projection and fragmentation within which the spectator is "fixed"—that is, positioned and re-positioned within a precise formulation of often conflicting codes and effects. The film's construction of identification processes is highly complex and related at a deep structural level to the ideological discourse produced within the film. For there is a sexualized or gendered system of spectatorship mobilized by the film which hinges upon the delineation of a male/female domain. It is

Wide Angle Vol. 4, No. 1 (1980). Reprinted by permission of the author and The Johns Hopkins University Press.

through this enunciation of sexual difference that the key term of the film—"notorious"—is constructed. This paper will disentangle the constellation of effects traversing the film which produces identification. A close reading of the film text is necessitated, for it is Hitchcock's consummate skill to imbed the signposts which channel our projections onto fictional characters in the aural and visual ensembles entering the perceptual system directly as imaged representations, thus avoiding the fuller cognitive efforts of censorship or reorganization attached to verbal articulation.[3]

A central question with regard to *Notorious*, at one level a romance-thriller coupling Cary Grant and Ingrid Bergman at its suspenseful close, concerns what Bellour has termed the successful Oedipal trajectory characteristic of the classical American cinema.[4] In brief, the assumption is that the vast majority of conventional narrative films are constructed within a pattern of male desire which is placed in crisis, then consummated at the conclusion, always at the expense of female desire whose subject is reduced to the object of the male drive. *Notorious*, on the other hand, is curiously anomalous in its patterning of desire, for there is a distinct bifurcation of the male function which is consistently reinforced, thus splitting identification between the agent of the Good Law, Cary Grant the American spy, and that of the Bad, Claude Rains, a post-war Nazi agent, leaderless and castrated by his mother. Yet it is only through the undermining of a unified male subject that the sexual discourse can be achieved with its ideological charge intact. What appears at first to be a fracturing of phallocentrism and a subversion of the successful male trajectory of desire emerges as the very basis for the subjugation and oppression of the female category within the film.

An appropriate point of departure for the analysis is with the paired activities of knowledge and sight which, as in all of Hitchcock, are crucial. They are also distinct, as evidenced by Madame Sebastian, mother of Alexander Sebastian (Claude Rains), as she responds in tragic tones to the unveiled treachery of Sebastian's wife (Bergman) near the end of the film: "I knew, but I didn't see." The film unfolds as an intricately crosshatched weaving of narrative and thematic voices whose engine is the desire to know, whose primary epistemological tool is the ability to see. For Hitchcock, these twin drives are wed by the camera which repeatedly provides the spectator with a single character's point of view in order to place that character upon a map of sight and knowledge which will terminate in narrative closure. The point-of-view shots are given almost exclusively to the principals of the romantic triangle—Grant, Bergman and Rains[5]—since it is they who are pursuing at least two levels of knowledge at any given time: 1) the facts pertaining to the espionage case and 2) the facts of romantic attachment—who truly loves whom. (It is only towards the end of the film that Rains full participates in knowledge level one.)

The second shot of the film is a point-of-view shot into the courtroom in which Alicia Huberman's (Bergman's) father is being sentenced for treason. The spectator is introduced to this function of the camera in its purest state—we identify with the sighted apparatus that peers through the crack in the door at the secret proceedings (and with the enunciator of images, Hitchcock himself), rather than with the imperfectly imaged and nameless reporter who nominally motivates the camera placement. The initial sightings of Alicia, then, are slightly rapacious. She is the source of great curiosity, her broad-brimmed hat casts a shadow over the face we seek to devour. This is the first move towards sexed spectatorship, at least implicitly, for the thematic—"mysterious and beautiful woman"—is introduced, whose subject is precisely our object—the object of our impassioned "male" gaze.

The second term of the romantic triangle to be introduced is Dev (Cary Grant) with whom a strong identification is immediately mobilized. If, so far, Alicia is defined as the object of the gaze, it is Dev who is encoded as the source of the look. In our first view of him, he is seated in the left foreground with his back turned to the camera, silent and in silhouette, while all others in the frame are bright and animated. This inert character is the spectator; his passive behavior throughout the film is founded in this initial pose. A contradiction resides in the gender of this master spectator, however, for it is his maleness that motivates his rapt gaze, yet it is this passivity which endangers the romantic discourse as the film progresses. How can this male spectator also fulfill the socially-defined role of active party in the love game? In part, it is the splitting of the male function that nurtures this fundamental contradiction of male desire in the cinema—the ineradicable split between viewer and actor.

Yet the knowledge game is predicated on more than sight. There are socially-generated systems which situate both characters and spectators within a carefully defined context. For beyond the romantic triangle, another configuration exists in *Notorious* in which Alicia as woman is exchanged and rigorously controlled by two male systems—the Law in its two Manichean manifestations—Good and Bad. Alicia is originally pursued by the Good Law, the American government in the persons of Dev, Captain Prescott (Louis Calhern), the group of officials in Rio who monitor her intelligence activities, the motorcycle cop who pursues her early on in the film and all other visible representations of American justice. The Bad Law is the body of expatriated Nazis, deformed by a harsh fate which has decimated their ranks and rendered them leaderless. The most visible manifestation of that deformity is Madame Sebastian's "unnatural" power over her son Alex. Dev's rescue of Alicia at film's end restores Sebastian to the Oedipal fold, ending his brief sexual emancipation. Within the arena of the Hollywood film, it is no coincidence that this character's loss of sexual power accompanies his imminent loss of life, for his desire has been exhausted. He has both lost its object and satisfied his masochistic urge to verify his mate's infidelity.

There is a distinguishable parallelism between the two facets of the Law resulting from an identical exclusion of women at the narrative level. When the Germans meet to decide the fate of the hapless Emile Hupka during the course of a dinner party, they do so amidst the brandy and coffee taken separately from their women. Captain Prescott *et al.* are equally dismayed by Alicia's presence among them, even though their discussions concern her life-endangering activities as a fellow spy.

Alicia exhibits marked resistance to the Good Law at the outset, but there appears to be no escape. It is through the agency of the pursuing motorcycle officer that she first discovers Dev's full identity. In this sequence, a knowing glance is exchanged between Dev and the cop which moves across Alicia who is pinioned between them, just as Dev's unimaged credential is passed *across* Alicia—an exchange which can be read as a mark of sexual difference in its exclusion of the centrally framed female character. Alicia's growing comprehension of this "male conspiracy" (never acknowledged as such) is equaled by a growing recognition by the spectator of the systematic differentiation between male and female (perhaps equally unacknowledged). Up until this point in the narrative, Alicia's connection to Dev has been a romantic one—it is here that she recognizes his dual character (as the Law as well as the object of her desire), for he strikes her and forces her to submit. The blow which Dev delivers (which is likewise a blow to the code of romantic behavior) is unimaged, concealed behind his back which dominates the frame. Alicia is wrestled to the seat of her car where she passes out. This is the moment at which the romantic discourse is most endangered, for no longer does the male protagonist *have* the phallus, he *is* the phallus.

In a number of ways, Dev is the functional equivalent of Alexander Sebastian. Both are primary agents of the Law, Good and Bad. Both are bound to Alicia through visually potent compositions of object exchange. Both men force Alicia to drink something—Dev's potion is a "healing" one which he compels her to drink when she awakens at home after the scene in the car. Dev is also associated with a bottle of champagne which functions as a prop within the romantic discourse. It is left behind when Dev receives the orders for Alicia's seduction of Sebastian, triggering the shift of emphasis from love to espionage. Sebastian offers rhyming objects to Alicia far later in the film—the poisoned coffee cup is strongly placed in the foreground, hovering over an unknowing Alicia. This time the champagne bottle, now attached to Sebastian, contains the sought after uranium ore, the film's MacGuffin. Through these object exchanges, the two male figures are defined as equal (functionally) and opposite (thematically).

Another strong connection between the two men operates through a shared epistemology. When Alicia comes to tell Captain Prescott and the others of Sebastian's marriage offer, she submits to Dev's double-edged questioning. "May I ask what inspired Alexander Sebastian to go this far?" Alicia answers, "He's in love with me." "And he thinks you're in love with him?" asks Dev. After a dramatic pause, "Yes, that's what he thinks." This formulation applies equally to Dev and to Sebastian since the crucial knowledge factor, Alicia's true feelings, is withheld. As the text yields itself, the two men are clearly conjoined.

If Dev and Sebastian are linked by an analogous relationship to Alicia, there is a more pervasive attitude towards the heroine shared by all the men in the film. It is here that another source of male/female differentiation can be located, for it is the collective male attitude that Alicia is "notorious." A kind of male hegemony looms over the term—it is only definable in its otherness to the male order. Alicia's notoriety hinges upon the flagrant character of the patterns of her desire which conflict with the patriarchal agenda. All the semic qualities which adhere to Alicia to produce this notoriety depend upon her gender for their impact. She is alleged to drink a great deal, although the champagne bottle is also Dev's romantic prop— the traditional tool of male seduction. Alicia's participation in the espionage activities is predicated upon her willingness to seduce a man she does not love in order to gain access to information vital to American interests. Despite the altruism of her efforts, Alicia is disparaged as a vamp, a guileful temptress. She is different from the men who undertake all manner of unscrupulous activity under the guise of intelligence activities (the suave demeanor of Dev and Prescott signifies their possession of the requisite male charms). She is also different from the wives in Washington "who sit around and play cards." It becomes clear that sexual difference overrides other alignments of national loyalties or ethics. The Law, both Good and Bad, separates Alicia from itself and the female category within its domain.

Alicia recognizes her moral status within the collective male context as evidenced by Dev's reluctance to trust her at the outset of their affair. "Once a crook, always a crook; once a tramp, always a tramp," she sardonically observes. The notion of female as eternal and unchanging is joined to the irreversibility of female virtue which is contradicted *and* sustained at the close of the film—a double movement to be analyzed later. With regard to sexual difference, there is a discrepancy between the clear separation between the categories of male and female practiced by the phallocentric system of the film and the inability of the male characters who live that system to recognize gradations within the female category. Much of the miscommunication and equivocation within the romantic discourse (which is a major source of the narrative energy of the film) is founded in the apparently unbridgeable "otherness" of the female. When Dev first hears of Alicia's assignment, his immediate response is "I don't think she's that kind of woman." Her willingness to undertake the assignment signals a victory of patriotism and peer status and a defeat as an exemplar of virtuous womanhood. Alicia is ideologically complicit in her remarks to Dev when he brings word of the assignment. "Did you say anything? That maybe I wasn't the girl for such shenanigans?" Dev's passivity in this scene (cf the male character of his passivity discussed earlier), his reluctance to assert love or possession, forces Alicia's hand. There is a shift of discursive levels, from that of the romance to that of espionage, in which Alicia assumes a male-assertive function. In the next scene, in which Alicia is to meet Sebastian on horseback in the park, an inversion of the gendered dress code occurs. Alicia wears a tie and snap-brimmed hat while Dev is open collared and hatless.

Alicia's functions in the paired discursive levels (romance and espionage) are antithetical. She can participate at the level of romance only through submission to male desire, which removes her from an active role in the espionage game but redeems her moral status. But Dev's unwillingness to perform the male function through the acquisition or domination of the female necessitates the shift to espionage in which Alicia is assertive and active but morally suspect.

Beyond the infraction of the dress code, there is little subversion of the patriarchal mode. Alicia's unstable status within the Good Law (of which she is a vestige) is evidenced in a meeting with Captain Prescott soon after her marriage to Sebastian. In this scene, she is repeatedly addressed as Mrs. Sebastian. Just as her reputation is derogated by the men who benefit from her seductiveness ("I don't think there can be any illusions as to what kind of woman we're dealing with"), her submission to the male nomenclature is equally assumed by those who have instigated the false marriage. Again the male/female division overpowers the Good/Bad or nationalist distinctions. More than excluded from the male grouping, Alicia's very sovereignty is denied, even in her naming.

Sebastian participates in a second erotic triangle, which is the Oedipal one formed by his dual role as son and husband. His strong attachment to the dominating Madame Sebastian is also subservience, for she controls the phallic imagery—the keys, the embroidery needles, the aggressive cigarette-smoking posture. It is only with great effort that Sebastian countermands his mother's disapproval of Alicia as marriage partner and wrests control of the keys. This movement to a more conventional domesticity appears to correct the deformed relations within the household, as Sebastian anticipates the love and devotion of his new wife.

A patterning of identification is constructed around the Sebastian character, for he is given a great number of point-of-view shots. Although Dev is the spectator-model at the film's beginning, more and more Sebastian assumes the role of knowledge-seeker. It is he who experiences the most marked gap between appearance and reality. Time after time, his gaze towards Dev and Alicia uncovers hints of double communication—they speak words belied by expression, they pass keys beneath conventional gestures. If the spectator is motivated by a desire to see and know, it is Sebastian who most clearly embodies the crisis of those desires.

As a castrated male, Sebastian is beset by suspicions and insecurity. He rightly suspects Dev's attentions from the outset ("You made a pretty couple"). The final moments of the film—Dev's archetypal resurrection of the doomed princess, the resuscitative kiss and the successful retreat from the Castle—are, on one level, the recognition of true love, the valorization of the impugned woman, the triumph of the Good Law over the Bad. But the final shot of Alicia's face as she drives away with Dev suggests a second reading of that scene. The wan smile of triumph is also the sign of cold contempt—evidence of the seme "notorious" which has been attached to Alicia throughout the film. "Once a crook, always a crook; once a tramp, always a tramp." She has stolen Sebastian's love and his secrets, indeed his life, and she has feigned her love "with those clinging kisses" while lusting for another. If it is every man's suspicion that his mother is right—that she is the only woman he can trust—that suspicion is borne out by Alicia and by the film.

There are, in fact, a range of reasons for identification with Alexander Sebastian whose fate is sealed by the sepulchral thud of the castle door at the fade-out. He dominates the closing images of the film, while subjective music accompanies his heavy steps. In the first instance, Sebastian has been constructed in a paired relationship with the romantic hero, sharing both Law-wielding function and epistemological relationship to the heroine. He is the legally bound mate whose mastery is accepted, in name at least, even by his adversaries. He is joined with Dev on the male side of the inviolable sexual schism. Sebastian is the castrated male whose sexual renewal is abruptly shattered by a faithless wife in an enactment of a primal male dread. He shares an equal status with Dev and Alicia as knowledge-seeker; a man for whom the gap between knowledge and sight is bitterly bridged. Finally, a plethora of point-of-view shots, particularly during the crucial party sequence, provides the spectator with a direct entry into Sebastian's visual field and cognitive processes.

If Alexander Sebastian is the mirrored image of Devlin, their functional equivalence is finally and irrevocably split by the shape which their respective modes of emplotment assume—Sebastian's is the mode of tragedy; Devlin's that of comedy.[6] Yet, the hegemony of patriarchal ideology is distinguishable in this bifurcation of comic and tragic, for these modes are alike determined within a male perspective. Dev's rescue of Alicia and their romantic union in the last scenes is reminiscent of the resolutions of the preponderance of "family dramas." But in this case, it is clear that Alicia has merely exchanged her submission to the Bad Law for submission to the Good. Her drugged passivity provides the impetus to thrust Devlin into the assertive role which he has avoided throughout the film. Her greatest animation in these scenes accompanies the lines, "Oh, you love me, you love me." She no longer wears the male garb, steals wine cellar keys or passes on state secrets. She is at last the passive recipient of male desire. So while the tragic emplotment attached to Sebastian depends upon the loss of the romance object while the comic assumes unification, it is important to recognize that these seeming opposites both exist within the patriarchal domain. For even the "happy ending" demands Alicia's submission to the Law.

But the key factor which marshals identification upon an otherwise merely pitiable Alexander Sebastian is that it is his perspective which justifies the title of the film and the ideological position towards women which absolutely controls the narrative. Alicia *is* notorious from Sebastian's point of view, his experience legitimates the semic ensemble which it has been the work of the film to attach to Alicia Huberman.

To review, there are multiple splits contained within the film. There is the Good Law and the Bad Law within whose respective fields Devlin and Sebastian can be situated. Each of these male figures becomes the object of identification processes through formal configurations (as with Dev's initial placement in the frame as master-spectator), the systematic structuring of point of view and the enactment of primal male dramas (castration, betrayal). The normally unitary and fully consummated desire of the central male figure is thus obviated, producing an unsettling conclusion in which Sebastian, for whom we have been made to care, experiences his worst sexual fears. Moreover, it is this tragic male perspective which completes the construction of Alicia Huberman as "notorious." For another more fundamental category of difference in the film is the sexual one. Alicia is defined in her alterity to the male regime which embraces motorcycle cops, judges, Nazi scientists and lovers. Ultimately, Alicia submits to male desire, exiting from the narrative in the arms of a man whose assertiveness has at last bound her to him. But at another perhaps deeper level of discourse, she is not at all redeemed by her submission, but instead proven beyond doubt to be the "marked woman" she calls herself in an opening scene. A spoiled, drunken flirt who hates cops, a woman with a past, "first, last and always not a lady" and one who betrays the vows of matrimony, Alicia is made to pay the price of female transgression against the male value system through the spectator's identification with Sebastian at the film's conclusion. Sebastian the Nazi criminal is overshadowed by Sebastian the deserted and betrayed husband. Sexual difference is energetically reinforced, displacing the clash of political or moral positions which appears to be the film's battleground.

This analysis of Hitchcock's *Notorious* does not attempt to account for the complex processes of identification and spectatorship in their totality, a project which can only be achieved in terms of a material audience experiencing the film in concrete ways. Yet it is the supposition of the analysis that the "fixing" of the spectator operates, at least in part, within the play of signifying processes residing in the text itself. Moreover, the film's ideological discourse can be fully evaluated only through the recognition of the plural structuring of identification which splits apart male projection. As a result, the male spectator, while sharing the successful romantic resolution with the "hero," can simultaneously share bitter hostility towards the "heroine."

The reading undertaken here is an attempt to comprehend the multivalence of spectatorship and the complex processes of identification in a single classical film. The recognition and manipulation of sexual difference in the film, far from functioning as a static condition within phallocentric representation, is here mobilized to explain the ideological repercussions of fragmented male spectatorship. The apparent subversion of the unified male trajectory of desire becomes instead the precondition for concurrent male projections of mastery over and hostility towards the female object of desire. Further analyses of films in their multiplicity as machines of desire and sexual identification may well begin to explain the complexity of emotional response to the narrative fiction film.

NOTES

1. Janet Bergstrom, "Alternation, Segmentation, Hypnosis: Interview with Raymond Bellour," *Camera Obscura*; No. 3–4 (Summer 1979), pp. 73–74.

2. Bergstrom, p. 76.

3. A further characteristic of the identification process concerns its ambivalent nature as outlined in Freud's *Group Psychology and the Analysis of the Ego*, ed. James Strachey (New York: Norton, 1975), p. 37. The introjective process we call identification can be an expression of tenderness or of hostility.

4. Bergstrom, p. 95.

5. For those unfamiliar with the film's narrative line, Bergman is the daughter of a Nazi sympathizer in post-war Brazil whose aid is solicited by American intelligence to crack the Nazi ring. Grant is her amorous agent/contact who must watch her seduction of and marriage to Rains, the love-starved weak link in the German chain of command. Bergman retrieves the necessary information and is rescued by Grant before she can be dispatched by her husband, whose doom she has sealed.

6. Mode of emplotment, a term associated with literary critic Northrop Frye, refers to the *type* of story which a narrative gradually reveals itself to be. For a concise evaluation of the term's critical utility see Hayden V. White's "Introduction" to *Metahistory* (Baltimore: John Hopkins University Press, 1973), p. 7.

Vertigo As Orphic Tragedy

ROYAL S. BROWN

. . . the continuous development of art is bound up with the Apollonian *and* Dionysian *duality—just as procreation depends on the duality of the sexes, involving perpetual strife with only periodically intervening reconciliations.*

FRIEDRICH NIETZSCHE

I aim to provide the public with beneficial shocks. Civilization has become so protective that we're no longer able to get our goose bumps instinctively. The only way to remove the numbness and revive our moral equilibrium is to use artificial means to bring about the shock. The best way to achieve that, it seems to me, is through a movie.

ALFRED HITCHCOCK

O f all the Greek myths, the story of Orpheus, the musician/poet of Thrace, remains one of the most pervasive in western society. One reason for this would seem to be that the myth and the religion that developed from it embrace the two extremes of Greek religion—the Dionysian and the Apollonian, extremes that still provide vital symbolism relevant to contemporary mythic behavior and, if one can believe Nietzsche, artistic creation. The Dionysian side of the Orphic tale is manifest in the hero's quest for his dead wife, Eurydice, in the underworld, and it is in this part of the myth that we see the fascination with death, as embodied in a female figure, that characterizes many recent versions of the story. The Apollonian side of the myth is inherent in a) Orpheus' loss of Eurydice by *looking* at her before he has brought her back to the surface from Hades, and b) his anti-female despondency and his preaching of the Apollonian religion (to all-male audiences) following the second loss of Eurydice. The continued singing by Orpheus' head once the poet/musician has been torn limb from limb by the female followers of Dionysus symbolically extends to both extremes. In these events, we see the Orphic desire to escape from the archetypal world of the female—and from the mortality implicit in the necessity of sexual reproduction—towards a more spiritually oriented immortality that in many ways foreshadows elements of Christian mythology. Because of its artist hero, and because of its mid-point symbolisms, the

Reprinted from *Literature/Film Quarterly*, Vol. 14, No. 1 (1986), 32–43. Copyright © Royal S. Brown.

Orpheus myth has dimensions that the more linearly conceived myths lack. As one author has put it, ". . . in this particular story, mythology is considering, in the person of the poet, the power and fate of poetry or thinking or myth. In the Orpheus story, myth is looking at itself. This is the reflection of myth in its own mirror."[1]

In none of his films does Alfred Hitchcock reflect not only the artist but the mythology of artistic creation more strongly than in his 1958 *Vertigo*. Coincidentally, the film is based on a French novel, *D'Entre les morts*,[2] in which the authors specifically allude not only to the Orpheus myth (by having the hero, Roger Flavières, call the heroine "my little Eurydice" on several occasions) but also to the story of Christ and to Kipling's Orphic and quite misogynistic novel, *The Light That Failed* (1890). Although *Vertigo*'s ending differs somewhat from that of *D'Entre les morts*, most of the principal elements of the novel's narrative structure remain in the screenplay, which immediately reveals its Orphic themes: the hero, John "Scottie" Ferguson (James Stewart), a former San Francisco police detective, is asked by an old college friend, Gavin Elster (Tom Helmore), to investigate the strange behavior of his wife, Madeleine, who, he says, is possessed by the spirit of her great-grandmother, Carlotta Valdez, a Spanish woman driven to suicide after being abandoned by her rich and powerful lover. Scottie follows the woman he believes to be Madeleine (Kim Novak) and at one point saves her after she has jumped into the San Francisco Bay. Having fallen in love with her, and trying to discover the key to her obsessions and suicidal impulses, Scottie takes "Madeleine" to an old Spanish mission, San Juan Batista, she has "seen" only in a dream. There, "Madeleine" breaks away and runs up the stairs of a bell tower. Unable to follow her because of an acrophobia that had led him to resign from the police force, Scottie hears a scream and sees a body fall past the tower window.

It is now Scottie's turn to become obsessed with "someone dead." In spite of time spent in a sanatorium to be cured, he continues to be haunted by "Madeleine" and reminders of her in San Francisco. Around a year after "Madeleine's" death, Scottie discovers a woman, Judy Barton (again Kim Novak), who strongly reminds him of "Madeleine."[3] Shortly after Scottie has won Judy's confidence, the audience is shown, via a flashback and letter/voice-over sequence, that Judy had been hired by Elster to impersonate his wife. This charade had allowed Elster to kill his wife and throw her body from the top of the bell tower at San Juan Batista, while forcing the acrophobic Scottie below to be a helpless witness to this "suicide." Unaware of what the audience now knows, Scottie proceeds, with the appropriate clothing and hair-do, to transform Judy back into "Madeleine." No sooner has this restoration taken place, however, than Scottie stumbles onto Judy's secret by discovering the Carlotta Valdez necklace she had worn as Madeleine. Taking Judy/Madeleine back to the scene of the crime at San Juan Batista, Scottie finally overcomes his vertigo by forcing Judy/Madeleine to accompany him to the top of the bell tower. There, frightened by the sudden apparition of a nun, Judy/Madeleine slips from the edge and falls to her death.

The Orphic story in the film is in fact doubled: Scottie saves "Madeleine" from death by pulling her out of San Francisco Bay (it is immediately after the parallel incident in the novel that the hero calls the heroine "Eurydice" for the first time), only to lose her at San Juan Batista for having too zealously pursued her secret. Unlike the original Orpheus, Scottie Ferguson is given a second chance when he is able to reconstruct "Madeleine" out of Judy. His beloved is taken from him again, however, and for much the same reason as the first time—not content to love Judy or even Judy/Madeleine on a sexual, human level, Scottie is compelled to "look" at her, i.e. to discover her secret and lay it bare, and in so doing loses her forever.

From this, or from a casual experiencing of the film, one might conclude that Hitchcock, in line with many modern adaptors of the Orpheus myth, intended the film as a romantic tragedy. Indeed, composer Bernard Herrmann, who did *Vertigo*'s musical score, maintained in an interview that Charles Boyer would have been a better choice for the male lead than James Stewart![4] But part of *Vertigo*'s richness resides, as it does in most of the director's best work, in the existence of various structures that move parallel to the narrative structure while at the same time contradicting it. One thinks, for instance, of the sequence in Hitchcock's 1935 *The Thirty-Nine Steps*, where Richard Hannay (Robert Donat) has brought "Annabella Smith" (Lucie Mannheim) back to his apartment, where he prepares a meal for her. The narrative sets up Hannay as the classic "wrong man" when Miss "Smith" is knifed to death. But two elements in the visual structure set up, at the very least, the relationship between Hannay and the killing as a murder/rape fantasy on the part of the "hero." These are a) the shot of Hannay holding the knife that will kill the woman, and b) the ambiguous editing, which establishes only the most tenuous cause-and-effect between two men seen in the street, an open window, and the murder.

Vertigo's hero is just as ambivalent. As a man obsessed with a mysterious woman whom he will twice lose to death, Scottie arouses audience involvement and sympathy. But Scottie also stands as an artist-hero who, on a first level, sucks the life, à la the husband in Poe's "The Oval Portrait," from the human being he has transformed into an artistic creation; he also, on a second level, acquires a knowledge of the mysteries of death with the light of a killing, Orphic gaze cast into the darkness of the eternal feminine. As a French critic notes, "Scottie is a light-bearer (Lucifer). Overestimating his abilities, he attempts to seize the fleeting shadow, to pierce and dissipate the Darkness (the night) once and for all, a night into which he boldly plunges and whose dangers he willingly ignores."[5]

Vertigo's final shot, with Scottie standing on the ledge outside the tower from which Judy/Madeleine has just fallen, does not simply show a tragic figure defeated by the death of a woman he has loved; it also shows a man who has defeated death through the quasi-ritualistic sacrifice of another human being.

The battles in *Vertigo*, then, are waged on two vastly different grounds, that of the tragic hero and that of the artist-hero. As a tragic hero, Scottie is guilty of a form of hubris that leads him to reject ordinary, life-affirming love and to seek an ideal love that is connected from the outset with "someone dead." Put another way, Scottie rejects existential reality in order to live within mythic non-reality. The contrast between these two domains can often be read, in *Vertigo*, in the oppositional way that certain sequences, or blocks of sequences, are set against each other, particularly the first nine,[6] which can be described as follows:

mythic	I.	TITLES (2'58")	
	II.	ROOFTOP (1'38")	PRELUDE
non-mythic	III.	MIDGE'S APARTMENT I (6'20")	
	IV.	MEETING WITH GAVIN ELSTER I (5'33")	EXPOSITION I
mythic	V.	ERNIE'S I ('39")	
	VI.	FOLLOWING "MADELEINE" I (13'52")	INITIATION I
non-mythic	VII.	HISTORY OF CARLOTTA VALDEZ (5'57")	
		A. Midge's Apartment II	
		B. Argosy Bookshop[7]	EXPOSITION II
		C. Return in Car to Midge's	
	VIII.	MEETING WITH GAVIN ELSTER II (2:00)	
mythic	IX.	FOLLOWING "MADELEINE" 11 (3'36")	INITIATION II FIRST HEROIC/ ORPHIC EXPLOIT

On the basis of action/non-action, one can see that the expository stasis of sequences III/IV and VII/VIII sets them apart from the exploration and/or action of sequences I/II, V/VI, and IX. The basic cinematic style likewise provides a point of strong contrast: sequences I/II, V/VI, and IX contain no or minimal dialogue and are almost continually supported by Bernard Herrmann's non-diegetic score. Sequences III/IV and V/VI contain extensive dialogue and either have no music or, in III, diegetic music (two brief exceptions to this are the sixteen-second, non-diegetic cue that accompanies Scottie's attack of vertigo at the end of III and the brief combination of themes that forms a non-diegetic, musical segue from VII to VIII).

Scottie's rejection of the ordinary also forms an important part of *Vertigo*'s narrative/thematic structure. This becomes immediately apparent in sequence III. Sequences I and II, with their absence of dialogue, their non-stop music, and their lack of *logical* continuity with the rest of the film, have created a kind of mythic time and space (or non-time and non-space) that stand in strong opposition to the extended verbal exposition, the ordinary setting (a San Francisco apartment) and the interrupted "classical" music of sequence III, which from the start evokes the kind of *static* mid-point the hero cannot abide: the Orpheus myth resides in the dynamics of the hero's moving from one pole to the other, and not in his stopping halfway between. It is in this sequence that Hitchcock and his scriptwriter made perhaps their most radical departure from the novel by introducing a third major character into the story, that of Margaret "Midge" Wood, Scottie's ex-fiancée, who fully embodies the ordinary and imprisonment within the world of the mother. This point has been stressed by several writers, most strongly perhaps by Robin Wood in an article entitled "Fear of Flying."[8] In the role of Midge, the bespectacled Barbara Bel Geddes is certainly attractive enough, both physically and as a personality, to more than satisfy most men, and it is only against the physical presence of a Kim Novak that her attractiveness, at least in *Vertigo*,[9] pales. As an actress as well, Bel Geddes, while always a highly respected talent, never reached the stardom enjoyed by Kim Novak, whose rare, sensual, physical beauty and star status made her a perfect complement to the Scottie/James Stewart persona. Midge is even an artist, but one who limits herself to the practical goals of a protective culture by designing brassieres. (In sequence VII, Midge is first seen polishing shoes, while, in sequence XII, her one attempt to rise, by painting her own head onto the body of Carlotta Valdez in a copy of the latter's portrait, to the level of the artist-hero falls tragically flat.) Even in the humorous and mildly risqué (for the time) bra symbolism, Hitchcock avoids the gratuitous. For the bra as a kind of restraint is reinforced by Scottie's discomfort at having to wear a corset, apparently the result of his rooftop accident (just how he was saved is never explained). Looking forward to the removal of it the next day, Scottie exclaims, "I'll be a free man." While Midge artistically plans containment, thereby supporting, in her motherly way, the superego, Scottie thinks only of breaking away. (In his book-length interview with

Hitchcock, François Truffaut notes, and receives the director's agreement, that Kim Novak, when first seen as Judy Barton, is not wearing a bra, which was fairly unusual at this time.[10] A close examination of the film does not seem to support this.)

The breast symbolism implied by the bra helps establish, along with several lines of dialogue and the very personality created for Midge, the character as a kind of mother/life figure who from most perspectives would be seen as positive but who becomes negative seen in the light of Scottie's hubris. The latter characteristic quickly shows up in the dialogue when Midge reminds Scottie, "You were the bright young lawyer that decided he was going to become chief of police someday." In leading Scottie away from the ordinary, this hubris will cause him to seek a woman who embodies death. Scottie's problems with Midge can also be seen from a Freudian perspective, which would certainly take note of two castration symbols, the corset and a small step-stool. Scottie reveals that he feels threatened by wearing this woman's apparel in the following lines of dialogue: "Midge, do you suppose many men wear corsets?" "More than you think," answers Midge in a classically Hitchcockian double-entendre. One is reminded of the leg cast that immobilizes the Stewart character in *Rear Window*. As for the step-stool, which Midge uses in this sequence to theoretically help Scottie "lick" his vertigo, here again Hitchcock offers a double-edged image. Midge's gesture may very well appear helpful; but the step-stool reduces to the absurd and insignificant the heights that Scottie has previously tried to conquer and will again tackle in the two climactic bell-tower sequences, with their obvious phallic implications. Here, there is a parallel with the miniscule razor Eva Marie Saint gives to Cary Grant in *North by Northwest*, a device that both helps him and belittles him. In *Vertigo*, it is also worth noting, with Robin Wood, that the cross-cutting generally allows Hitchcock to avoid showing Midge and Scottie in the same frame.

The initial Midge/Scottie sequence, then, gives the audience a strong dose of reality after the jolting unreality of the first two sequences: the dialogue is expository, the camera work unspectacular (save at the end), the editing fairly "invisible"; and while at the outset there is still music, it too is realistic, since it is diegetic music—an anodyne, minor-mode, "classical" *Sinfonia* by Johann-Christian Bach—coming from Midge's phonograph. Scottie's rejection of Midge's world includes a rejection of her music: shortly after rather piquedly telling his ex-fiancée, "Don't be so motherly. I'm not going to crack up," Scottie complains about the music, which Midge turns off. And when, following "Madeleine's" fall from the tower, Midge tries to use a recording of similar if more interesting and sophisticated, music—the second movement of the Mozart Thirty-Fourth Symphony—to draw Scottie back from the depths of nightmare and depression, Scottie does not even react.

Scottie, then, will allow himself to be drawn out of the world of the present, the known, and the ordinary into a universe bound up in the past (Carlotta Valdez), mystery, and the hispanically exotic (the latter is reinforced by Bernard Herrmann's use of a habanera motive in the music). In his Orphic attempts to bring light into the latter domain, he will set off tragedy, his punishment for which will be a sense of guilt common to both Greek mythology and Christian religion. As the stern coroner (Henry Jones) says following the inquest after the first tower scene, "It is a matter between him and his own conscience." In this sense, Scottie becomes a tragic hero, a man several cuts above the ordinary, both in James Stewart's status as a movie superstar and as a character, who, like Orestes, is pursued by the furies of guilt for a "crime" the gods led him to commit. Certainly, the presence of the gods is felt quite strongly in *Vertigo*. The first of the gods is obviously the wealthy shipping magnate, Gavin Elster, whom Scottie has initially thought to be on the skids and who, profiting from both the vertigo and the detective inclinations that pre-exist in his former acquaintance, needs only set the wheels in motion and oil them once or twice while remaining a dispassionate (and, for the most part, absent) observer. But following the inquest after the death of "Madeleine"/Madeleine, Elster bows out of the picture, telling Scottie he is going far away. At this point, it is Hitchcock who briefly takes over as both manipulator and as the prototypical artist-hero.

If this seems farfetched, it should be remembered that one of the director's distancing techniques has always been the brief appearance he makes in almost every film he has shot. Even though fleeting, Hitchcock's apparition in his own work subtly signals the presence of a force guiding every move made by every character and shaping every photographic frame in the film. A film such as *Vertigo* strengthens the artist/characters = gods/mortals analogy by actually having the actors play roles within their roles: Elster puts on an act for Scottie; Judy plays Elster's wife and then, under Scottie's control, accepts to play the role again, up to and including her own death. (In Hitchcock's next film, *North by Northwest*, role-playing reaches a dizzying apogee within the director's *oeuvre*.) Furthermore, it is just before Scottie enters Elster's office that Hitchcock makes his appearance in *Vertigo*. Elster's British accent further puts him in the domain of the English-born director (as "Madeleine," Kim Novak also affects a British accent). Elster more or less becomes, in the first half of the film, a surrogate Hitchcock directing the movements of his player/victims. This makes the character's cocksureness concerning Scottie's behavior much less outrageous than it would be in a non-mythic narrative, even though Hitchcock himself has objected to the improbability of Elster's *knowing* Scottie would not make it to the top of the tower.

The first half of the picture is shot essentially from Scottie's point of view; as soon as Elster disappears from the action, though, Hitchcock becomes much more strongly the "omniscient director." In the sanatorium, for instance, Hitchcock shows Midge, once she has left Scottie's room, talking to a doctor and then leaving, a lonely figure in an abandoned corridor (this is the one point in the film when Midge gets her own non-diegetic music; earlier in the film, the camera had stayed briefly with Midge at the end of sequence XII). Later, we are given Judy's point of view, to which are added the devices of the flashback and the letter/voice-over that further show the presence of the film director at work. Even more important, it is not long after the second half of the film is underway that Hitchcock reveals to the audience the key to the Judy/Madeleine mystery. It is in this manner, as Hitchcock has often explained, that the director is able to stress the element of suspense, thus relying on the much stronger aesthetic effect of expectation rather than surprise.[11] And the audience, having seen the work of the gods, becomes fully aware of the inevitability connected to the story-line.

Following the "revelation" scene, however, the camera again begins to mirror Scottie's subjectivity. Following through on his hubris to the hilt, Scottie accomplishes the god-like function of bringing "Madeleine" back to life—more as a work of art than as a human being, or, to be more precise, as a work of art to the second degree, since "Madeleine" never was a full human being, within the narrative context, to begin with. No sooner has he accomplished this than Judy "Madeleine" makes the fatal slip of putting on the Carlotta Valdez necklace. Indicatively, Scottie perceives this not on Judy/"Madeleine" the human being but in her reflection in the mirror (it might be recalled here that the character of Orphée in Jean Cocteau's 1950 film of the same title loses Eurydice by looking at her in the rear-view mirror of Death's automobile). And the camera work—a track-in to Scottie's face; cut to a track-in to the mirror showing the necklace worn by July/"Madeleine"; cut to a track-out from the necklace on the portrait of Carlotta Valdez, ultimately giving the audience a quick flashback of the museum scene (Bernard Herrmann's habanera also is suggested on the music track); dissolve back to a close-up of Scottie's face—perfectly communicates the drama inherent in the Orphic gaze while also bringing back Scottie's subjectivity and recalling his vertigo, which is set off by the hero's suspension not only between high and low (camera work), between life and death (narrative structure), but also between past and present (editing). Juxtaposed as a mirror image with the recalled portrait of the long-dead Carlotta Valdez, Judy/"Madeleine" now joins Carlotta as a portrait of "someone dead."

"Madeleine," then, is now dead for Scottie: dead because she has already been murdered, dead because she has been revealed as a veneer, a work of art, dead because she has joined Carlotta Valdez in the past. Scottie/Orpheus' tragedy is apparently over. Why, then, does *Vertigo* continue and return a second time to San Juan Batista? The answer is that the tragedy is only half the picture at best. For if Scottie can be seen as the victim of god-like machinations, he also, in quite another vein, represents the third in a line of men—following Carlotta Valdez's lover (as defined in the story told by Pop Leibel in sequence VII) and Gavin Elster—who were able to exercise the power of life and death through the sacrifice of three women—Carlotta, Madeleine Elster, and Judy Barton. Within this perspective, Scottie aligns himself with the male-dominated forces of the Apollonian in an ongoing struggle with the female-dominated forces of the Dionysian. Each of the Apollonion combatants implicit or explicit in *Vertigo*'s narrative will wield his power in a different way: Carlotta Valdez's lover by exercising a kind of frontier "power and freedom," Gavin Elster through the perfect murder, and Scottie Ferguson via art. Each will be victorious.

Even in *Vertigo*'s title sequence (I), ingeniously designed by Saul Bass (who also did the titles for *North by Northwest* and *Psycho*), the mask-like appearance of the face of a woman with no diegetic relationship to the film acts as a visual generator for *Vertigo*'s definition of the artist-hero's Apollonian goal, namely to take the living, sexual female and transform her into a cold, dead *objet d' art*. As in Greek tragedy, this actually begins in a distanced, Apollonian, formalistic mirroring of Dionysian ritual. For, in the title sequence's cinematic poetry, the woman is visually dismembered: not only do we see only her head, we see only half of her face, then the lips, then the eyes (which, by the way, look in each direction), and then a single eye; she is finally transformed with a blood-red monochrome (towards the end of the film, as Judy Barton is being transformed at the beauty parlor, a similar dismemberment takes place). We are then allowed to penetrate, via the woman's eye, into the mysteries of darkness, out of which emerge a series of perfectly geometrical figures that are the visual essence of Apollonian order and abstraction. Behind all of this, Bernard Herrmann's musical score, if not stereotypically ritualistic, reflects, in its series of non-resolving, broken seventh-chords, the darkness,[12] while the titles inform us of the artists who have created the audio-visual cosmos we are about to experience. At the end of the title sequence, the woman's face returns to re-establish the presence of the eternal feminine in a manner that foreshadows Robbe-Grillet's 1963 *L'Immortelle*, a film that has a remarkable number of points in common with *Vertigo*, not the least of which is its doubled Orphic structure.

The abstraction of *Vertigo*'s "overture" resolves only partially into the concrete in the post-title sequence. Departing from the novel's initial action, which has Flavières, a lawyer, being hired by his friend to follow "Madeleine," the lawyer's wife, Hitchcock establishes Stewart as a man who, failing in his attempt to establish *order*, hangs suspended between the heights and the depths, between life and death, while another pays the price for his gropings towards the light. After the opening shot, which shows a pair of hands grabbing hold of a horizontal bar, followed by a rack-focus that brings a San Francisco panorama into perspective, a man who is apparently a lawbreaker is seen being chased across the rooftops by a police officer in uniform and a plain-clothed James Stewart. Stewart slips and is left hanging onto a gutter high over the streets below. Unable to help himself because of an attack of vertigo, Stewart is assisted by the police officer, who suddenly loses his grip and falls, screaming, to his death. (A close examination of this sequence reveals all sorts of impossibilities, not the least of which is that the rooftop offers nothing whatsoever to grasp onto.) The entire Orphic ambivalency is abstracted in the hero's acrophobia, which Hitchcock turns into a cinematic motif. This is accomplished first of all in the use of a vertical track-out/zoom-in shot, which gives the feeling of two opposite motions experienced simultaneously, and which somewhat mirrors the more dreamy in/out motion of the title sequence's whorls. Complementing the visual depiction of the acrophobia motif are dissonant chords, alternating high and low, and harp glissandi on the music track. Hitchcock definitely makes the association, noted by Robin Wood,[13] between acrophobia—the desire to fall versus the dread of falling—and the death wish—the love of death versus the dread of death—that will become quite apparent in Scottie's relationship with "Madeleine."

The "Rooftop" sequence offers the possibility of at least four different readings, each of which interacts and overlaps with the others. On the most obvious level, Hitchcock uses the sequence to visually and viscerally set up the tragic theme of Scottie's guilt, a guilt from which he tries to escape only to have it re-created twice more under similar circumstances involving a falling body and a scream (in Robbe-Grillet's *L'Immortelle*, a scream likewise punctuates each of the three "accidents," with the opening accident, experienced only as a lateral tracking shot and sound, serving an encapsulating function that parallels that of the "Rooftop" sequence in *Vertigo*). A second, more Oedipal level is well described by Wood in "Fear of Spying"; speaking of the three characters and their interconnection, Wood notes that

> They can be taken to represent the fundamental Freudian triumvirate id-ego-superego. The id is associated with unrestrained libido, pursuit of pleasure, which is—in our surplus-repressive culture—commonly associated with criminality. The superego is conscience, the law, the internalized authority of the father our psychic police officer in fact. The ego is the self, within which the struggle for dominance between the id and the superego is played out. At the opening of *Vertigo*, then, the symbolic father is killed and the "son," if not the actual agent of his death, is responsible for it. The id escapes to wander freely in the darkness, reflected—at the end of the film—in the fact that the murderer, Gavin Elster, is never caught. (pp. 32–33).

A third level has more initiatory implications: trying to enter, as an adult male, the world of the father, the world of (law and) order, the world of the superego, Scottie fails precisely because he is still too strongly drawn back towards the world of the mother, where he will end up (Lord knows how) in the next sequence. In other words, the "Rooftop" sequence stands as an initiation manqué; yet Scottie, in telling Midge he knows he can "lick" his vertigo, is all ready to try again: sequence IV (Scottie/Elster I) will start him out on a much more cinematically elaborated second attempt, which will also be manqué, since it is "Madeleine"/Eurydice who precedes Scottie/Orpheus in the ascent, which negates Scottie's Orphic destiny. Contrary to her own, play-acted prediction ("I know that when I walk into the darkness, then I'll die"), it is by rising towards the light that the Madeleine incarnated by Judy Barton is lost (temporarily) to Scottie, while the murder of the "real" Madeleine (paradoxically never seen as a character in either the movie or the novel) is rendered "perfect." After the rooftop sequence, the initiation here amounts to a kind of second rehearsal, with Scottie a surrogate Elster and Judy a surrogate Madeleine (which creates a symbolic bond of marriage between this Orpheus and this Eurydice). Scottie must start yet once again from the bottom.

Finally, a fourth, Orphic level allows us to look at Scottie as a character forever "wandering" between the Apollonian and the Dionysian while seeking his destiny, which will not be found as a member of the collective superego (the police force) or as a "private" detective working for a single individual but as the solo artist-hero working for himself—by transforming Judy Barton into "Madeleine," Scottie will remarkably mirror precisely what Hitchcock did with his famous "blondes." Seen within this perspective, *Vertigo*'s Orphism mirrors the sexism inherent in the patriarchal, American culture. And thus, the police officer in the "Rooftop" sequence can also be seen to stand as just the opposite of a father figure: being uniformed, he is inferior in status to Scottie, who is in plain clothes; being inferior, he is just as sacrificeable as the women, with whom he shares the same audio-visual fate.

In light of the above, the first sequence between Scottie and Elster (IV) likewise offers more than one perspective. As Wood notes, this "sequence . . . is also built on alternation patterns, but the series are interrupted much more frequently by two-shots. The main purpose of these is to under-line—with the additional emphasis of a low angle—Elster's growing domination of Scottie as he imposes his story on him. Scottie sits, Elster stands; when Scottie rises, Elster moves to the room's higher level, dominating even in long shot" ("Fear of Spying," p. 34). But the very fact that Scottie and Elster are often seen in the same frame while Scottie and Midge rarely are emphasizes the male orientation of both the *ethos* and the *mythos* in which Scottie is involved. This is even more apparent in the second (and last) pre-tower meeting between Elster and Scottie (sequence VIII), which seems to take place in a male-only club. As Elster compliments Scottie on a job well done, we have a long (1'14") two-shot in which the men, both seated, appear exactly the same height. A nearly perfect symmetry likewise characterizes the shot: two identical glasses sit on a table between them, while in the background, two other men can be seen between two pillars. The second half of the sequence, which begins as the conversation becomes dramatic ("She never heard of Carlotta Valdez"), offers a totally different form of symmetry that is created by the editing. In some forty-six seconds, Hitchcock cross-cuts nine times between over-Scottie's-shoulder shots of Elster and over-Elster's-shoulder shots of Scottie, ending, in a tenth shot, with a solo shot of Scottie taking a drink ("Boy, I *need* this!") without ever returning to the two-shot. In almost every cinematic way, Scottie and Elster are set up not only as equals but as two sides of the same male-oriented, order-pervasive coin. Scottie is now ready to save "Madeleine" from the depths (San Francisco Bay) and to make a second attempt to carry his knowledge back to the heights. For Scottie will *know* death again, not only in the sense of having plunged into its waters but also, if one can believe the necrophiliac sub-text given to *Vertigo*, by Hitchcock and others,[14] in the Biblical sense of the word.

In order to accomplish the final stage of his initiation and/or ritual, Scottie must rise to a level that is not only more purely Orphic but, ultimately, Narcissistic. In her role as a woman haunted by a figure from the past, "Madeleine" is also the mirror image of Scottie himself, as is La Mort for Orphée in the Cocteau film. In Jungian terminology, these two females are anima figures vis-à-vis the respective heroes. As Douchet puts it, Scottie's "love for Madeleine is necessarily a lie, since it is essentially Narcissistic. Our hero is attracted only by the reflection she gives him of his own self" (p. 26). Interestingly, it is only in the final part of the film that Scottie is seen reflected in a mirror. This occurs in a dramatic shot at the dress-shop (sequence XIX), in which both Scottie and Judy are doubled in a modeling mirror. This doubling, incomplete vis-à-vis the policeman, allows Scottie, via the phoney Madeleine's faked suicide, to experience his own death, which is very much the principal function of initiation rites. But if Midge is a "life mother," Judy/"Madeleine" must be seen as a "death mother" (the green she wears when first seen in the second half of the film supports this) from whom Scottie must also free himself (in the Cocteau film, Death is not just *la* Mort but *ma* Mort—my death—which in French sounds very close to *maman*).

It is in the final part of the film that Scottie's hubris fully defines itself. In his total despondency at the loss of "Madeleine," Scotty mirrors Orpheus who, once having lost Eurydice to Hades, turns to the Apollonian religion, with its goal of a "fixed and changeless immortality which Olympian theology ascribed to its gods."[15] So thoroughly does Scottie now reject existential reality that he refuses to accept its major premise, that of mortality. Where Orpheus had his music, Scottie brings "Madeleine" back to life like a stage or film director, as has been suggested. But not only is "Madeleine"/Eurydice brought back from death via art, she becomes a work of art, a transformation that is made most dramatic when the "completed" Madeleine steps out of her bathroom surrounded by a green haze. This is her destiny, just as it is Scottie's to become the artist, a destiny made evident as of the very first time we see "Madeleine"—(sequence V). In this first encounter, "Madeleine" is at first aestheticized not by Scottie's gaze but the oftnoted, lyrical arc and track-in, accompanied by Bernard Herrmann's slow, sad waltz; this is Hitchcock's gaze, not Scottie's. For the latter has been leaning back to look at "Madeleine," and when, after a rather confusing cut, we get his point of view, we see "Madeleine" framed like a painting in a doorway. Both Hitchcock's and Scottie's points of view merge as "Madeleine," leaving the restaurant, pauses for a close-up profile shot as Hitchcock raises and then lowers the lights on the background wallpaper.

Once re-introduced to Scottie, Judy/"Madeleine" becomes the strangely cyclical double of the Scottie of part one of *Vertigo*—she is in love with a person haunted by the death of somebody from the past ("Madeleine") while at the same time *being* that person from the past who herself has been in love with a man (Scottie) haunted by another being (the police officer) further from the past. Having freed himself from the life-mother world of Midge, and having freed himself from the death-mother world of "Madeleine"—both by freezing her as a work of art and by "looking" at her—Scottie continues to move simultaneously in two parallel directions. As an initiate, he must free himself from the humiliation of the initiation by accomplishing on his own an exploit similar to Elster's. We now know that "Madeleine" is his by the music, which, instead of repeating the "Rooftop" music, as has the first tower sequence, now offers various parts of the love theme. We also see a bit of explicit rivalry when, alluding to Elster, Scottie tells Judy/"Madeleine," during the final tower scene, "He made you over, just like I made you over, only better." The "only better" attitude can be erased only by Scottie's carrying the act to the same point Elster had carried it. But by having this ordeal undergone at the same place as the original ordeal, San Juan Batista, and one that strongly evokes religious ceremony, Hitchcock considerably heightens the ritualistic implications of Scottie's final act, which, instead of simply allowing him to attain "manhood" by "knowing" a woman, sets him within the framework of a series of male upholders of the patriarchal culture. At the end *leading* Judy/"Madeleine" up the final flight of stairs, Scottie completely becomes the Orphic hero by attaining a symbolic, god-like immortality, living his own death (that of his double) while not dying himself, so that Judy/"Madeleine's" demise becomes a sort of sacrificial murder. In fact, at this final moment, Scottie, Judy and the audience actually "see" death in the unsettling apparition of the nun, which leads Judy to what can be seen as suicide. (The novel considerably weakens the final scene by having it set in a Marseilles hotel room where Flavières actually murders Renèe Sourange, who had played Madeleine, by strangling her.) This certainly corresponds with one of the possible interpretations of Orpheus' loss of Eurydice and is fully in keeping with the preaching of sacrificial murder often attributed to the post-Eurydice behavior of Orpheus. Scottie is now free from everything, including his own death. The woman's head seen in the title sequence becomes his head which, like Orpheus, will continue to sing even after the hero has been torn limb from limb by the Maenads.

If, then, the final part of the Orpheus myth suggests the aspiration towards the Apollonian and towards an immortality tied in with a linearly conceived temporality and ultimate transcendence unrelated to the earth state, the Eurydice part of the Orpheus myth implies the necessity of a communion with an earth-oriented life-death cyclism in which male-female sexuality plays a key role (with this in mind, the use of the extremely sensuous Kim Novak, who was a second choice after Vera Miles, seems a particularly fortunate accident for *Vertigo*). The overwhelming equivocacy of the Orpheus myth stems from the murder, symbolic or otherwise, of the female double, allowing the Orphic hero a communication with a sex(life)/death totality that he assimilates with himself, thereby creating the illusion of an individualized, god-like transcendence and oneness that can somehow remain earthbound. Because it loses strength with the passage of time, the illusion needs periodic renewal, and this is particularly stressed in *Vertigo*'s cyclical structure, which leaves Scottie in the same position at the end of the film that he occupied in the beginning. Because Orpheus is a "god who remembers Dionysus and looks forward to Christ,"[16] his myth allows for the stressing of either side. It takes the entire film for Scottie to break free of the female-based darkness of the title sequence in order to reach the god-like, male-oriented isolation of the film's final shot. If mythic cycles continue, re-integration with the female will again become necessary, thus bringing together in an ongoing ritual the Hitchcockian *immortal* with the Robbe-Grilletian *immortelle*. Yet, unlike Robbe-Grillet, whose cyclicity leaves *L'Immortelle* in a very open-ended state, Hitchcock in *Vertigo* seems to suggest, as does Aeschylus in *The Eumenides*, that, if the Apollonian world of the father and the Dionysian world of the mother are on nearly equal footing, the patriarchal culture for which he speaks gives just the slightest edge to Apollo, as does Athena in *The Eumenides*.

Starting, as he has in almost all his films, with a work of popular fiction, Hitchcock was able, in *Vertigo*, to immediately draw his audiences into the drama by mystifying them and shocking them. Then, creating a hero of tragic dimensions, Hitchcock raised *Vertigo* to a level with which occidental audiences can rapidly identify, both because of the very character of the hero and because of the ethical guilt inherent in his suffering. Another level is suggested by Robin Wood's Freudian interpretation of *Vertigo* as a "dramatization of fundamental sexual anxieties." Wood's reading of *Vertigo* does not exclude, however, the mythic perspective so basic to the film. Mircea Eliade has noted that "sexuality never has been 'pure'" and that "everywhere and always it is a polyvalent function whose primary and perhaps supreme valency is the cosmological function: so that to translate a psychic situation into sexual terms is by no means to belittle it; for, except in the modern world, sexuality has everywhere and always been a hierophany, and the sexual act an integral action (therefore also a means to knowledge)."[17] Although a manifestation of the "modern world," *Vertigo* transforms the sexual content expressed on diverse levels of the cinematic language into hierophantic content. By allowing the audience to feel the presence of Scottie as an isolated, godlike (and rather dangerous, in the manner of quite a number of Hitchcock's male leads) egotist thriving on the sacrifice of human lives in order to guarantee the illusion of his own immortality, Hitchcock maintains, through the equivocal good-evil nature of his hero, the essential multivalency of mythic symbolism, a multivalency that can be felt on almost every level of the cinematic style as well. *Vertigo*'s Orphic ambiguities seem particularly appropriate to Hitchcock's Roman Catholic religion, which, with its rituals and cult of the Virgin, incorporates much more of the Dionysian than most other forms of Christianity.[18] In many ways, *Vertigo* is the director's sexual, artistic, and metaphysical testament while also remaining solid, cathartic entertainment. While showing the role of the Orphic/artist-hero, *Vertigo* is also a meditation on the two poles towards which mythic man continually aspires while remaining on a mid-point tightrope, the principal dangers of which are stasis and fall.

NOTES

1. Elizabeth Sewell, *The Orphic Voice, Poetry and Natural History* (London: Routledge and Kegan Paul, 1961), pp. 40–41.

2. *D'entre les morts* (literally "Amongst the Dead") is by Pierre Boileau and Thomas Narcejac (Paris: Denoël, 1956), who have had a remarkable number of their novels turned into films, including Clouzot's 1955 *Les Diaboliques*. *D'entre les morts*, later retitled *Sueurs froides*, after the initial French title for *Vertigo*, in its paperback reissue (Paris: Collection Folio), appeared in a translation by Geoffrey Sainsbury under the title of *The Living and the Dead* (London: Hutchinson, 1956). The Boileau/Narcejac team apparently wrote the novel with Hitchcock in mind, after the latter was unsuccessful in his attempts to acquire the rights to *Les Diaboliques*.

3. In a plot twist wholly characteristic of the intra-aesthetic French, Boileau and Narcejac have Flavières rediscover Madeleine by catching a fleeting glimpse of her in a movie newsreel shown in a Paris theater. Leaving the hell of a German-occupied Paris, Flavières goes to the sunny climes of Marseilles in his attempt to retrieve Madeleine.

4. See my "An Interview with Bernard Herrmann (1911–1975)," *High Fidelity*, 26, No. 9 (1976), 64–67.

5. Jean Douchet, *Alfred Hitchcock*, l'Herne Cinéma Series, No. 1 (Paris: Editions de l'Herne, 1967), 16, my translation.

6. As is often the case in the cinema, *Vertigo* defies, at certain points, a clear-cut delineation of its sequences. In addition to the nine sequences suggested in the main text above, I would propose the following as the remainder of *Vertigo*'s sequences: X. PORTRAIT OF MIDGE (3'05"); XI. SAN JUAN BATISTA I (9'42"); XII. INQUEST (5'15"); XIII. NIGHTMARE (1'54"); XIV. SANATORIUM (3'37"); XV. LOOKING FOR MADELEINE AND REDISCOVERY (13'19"); XVI. NEW LOVE (3'07"); XVII. TRANSFORMATION (6'37"); XVIII. RE-EMERGENCE OF MADELEINE (5'24"); XIX. REVELATION AND SAN JUAN BATISTA II(1'44"). Titles are mine and timings are approximate.

7. Besides its broader mythic overtones, the name "Argosy" becomes doubly appropriate when one recalls that Orpheus, in later versions of the Jason myth, is supposed to have been a member of the crew.

8. *American Film*, 9, No. 2 (1983), 28–35

9. In his "Films in Focus" column, Andrew Sarris, in a piece entitled "Hitchcock's Split Vision" (*The Village Voice*, 3 January 1984, p. 47), recalls, in opposition to this vision of Bel Geddes, "the slip-clad tigress played by Bel Geddes in the original New York stage production of *Cat on a Hot Tin Roof*."

10. See *Hitchcock*, rev. ed. (New York: Simon and Schuster, 1984), p. 248.

11. Leonard B. Meyer, in his *Emotion and Meaning in Music* (Chicago: University of Chicago Press, 1956), stresses "active expectation," rather than surprise, as a key element of musical aesthetics (see p. 29). The musical structure of Hitchcock's films, which deserves a separate study, certainly adds to their mythic quality.

12. For a more detailed discussion of the relationship of Herrmann's music to Hitchcock's films, see my "Herrmann, Hitchcock, and the Music of the Irrational," *Cinema Journal*, 21, No. 2 (1982), 14–49; rev. rpt. in *Film Theory and Criticism*, 3rd ed., ed. Gerald Mast and Marshall Cohen (New York: Oxford University Press, 1985), pp. 618–49.

13. See *Hitchcock's Films* (London, New York: A Zwemmer Ltd./A. S. Barnes and Co., 1965), p. 74.

14. See Truffaut's *Hitchcock*, p. 245.

15. F. M. Cornford, *From Religion to Philosophy, A Study in the Origins of Western Speculation* (New York: Harper Torchbooks, 1957), p. 185.

16. Joseph L. Henderson. "Ancient Myths and Modern Man," in *Man and His Symbols*, ed. Carl G. Jung (Garden City, N.Y.: Doubleday, 1961), p. 145.

17. Mircea Eliade, *Images and Symbols. Studies in Religious Symbolism.*, trans. Philip Mairet (New York: Sheed and Ward/Search, 1969), p. 14

18. It is interesting that in Italy, where the Roman Catholic cult of the Virgin is perhaps the strongest, the title given to *Vertigo*, *la Donna che visse due volte* (*The Lady Who Lived Twice*), stresses the female element.

North by Northwest and Romance

LESLEY BRILL

When Roger Thornhill (Cary Grant) arrives at "Prairie Stop" to face attempted assassination by crop-duster plane, the landscape turns a desiccated, lifeless brown. The camera surveys the desolate scene from a high panoramic viewpoint. The audience is unlikely to find anything notable about either of these facts; and, if it does notice them, it is unlikely to find them awkward. Yet for a viewer with realistic expectations, both the scorched countryside and the camera placement could be jarring. The foliage elsewhere—in New York, Long Island, and South Dakota—is lush and verdant; the elevation of the camera in the Prairie Stop scene provides a point of view that nobody in the film, including the men in the moving airplane, could possibly have. A viewer with realistic prejudices might feel other qualms as well. Why does the plane, so maneuverable throughout the rest of the scene, crash awkwardly into the gasoline truck at the end? Why does it first buzz Thornhill and begin firing at him only with its second pass? What sort of fool would lure someone to the country and try to run him over with an airplane, anyway? Surely a gun, rope, or knife would be more efficient, more plausible.

One can answer such questions only by pointing out that they are largely irrelevant. Phrased as logical objections, they have little to do with the sort of film *North by Northwest* is, and trying to explain them away obscures more than it clarifies. To ask why such questions miss the point, however, tells us a good deal, not only about *North by Northwest* but about Hitchcock's work in general. . . .

Nobody, so far as I know, has objected in print to the Prairie Stop scene in *North by Northwest*, but complaints about implausibility have been a general motif in Hitchcock criticism for half a century. The obvious rear projection in *Marnie* and *Spellbound*, the painted backdrops and artificial sets of *Under Capricorn*, the trainwheels that whisper "save Ashenden" in *Secret Agent*, the comically speeded-up fireworks of *To Catch a Thief*, the anxious fantasy of Markham sinking into impossibly plush carpet in *Murder!*—these and similar moments in Hitchcock's work could be (and many have been) criticized as gross disruptions of the realistic illusions of the films in which they appear. The description is accurate, the complaint unjust. Though their importance varies from movie to movie, anti-representational techniques in Hitchcock's films express the basic assumptions

Reprinted from Lesley Brill, *The Hitchcock Romance: Love and Irony in Hitchcock's Films*, 4–21. Copyright © 1988 by Princeton University Press.

of much of his work. They signal a romanticism, a self-conscious sense of the fiction as a story of a certain kind, that is the dominant mode of many Hitchcock films and an important element in almost all of them.

I will often be using the word "romance" in a limited sense to talk about the sort of story that forms the core of most of Hitchcock's movies, so a brief definition will be useful.[1] By romance I mean to indicate the relatively fabulous kind of narrative that we associate with folklore and fairy tale and their literary and cinematic offspring. In film, such narratives may be as clearly related to their mythic and folkloric forebears as Cocteau's *Beauty and the Beast* or Murnau's *Nosferatu*; they may be modernized fairy tales like *The Gold Rush* and *Star Wars*; or they may underlie such rationalized and relatively distant relations as *Grand Illusion* or *She Done Him Wrong*.

In the world of romance, whether in film or in other narrative media, the ordinary constraints of natural law are loosened. As in dreams and nightmares, reality mixes with projections of desire and anxiety. This mixture produces an animism and a psychological transparency considerably greater than are found in more realistic fictions. As folk tales swarm with talking plants and animals and vindictive or grateful landscapes, the romantic world of more sophisticated fiction is peopled with extreme and relatively pure human traits. Heroes are brave, handsome, and unentangled by previous commitments; they seek and serve women who are lovely and pure of heart despite dreadfully compromising circumstances; and they oppose villains who reek of carrion and the smoky fires of hell. Characters fit epithets right off the rack: good old king, unjustly disinherited prince or princess, evil magician, wicked stepmother. But for all its sympathetic clarity, the characterization of romance is not drawn in the pitch blacks and unsullied whites of melodrama. Circumstances are frequently perplexed; and characterization, though uncomplicated by abundant detail or delicate shading, avoids simple uniformity. The hero or heroine does something equivocal. The villain attracts justifiable sympathy.

The plot of romance leads to adventure, with the killing of a hyperbolically evil figure the usual penultimate action and the winning of a mate the conclusion. In fairy tales, the destruction of a wicked king, dragon, or troll precedes a wedding to a prince or princess. In the more realistic but still romantic world of most of Hitchcock's films, the grouping of characters is analogous but the stratifications take modern symbolic forms—the upper class background of the hero in *Murder!*, for example, the beauty of Grace Kelly and Ingrid Bergman, or the association of villains with lower classes, foreigners, or sexual deviates. The plot normally revolves about a quest (often thrust upon the protagonist rather than chosen) and entails perilous journeys, violent struggles, mountaintop epiphanies, disappearances and apparent deaths, and triumphant returns. Rather than being rationalized or made plausible, such plots emphasize lucky coincidence and exhibit a high degree of conventionality and artificiality. Human wishes and their enemies and obstructions are anatomized and segregated more sharply in romance than in ironic fictions. Good and evil figures embody radically competing world views. Frye characterizes the conflict as a struggle to maintain "the integrity of the innocent world against the assault of experience."[2] This innocence is partly manifested by the prominence of the miraculous, which, along with an accompanying emphasis on the fictionality of the narrative and an occasional anti-representationalism, clusters with other romantic elements.

Since the terms romantic and ironic are relative, one cannot speak of pure romance or pure irony. Hitchcock's most romantic works include *Young and Innocent*, *To Catch a Thief*, and *North by Northwest*; his films often become more ironic as the importance of their political content increases, as in *Secret Agent*, *Notorious*, and *Torn Curtain*. Yet the first three films all contain some politics and considerable ironic realism, whereas in the latter there remain elements of the miraculous quest with a bride or a husband to be claimed at its completion. Romantic and realistic elements mix in all Hitchcock's films, with one or the other usually providing a dominant modality. If we exaggerate either element, we distort our account of his work. Such distortion will be evident in parts of the argument of this chapter, which is devoted chiefly to defining the romantic core at the center of Hitchcock's cinematic vision. I will consequently give less emphasis to ironic tensions in the film than I would if my aim were simply to provide a comprehensive interpretation.

The story line of *North by Northwest* illustrates the sort of outlandish adventures that often make up the plots of romantic narratives. It coils and recoils intricately and exemplifies the exuberance of plot that characterizes many such stories. Like Sinbad the Sailor, Thornhill sails from adventure to adventure. In fact, a ship is practically the only common conveyance that he does not travel on. When things grow most desperate, he runs— away from his assassins in the elevator, out of the United Nations building, back and forth over the dusty fields of Prairie Stop, through the woods, and across the Mount Rushmore monument. Airplanes, which threaten both Eve (Eva Marie Saint) and Thornhill, play the role of modern Orc to Thornhill's Sinbad. (The creator can send his hero on such electrifying peregrinations, but he cannot accompany him, as the film suggests in the wry cameo appearance of Hitchcock with bus doors closing in his face.)

All Thornhill's rushing about emphasizes the centrality to the film of his quest. The "MacGuffin," a well-known idea in Hitchcock criticism, refers to the nominal goal of a film's characters. It is only partly relevant to the real concerns of the movie, but it provides an excuse for them.[3] In *North by Northwest* the MacGuffin is unspecified information, both that being smuggled out of the country by Vandamm and the knowledge of Vandamm's organization being sought by the Professor. Like the Grail quests of medieval romances, the MacGuffins of Hitchcock's films give motive force to the characters—get them out having adventures, falling in love, slaying dragons. Although Hitchcock maintains interest in Vandamm and in his information through the end of the film, the fundamental object of the quest in *North by Northwest* lies elsewhere, in Roger Thornhill's search for identity and a proper mate—two aspects, it usually turns out, of a single goal.

Thornhill's continuous wayfaring epitomizes his personal rootlessness. With the exception of his last trip home as a newlywed, Thornhill crosses the country in a series of conveyances that are stolen, forced upon him, or associated with deceit. The taxi he takes from its rightful passenger in the first sequence, Vandamm's limousine, "Laura's Mercedes," the taxi he gets by brushing ahead of a waiting couple at the Plaza, his ticketless ride on the 20th Century Limited, the bus he is lured into taking to Prairie Stop, the truck he steals to get back to Chicago, the police car he "summons" to escape the auction, the ambulance that carries him away from the faked shooting in Rapid City, and the Ford sedan in which he effects his last-minute rescue of Eve—together all suggest the extent to which he is uprooted, dispossessed, and unable to establish his real identity. That Vandamm and his underlings insist on taking him for Kaplan further underscores the tenuousness of his existence as Thornhill.

As befalls innumerable folktale heroes who leave home to seek their fortunes, Thornhill ends up with a wife and something that looks suspiciously like a "happily ever after." The defects in his character and circumstances have been discussed by several other critics, so I will only sketch them here. Incipient alcoholism, frivolous and perhaps promiscuous relations with women, prolonged dependence upon his mother, and a readiness to lie to and impose upon other people are among his shortcomings hinted at in the opening scenes. In describing Thornhill's deficiencies, however, it is easy to misrepresent the tone of the film, which makes its hero a strongly sympathetic figure from the beginning. Indeed, he may be the more sympathetic for his venial sins. His marriage to Eve represents a maturing and a serious mating—the making of his fortune.

Eve shares Thornhill's personal defects and emotional voids. She, too, is deceitful and frivolous about sexual relations; but more than Thornhill, she seems conscious of the pathos in her life and of her anemic self-esteem. "I had nothing to do that weekend, so I decided to fall in love," she says by way of explaining her relationship to Vandamm, a man who seems more a father than a lover. Like Thornhill, she is too old to be unmated: "I'm twenty-six and unmarried. Now you know everything." When she marries Thornhill, she finds an identity and a legitimate place in the world. It is typical of Hitchcock, and of romantic fictions, that the concluding marriage should resolve the problems of both partners. There is a structural logic behind such plot configurations. Humans, injured and deficient by nature, can be healed and made whole only by the mundane miracle of love. It follows, since the love must be reciprocal and not adulterous, that both partners before their meeting are to some degree ill and in need and that their redemption must be mutual.

An odor of dragon-killing lingers in the deaths of Vandamm's knife-throwing gardener and Leonard, from whom Thornhill saves Eve with the providential aid of a sharpshooting state trooper. Leonard's death is of particular interest, in part because Hitchcock has spoken with satisfaction of dividing the villain's role among Vandamm and his associates.[4] By splitting the villain, Hitchcock presents evil as demonic and worthy of extirpation while at the same time he shows it as human and pathetic. With their dark suits and cold refinement, Vandamm and Leonard are strongly linked when they first appear in Townsend's library. Thereafter they are increasingly discriminated. Leonard, left behind in the library as Vandamm goes to join his guests, becomes an angel of death. He administers a gargantuan "libation" to Thornhill at Townsend's house, orchestrates attempts to kill him at Prairie Stop and the auction, and pushes Eve off the face of Mount Rushmore. He also commands the two thugs who seize Thornhill in the Plaza Hotel.

Leonard as dragon, moreover, shows traces of the deviant or equivocal sexuality that Hitchcock typically assigns to the thoroughly wicked figures who are killed or captured at the end of his films. Similarly sexually distorted antagonists include the androgynous Fane in *Murder!*, the hyperlibidinous General in *Secret Agent*, Squire Pengaltan in *Jamaica Inn*, Uncle Charles in *Shadow of a Doubt*, Norman in *Psycho*, and the fruiterer-rapist in *Frenzy*. Suggestions of effeminacy arise with Leonard ("Call it my woman's intuition," he says at one point), and there are indications of homosexual feeling between him and Vandamm. When Thornhill, for example, is disguised as a redcap and walking with Eve from the train to the station in Chicago, he lightly remarks that she is "the smartest girl I ever spent the night on a train with." Eve looks away rather tensely because, no doubt, she is aware both of her growing affection for Thornhill and of her duplicitous role. At this moment the soundtrack reintroduces the "lover's theme," a motif associated with the tenderest moments of the couple's unconventional courtship. Simultaneously, the camera pans from Eve's face to Vandamm and Leonard who are shadowing Eve and Thornhill. The "lover's theme" continues as the camera returns to Eve's face, then once more shows Eve and Thornhill together. The camera movement and cutting emphasize Eve's connection with Vandamm (which the audience learned of earlier); but the continuous playing of the "lover's theme" on the soundtrack during the shots first of Eve and Thornhill, then of Vandamm and Leonard, then of Eve and Thornhill again, obliquely suggests an amorous attraction between the two men as well as between the man and the woman. Vandamm and Leonard are shown similarly paired in parallel with Thornhill and Eve on the 20th Century Limited and at the Mount Rushmore cafeteria.

Leonard's uncertain sexuality, and that of other evil figures in Hitchcock's work, should not be dismissed as a reflection of the director's prudery. As I will argue later, true heterosexual love between well-matched partners approaches divine grace in many of Hitchcock's films. Deviance, therefore, is generally demonic; and it is artistically consistent that Hitchcock's villains often show signs of sexual perversity.

The love of Vandamm for Eve cannot accurately be called perverse (unless we emphasize its muted suggestion of father/daughter incest), but it is egotistical and possessive and thereby antithetical to the selflessness Hitchcock associates with true love and lovers. Vandamm nonetheless attracts considerable sympathy, for his wit and affection are genuine, if menacing, and his loyalty to Eve is deep. He does not even appear to consider Thornhill's proposal that he "turn over the girl," and he suffers intense anguish when he learns of his mistress's double agency. In his last appearance, standing beside the Professor as Leonard is shot, he preserves an urbanity under pressure that he shares with his chief adversary. "Not very sporting," he murmurs, "using real bullets." As Eve's lover, he opposes the murderous Leonard to the extent of slugging him when Leonard uncovers the truth of the sham shooting of Thornhill. But his rebellion against his evil side, expressive as it may be, is momentary. He remains of the devil's party, willing to murder Eve for political advantage and unredeemed by his love for her. Since the monstrous side of the villain has been partially split away from him and attached to his secretary, Vandamm gives rise to more pity than terror, even though we are never allowed to forget the ruthless intelligence that makes him, in the Professor's apt phrase, "rather a formidable gentleman."

The leader of the spies finds a surprising comrade in his adversary from the United States Government. For all the sympathy he attracts, Vandamm remains identified with a world that is low and cynical when contrasted with that inhabited by Thornhill and Eve after they have fallen in love. The ideology and actions of the Professor link him with the world of cynical expediency inhabited by Vandamm and guarantee that the U.S. agency also will eventually become inimical to the lovers. Both Vandamm and the Professor, although they have considerable affection for Eve, are willing to sacrifice her. Vandamm decides to murder her after he learns of her treachery, and the Professor wants to send her off with Vandamm probably, as Thornhill says accusingly, "never to come back." "Much more than her life is at stake," the Professor exclaims after he has revealed to Thornhill that Eve "is one of our agents." For Thornhill, of course, nothing could count for "more than her life."

The Professor and Vandamm share vaguely academic identities, the Professor by virtue of his name and Vandamm because of the newspaper photo that shows him on what appear to be the steps of a university library. Both deal in information: Vandamm exports government secrets and the Professor refuses to have him arrested because "there's still too much we don't know about his organization." In contrast to the intelligence traded in by the Professor and Vandamm, Thornhill has the wisdom bestowed by love and a clear sense of the value of human life. "War is hell, Mr. Thornhill—even when it's a cold one," intones the Professor complacently. "Perhaps we'd better start learning to lose a few cold wars," Thornhill replies.

Thornhill does not dwell in this more gentle and innocent world at the beginning of the film; he attains it in the course of his adventures. Somewhat later, so does Eve. Their love lifts them above the soiled worlds of business and espionage. The crucial scenes en route to their final state of gratified desire take place, characteristically for both Hitchcock and romantic fictions, in elevated settings. In his quest for the truth, Thornhill ascends. He goes up to Kaplan's room at the Plaza and up to confront Townsend at the U.N., but both of these unsuccessful attempts at clarification soon find him on ground level again. His most important encounters with Eve take place in elevated settings: her fourth-floor hotel room in Chicago, the mountainside pine forest after the fake shooting, her upstairs bedroom at Vandamm's, the top of the Mount Rushmore monument, and finally an upper berth on the 20th Century Limited. These climbs to illumination and love symbolize ascent to a higher plane of existence. Indeed, the vertical movement in the film may be more important than the horizontal northwesterly movement to which its title refers.

Though they are neither static nor uncomplicated, the central characters of *North by Northwest* have the moral and empathetic transparency and the oversized quality that we expect from figures in romance. Human in their failings, Thornhill and Eve are slightly greater than human in their virtues. For Vandamm, the reverse applies; he has attractive human qualities, along with vices magnified to the demonic.

Roger Thornhill is the sort of man who thinks of the perfectly aimed reply immediately, not later while brushing his teeth before bed. Although he has the defects of an ordinary man, he is handsomer, wittier, "better tailored," and more persistent than an ordinary man could be. His wit is partly that of a quick-thinking rogue, and its comic gaiety is important to his survival. A boyish playfulness inspires his escapes from the elevator at the Plaza and from the auction—where, even as the police lead him away, he insists on reiterating his absurd bid. His light touch seems partly to control a hazardous world. It keeps tragedy at bay and the fortuitous escape and happy ending in sight. Taller than anyone else in the film, he is capable of such feats of strength as surviving uninjured a collision with a truck and holding Eve above a precipice with one hand while hanging on to a cliff face with the other—while Leonard stamps on his fingers. His persistence, above all, raises him to heroic proportions. He never flags in his determination, never retreats in the face of fear, self-doubt, or exhaustion. This doggedness, as it has for romantic heroes since Odysseus, eventually rewards him with a wife and a return home.

"Where will I find you?" Thornhill asks Eve, a bit desperately, as they are parting in the train station at Chicago. Eve does not answer, but the movie eventually does, and just as one would expect of a fairy tale: in the dragon's lair, needing to be rescued. "The reward of the quest," writes Frye, "usually is or includes a bride . . . often to be found in a perilous, forbidden, or tabooed place . . . often rescued from the unwelcome embraces of another and generally older male or from giants or bandits or other usurpers."[5] Vandamm, an older male who is also a bandit and usurper (as his appropriation of Townsend's home suggests), offers Eve embraces that are not only unwelcome but about to become lethal at the end of the film. At the auction the close-up of Vandamm's hand threateningly encircling the back of Eve's neck suggests that even before he learns of her double role his affection may be dangerous.

Like most of Hitchcock's heroines, Eve retains hints of Persephone, the goddess of flowers and vegetative fertility kidnapped by the king of Hades and finally rescued through the agency of Demeter and Zeus. She is shown with flowers on the dining car of the 20th Century Limited, on the bureau of her hotel room in Chicago and on the wallpaper there as well, and in the spectacular floral gown she wears to the auction. She resembles Persephone most, however, in her association with Vandamm who, along with Leonard and his thugs, persistently attracts demonic imagery. Shadow and dark colors are regularly associated with Vandamm, and we sometimes have a sense of him as a temple robber. Eve, his captive for all practical purposes, plays the part of Persephone in Hades or Scheherazade in her thousand and one nights, or any of a multitude of romantic heroines whose wits keep them alive in dens of danger until their true loves arrive to carry them away.

The names of its central characters illustrate the tendency of *North by Northwest* to evoke their archetypes. If my sense of the film is accurate, Vandamm, Eve, and Thornhill retain some qualities of the devil, the biblical Eve, and the savior who wore a crown of thorns and was crucified on a hill. To represent *North by Northwest* as a religious allegory would convince few of its viewers, but to argue that some of its resonance derives from its embodiment of a struggle between good and evil for the heart and life of a woman named Eve is not fundamentally antithetical. That Eve's rescuer "dies," disappears, and returns to save her enforces further an archetypal interpretation, as does the fact that Thornhill spends precisely three days and nights among the demons of international espionage in a kind of harrowing of hell.

Like its characters, the settings of *North by Northwest* are stratified and moralized. Counterpoising Thornhill's ascents to love and illumination are declivities in which he confronts confusion, evil, and danger. The first time we see him he is emerging from an elevator that has just descended to ground level; a little later he is hustled down the stairs of the Plaza and into his kidnappers' limousine; later still he is almost trapped by Vandamm's assassins in another descending elevator. The depth of the film's lower worlds is often established by an elevated camera looking conspicuously down on the action. After Townsend's murder, Thornhill flees the U.N. Building and we peer down the facade at a tiny speck far below, running for a cab. The scene in the conference room of the U.S. intelligence agency is photographed partly from an elevated camera position, a perspective that becomes emphatic at the end of the sequence, when we hear Thornhill rather pitilessly consigned to his fate: "Goodbye, Mr. Thornhill, wherever you are." Cut to Grand Central Station where more elevated camera placements give the scene a distinctly subterranean appearance. The high camera angles in the train station at Chicago warn us that Thornhill will neither find Kaplan nor escape danger there. The startlingly elevated point of view at the opening of the Prairie Stop sequence confirms the foreshadowing in the station and establishes the landscape below as dangerous and infernal. When Thornhill looks down from the second floor of Vandamm's home at Eve far below in the living room, we are presented with a particularly clear image of her entrapment in a lower world that threatens to destroy her.

The fact that airplanes are uniformly associated with danger may be one of the reversals of this intermittently ironic film; or, since we never see anyone in an airplane, their association with mortal hazards may serve to reflect the menace conveyed by elevated camera angles. In either event, the main pattern is not seriously disrupted; heights are associated with truth and love, depths with deceit and hostility. Two of the most desperate conflicts in the film, Thornhill's struggle not to succumb to his enforced drunkenness and the whole of the sequence on the face of Mount Rushmore, center on Thornhill's (and later Eve's) attempts to avoid being thrown off high places. Cinematographically and geographically, *North by Northwest* sets Thornhill and Eve the task of climbing above a corrupt world and resisting the people and circumstances that would pull them back down.

Within the romantic contexts of *North by Northwest*, the apparent anomalies of the Prairie Stop episode appear as consistent developments of emblematic patterns. The bizarre assassination attempt, Thornhill's journey to meet Kaplan and learn the truth of his inexplicable circumstances, the downward-looking camera, and the nightmare quality of the whole incident echo and anticipate similar events and settings throughout the film. The sere vegetation that contrasts with other verdant landscapes may perhaps be explainable as an early maturing corn crop, but it functions more importantly to emphasize the infernal world to which Thornhill has been sent. Dusty and desolate, Prairie Stop is hot as hell and as dangerous. It is a wasteland of the sort familiar to modern readers from T. S. Eliot's poem or the stretch between West Egg and New York City in *The Great Gatsby*. Hunted for murder by the police and for counterespionage by Vandamm's spies, abandoned by the Professor and his agency, deceived by the woman he is in love with, isolated and exposed, Thornhill sinks to the nadir of his journey at Prairie Stop. After he returns to Chicago, his isolation begins to decrease and his ignorance is gradually replaced by understanding. But for the moment he can fall no lower, and the desolation of the place reflects the desolation of his fortunes.

Characteristic of romantic narratives, of Hitchcock's romantic films generally, and of *North by Northwest* in particular is an intermittent antirealism that takes three main forms: (1) explicit references within the work to its own fictionality and to ideas of fiction generally, (2) the frequent use of marvelous plot elements, and (3) conspicuous artificiality. The first of these forms of antirealism, often called "self-consciousness," is less specific to romance than the other two but seems to be associated with them in romantic narratives. In *North by Northwest* it takes the form of a pervasive concern with acting and assuming false identities.

The unfolding of the plot is determined largely by the conflicting and mutually misunderstood roles and the concealed aims of its main characters. His abduction having prevented him from going to the "Winter Garden Theater," Thornhill is told by Vandamm that his "expert play-acting make[s] this very room a theater." As it happens, Vandamm is wrong in this particular case, but the accusation nonetheless rings broadly true for all the major and many of the minor characters in the film. Vandamm, by taking over Lester Townsend's estate, plays the role of the true owner. He also plays the role of art collector and, after he has discovered Eve's real identity, the continuing but no longer sincere part of devoted lover. Those about him act supporting roles: his sister as Mrs. Townsend, the knife-throwing assassin as a gardener, the thug's wife as a housekeeper, Leonard as private secretary. Eve plays Vandamm's mistress while spying for the American intelligence agency; she also adopts the role, for Vandamm, of a *femme fatale* on the 20th Century Limited. The Professor appears as an onlooker at the auction in Chicago and as a passing doctor in Rapid City.

Most versatile as an actor is Thornhill, the majority of whose parts are thrust upon him. For much of the film he plays, however unwillingly, George Kaplan. But he is also, as Vandamm says, "the outraged Madison Avenue man," "a fugitive from justice," and "the peevish lover, stung by jealousy and betrayal." In Chicago he plays a redcap, an expected visitor to Eve Kendall's hotel room, and the drunk and disorderly disrupter of a genteel auction; in Rapid City he dies in the cafeteria and is reborn in the hospital, where he manages to convince the Professor that "I'm a cooperator" in order to escape.

That this role-playing is at least partly to be taken as theatrical is made evident by the frequent allusions to acting and the theater that permeate the dialogue. "What a performance!" says Thornhill of Vandamm's sister at the Townsend mansion. "You fellows could stand a little less training from the FBI and a little more from the Actor's Studio," remarks Vandamm at the auction; but he later congratulates Thornhill on his "colorful exit" from that scene. Eve offers a critique of Thornhill's performance as shooting victim in the Mount Rushmore cafeteria. *North by Northwest* is rich in allusions to other kinds of fictionality and artifice as well. As Marian Keane points out, its title alludes to the entrance of the traveling players in *Hamlet*. She further shows that shot composition often depends on frames within the larger frame of the screen and that the film exhibits a persistent concern with "its very nature as a film."[6] The housekeeper at Vandamm's Rapid City home discovers the lurking Thornhill when she sees his reflection in a television screen. Finally, the government secrets that Vandamm is smuggling out of the country are recorded, appropriately, on a strip of film concealed inside a work of art.

The plot of *North by Northwest* progresses through a series of playlets scripted and staged by its characters but never wholly controlled by them. The first consists of the death-by-drunk-driving arranged for George Kaplan/Roger Thornhill; the second is the performance that Vandamm's sister mounts to reassure the police the next day. Thornhill then bribes his mother to "put on that innocent look you do so well" in order to get the key to Kaplan's hotel room. The sequence on the 20th Century Limited, another play-within-the-play that takes an unforeseen turn (its cast falls in love for real), is followed by the elaborate scenario of Prairie Stop and by further charades at the auction that evening. There the main players congregate to perform and to misinterpret each other's performances. Thornhill plays a rejected lover and a fugitive from justice—both parts he wrongly believes to be truly his—then consciously adopts the role of "drunk and disorderly." The Professor plays a member of the crowd. Eve is attempting to play Vandamm's mistress and Thornhill's antagonist, the latter a role that she is fast becoming unable to maintain with conviction for anybody but Thornhill, who mistakes her entirely. Vandamm plays an art collector and joins Thornhill as a peevish lover. The collision of these mutually deceived and deceiving figures leads to a complex confusion that, like many of Hitchcock's plots, has a touch of the intricacy of Restoration comedy. The next day at Rapid City, the Professor casts Thornhill and Eve as victim and murderess for the benefit of Vandamm in the last of the major internal productions of the film. Only in the final sequences, for the first time in *North by Northwest*, is everyone both playing and being perceived as himself.

It ought to be added that in this film playacting and other feigning are not necessarily equated with falsehood. Role and reality melt indistinguishably together. Eve Kendall the real lover of Vandamm becomes Eve Kendall the agent pretending to be a lover; Eve Kendall the sham lover of Roger Thornhill becomes Eve Thornhill. Vandamm may really collect art, and his associates doubtless perform their domestic duties along with more violent and exotic ones. For much of the film Thornhill almost seems to become George Kaplan, a role so pure that it needs no actor. It is an "expedient exaggeration," but not a very wild one, to say that in the world of *North by Northwest*, like that of advertising, "there are no lies." The fact that characters are most likely to accuse each other of lying at precisely those times when they are being unequivocally truthful indicates the plasticity of the relation between truth and fiction.

Associated with its theatricality and more specifically typical of romantic fictions is the conspicuous artifice and artificiality of *North by Northwest*. The spectacular abstraction of intersecting lines on which the titles appear draws the viewer's attention, from the first frames, to the film's dazzling technique. The opening also serves to introduce the important compositional principle of strong vertical lines, a motif that will reappear throughout the film, most notably perhaps in the U.N. sequence and in the pine forest meeting of Thornhill and Eve. Like the intersecting rails at the start of *Strangers on a Train*, the intersecting lines during the titles of *North by Northwest* serve as an emblem of the coincidences by which separate human paths come together. What is finally most notable about the opening is also most obvious: the conspicuous virtuosity by which it shows the real world with its quotidian shapes and sounds emerging almost insensibly from graphic design and music. This blending of real world and artifice anticipates the theme of fictionality in plot and language and the persistent interpenetration of the made-up and the real. An introductory voiceover that was written for the screenplay but abandoned somewhere in production may have had a similar intent.[7]

North by Northwest flaunts its polish and deftness. It is the opposite of that art that modestly conceals itself from its audience. Rich interior sets, such astonishing exterior scenes as the (recreated) Mount Rushmore Monument, the florid wit of the dialogue, attention-getting camera angles and movements, laboratory razzle-dazzle like the subjective double images of the drunk-driving sequence, opulent technicolor crashes, explosions, and cliff-hangings: the continuous glittering parade gives the film an atmosphere of technical exuberance.

The cinematic *tour de force* of *North by Northwest* draws attention as much to the style of its presentation as to what it presents. Stylization and emotional intensity, furthermore, increase together. The most technically arresting scenes—the U.N. sequence, Prairie Stop, the final chase—are also the most emotionally gripping. Among the artistic effects that become more conspicuous as emotional intensity increases, we may include the sound track. The lovers' theme, for instance, from its introduction on the train to its resolution as the returning 20th Century Limited enters the notorious vaginal tunnel, recurs with increasing emphasis while the love between Thornhill and Eve grows.

Plot development proceeds mainly by way of marvelous coincidence and elaborate obliquity. The quality of the action is thus associated with the antirealism implicit in the film's conspicuous artificiality and its emphasis on themes of pretense and the theater. Once we, like Thornhill, are compelled to accept the initial improbability of his mistaken identity, we are unlikely to protest any of the implausibilies by which the rest of the plot develops—so long as they bear with superficial consistency some relation to preceding events. Thus the theft of "Laura's Mercedes" and the damage to several other vehicles are cleared up for "two dollars" and pursued no further by the Glen Cove Police Department. The errant knife meant for Thornhill skewers Townsend just as he looks at Vandamm's picture; a photographer flashes Thornhill holding the weapon in an action so contrived that audiences invariably forget the innocent Townsend's death to laugh at the impudence of a film that frames its hero so shamelessly. Eve manages a seductive meeting with Thornhill on the 20th Century Limited, another coincidence whose fortuitousness is emphasized by the frantic improvisation of the fugitive's flight through Grand Central Station. And so it goes: when Thornhill needs quick transportation back to Chicago, a pickup truck presents itself; Eve writes the address of the auction on a pad that retains the impression of her writing; Thornhill overhears Leonard disclose Eve's real connections to Vandamm; the gun the housekeeper levels at Thornhill is Eve's, loaded with blanks; another vehicle presents itself for the planeside rescue. The world of *North by Northwest* is one of miraculous coincidence, not always happy but finally beneficent. It is a world in which the maker not only disdains to conceal his hand but insists on showing it through improbable plot manipulations, breathtaking artifice, and continuous musings on the interpenetration of the fictional and the true.

To what does the romantic journey of *North by Northwest* lead? Generally speaking, critics of Hitchcock's films have answered, "entertainment"—"mere" entertainment if they are hostile, and "superior" entertainment if they are friendly. Arguing that romantic fictions are more amusing than ironic seems to be a dubious enterprise; some of Hitchcock's ironic films—*Blackmail*, *Psycho*, or *Frenzy*—have been as popularly successful as his most romantic ones. The romantic mode of *North by Northwest*, and of similar films, is crucial not for entertainment value but because it determines the sort of world and human nature the films represent, the moral ideas they embody, and the relation they imply between themselves and the rest of the universe.

To judge by the condition of all the characters at the beginning of *North by Northwest*, humans are personally fragmented, anomic in crowds, and ruled by laws that regulate their disorder but do not meliorate it. To judge by the condition of Thornhill and Eve at the end of the film, the maladies of being human are not beyond remedy. The cure is love, the most miraculous and unreasonable of the implausibilities of romance. And, of course, the most common. As in Shakespeare's *Tempest*, in which not only does Ferdinand find a wife, but also "all of us ourselves/When no man was his own," so in *North by Northwest* Thornhill and Eve find not only each other but also themselves and their place in the world.

Before they achieve their love, both Thornhill and Eve wander unmated and misplaced among crowds and confusion. We first see Thornhill as one of the rush-hour mob, and it quickly becomes evident that despite his two previous marriages he is still under the aging wing of a domineering mother. He will spend most of the film establishing, literally, his right to be himself. Eve is twenty-six and unmarried, the mistress of a man she no longer cares for, and the employee of an agency that cares nothing for her. The sex lives of both Thornhill and Eve are trivial and loveless, at best. Early in the film Thornhill instructs his secretary to send goldfoil-wrapped candy, like money, to an unnamed mistress: "For your sweet tooth and all your other sweet parts." In addition to her treacherous relationship with Vandamm, Eve uses her sex appeal for hustling Thornhill on the train. But true love is fated, and not even the worst motives of counterespionage and frivolous promiscuity can thwart it. Eve and Roger begin by playing at love on the 20th Century Limited and end as Mr. and Mrs. Thornhill, homeward bound on the same train.

For Aristotle, tragedy did not need to be true but plausible, probable, necessary. For Hitchcock's romantic narratives, the opposite spirit presides. His art is implausible, improbable, and true. In the world of his romantic fictions, human life achieves integrity and joy through the miraculous coincidences and irrational feelings that make people more than a series of premises and conclusions. The antagonists to the world of innocence—Vandamm, the Professor, and the crowds of workers following their enlightened self-interest—live in conditions as infernal as they are logical. It is significant that Hitchcock, who very rarely responded with public impatience to even the most provocative imbecilities about his films, regularly aimed sarcastic blasts at "the logicians" and "our friends the plausibilists." Such critics reject the deepest convictions of Hitchcock's art; they judge it, indeed, by the standards of his villains rather than by those of his heroes. Even in love and madness, Hitchcock's villains are logical. For all that he treasures Eve, Vandamm decides to assassinate her when he learns of her true status. Thornhill, who has been quite as badly injured by both Eve and the agency she works for, comes to her rescue when he learns the truth.

Love between men and women, the most illogical and most common of the miracles of romantic fictions, is the central subject of nearly all

Hitchcock's films. Like divine grace, love cannot be earned or deserved; it must be "amazing." And like divine grace, it brings clarity and purpose to a desperately corrupt world. The strongest indications that a quality of grace attaches to love in *North by Northwest* come negatively, from the demonic egotism to which it is opposed. Vandamm and his henchmen, and to a considerable extent the Professor and his aides, wage their struggle in conditions of conflicting self-interest and cynicism that are opposed to the higher world of innocence attained by Eve and Thornhill. As heterosexual love in Hitchcock's films tends to be an analogue of divine grace, demonic figures like Vandamm collect tinges of perversion.

Even when it is "normal," the love of such figures is distorted by egotism and possessiveness. Vandamm cherishes Eve as one of the accouterments of his refinement, and he uses her as he uses Leonard and the other people around him. In the latter respect, his relationship to Eve resembles the Professor's callous use of her as his agent. Hitchcock's famous aversion to police, whatever the truth of the anecdote of his father's having had him briefly confined at age five, has more to do with the romantic mode of his fictions than with early childhood trauma. The police, like Hitchcock's villains, embrace the world of experience and judge people with logic rather than love. Like their associates the criminals, the police are fixtures of a world of law, necessity, and evil; and like the stony faces of the Mount Rushmore monument, they are the stuff of earth itself, passive and indifferent. Love, spontaneously given and accepted with wonder, has nothing to do with laws, or force, or logic. It redeems a world that law and reason abandon by accepting.

Love heals. In some of Hitchcock's films the central figures are literally ill before they are cured by love; in *North by Northwest* Eve and Thornhill are alienated, uncertain of their identities, and in need of mates. Each for the other fills voids and ends idleness. As they ride back at the conclusion of the movie, they go neither up nor down but straight through a mountainside. Unlike the shots of the 20th Century Limited on its journey west—shots that showed landscapes so similar as to seem unchanged and thereby suggested a voyage going nowhere—the eastbound train is making progress, going home. The startling dissolve from monument ledge to upper berth draws our attention to the artifice of the film at its moment of greatest tension and release. That dissolve and the comically exaggerated symbolism of the train clattering into the tunnel as "The End" appears on the screen reasserts the power of the jolly director to impose a happy outcome on his story.

In the last sequence we may notice a delicate detail: the fingers of Thornhill's right hand are neatly taped where Leonard stood on them. In *North by Northwest* (and in Hitchcock's films generally), hands are an emblem of intimacy, sometimes frustrated or only potential. On Mount Rushmore they link Thornhill and Eve and, in that linking, save her life.

The ending retains a few dissonant undertones: the tunnel raises ironic suggestions, and we may pause to hope that the new Mrs. Thornhill will fare better than her predecessors. But romantic cadences dominate. Thornhill's proposal to Eve on the stone face of the monument comes at a moment in this comic romance that is as convincing as it is implausible. As the movie concludes, his abraded hand is bandaged and healing. Not only is he married, but he has learned to "believe in marriage"—a point to which the film has been conveying him, and us, from its beginning.

NOTES

1 My conception of romance in this book relies heavily upon Northrop Frye, *Anatomy of Criticism* (Princeton: Princeton University Press, 1957; rpnt. New York: Atheneum, 1967) and *The Secular Scripture* (Cambridge, Mass., and London: Harvard University Press, 1976) by the same author.

2 Frye, *Anatomy of Criticism*, p. 201.

3 Hitchcock's explanation is recorded in François Truffaut, *Hitchcock/Truffaut*, rev.ed. (New York: Simon and Schuster, 1984), pp. 138–39.

4 Truffaut, *Hitchcock/Truffaut*, p. 107.

5 Frye, *Anatomy of Criticism*, p. 193.

6 Marian Keane, "The Designs of Authorship," *Wide Angle* 4, no. 1 (1980): 44–52. Ms. Keane's argument is echoed by George Wilson in *Narration in Light* (Baltimore: The Johns Hopkins University Press, 1986). Stanley Cavell, in "*North by Northwest*," *Critical Inquiry* 7 (1981): 761-776 takes Hitchcock's allusion to *Hamlet* considerably further, seeing in it an important indication that Hitchcock thought of *North by Northwest* as central to his own career and embedded in it particularly revealing signals of how he regarded himself as a director. See also William Rothman, "*North by Northwest*: Hitchcock's Monument to the Hitchcock Film," *North Dakota Quarterly* 51, no. 3 (Summer, 1983).

7 Ernest Lehman, *North by Northwest* (New York: The Viking Press, 1972), p. 1.

The Metafictional Hitchcock: The Experience of Viewing and the Viewing of Experience in *Rear Window* and *Psycho*

R. BARTON PALMER

irst lauded as a master of suspense whose art consists in the expert manipulation of the twists and turns of complex narratives, then recognized as an "artist" struggling to give shape to his intellectual, religious obsessions, Alfred Hitchcock is now being recuperated for a generation raised on Brecht, which values self-reflexivity more than either storytelling virtuosity or thematic profundity[1] Actually, current work on Hitchcock gives us two different, but related portraits of the director. On the one hand, poststructuralist and psychoanalytically-oriented critics such as Raymond Bellour and Bill Nichols have seen in Hitchcock's films (especially those of his later American period) a "classic realism" whose strategies of containment can be readily stripped away to display their psycho-social discontents. Thus *Psycho* and *The Birds* are made to "speak of themselves" despite the director's conscious intention to hide all traces of the enunciation process.[2] On the other hand, Robert Stam has argued for the view that Hitchcock was a subtle critic of his institutional apparatus, a filmmaker who deviously undermined the premises of the medium (such as the scopophilic interpellation of the spectator) and the thematic/narrative conventions of realist narrative. Hitchcock, Stam suggests, bears comparison with more self-conscious creators such as Luis Buñuel.[3]

I will not argue that there is no truth in these new ways of looking at Hitchcock's later American films. Adopting a *multum in parvo* approach that depends on the symptomatic analysis of individual sequences, Nichols and Bellour have revealed much about the director's sexual politics and his use of the Hollywood storytelling "machine." And Stam, with a number of suggestive thematic parallels, does in turn demonstrate that Hitchcock, an institutional filmmaker, and Buñuel, a self-avowed modernist with a disdain for the banalities of commercial moviemaking, have produced surprisingly similar bodies of work; such similarities, as Stam rightly infers, mean that the ease with which the Hitchcockian narrative deconstructs and displays its own premises to view is, at least in part, an index of the director's intention, his compulsion to undermine the working of narrative/representational structures toward ideological invisibility. I would

Reprinted from *Cinema Journal* Vol. 25, No. 2 (Winter 1986), 4–19. Copyright © University of Illinois Press.

argue, however, that Bellour and Nichols, on the one hand, and Stam, on the other, have usefully identified elements in the Hitchcockian *oeuvre* which exist within the films themselves as a source of creative tension; Hitchcock's later American films, in short, are neither "classic" nor "modernist," but rather "metafictional" in the sense described by Patricia Waugh: "Metafictional novels tend to be constructed on the principle of a fundamental and sustained opposition: the construction of a fictional illusion (as in traditional realism) and the laying bare of that illusion. . . . The two processes are held together in a formal tension which breaks down the distinctions between 'creation' and 'criticism' and merges them into the concepts of 'interpretation' and 'deconstruction'."[4] As Waugh demonstrates, multilayered, metafictional narrative constitutes one aspect of both the modernist and postmodernist movements; unlike other forms associated with these movements, such as surfiction and the *nouveau roman*, metafiction embodies a connection to the realist tradition and simultaneously turns the premises of that tradition into part of the content for the fictionalizing enterprise itself.

In this essay I intend to argue that Hitchcock's later American films, particularly *Rear Window* and *Psycho*, are metafictional in the senses described above. If this is so, then Hitchcock's foregrounding of the structures of realist narrative through their violation or his transformation of those structures into content must be traced in the viewing experience offered by those films; it cannot reveal itself in either symptomatic analysis or any global approach that ignores the syntagmatics of the narrative process. It is, to put it aphoristically, the viewing of experience that delineates the experience of viewing, the levels of fiction and interpretation mutually informing one another. To understand the metafictional Hitchcock we must therefore return to the Leavisite emphasis on "experience," whose usefulness as an approach to Hitchcock has been so well established by Robin Wood's pioneering study of the director.[5] We must assert the continuing relevance of those features of Hitchcock's art which so attracted earlier critics: his narrative consciousness and thematic preoccupations. At the same time, however, we must remember that the viewer's experience constitutes, in large measure, a category distinct from the experience of which she or he is a spectator. To underline this distinction I have in the two analyses that constitute the remainder of this essay made use of a number of related and mutually informative critical methods. I offer no apology for this diversity of method except to state that the multileveled nature of the two films demands a complex critical response.

Rear Window. A recent and closely argued study of *Rear Window* by Roberta Pearson and Robert Stam convincingly demonstrates how it thematizes the voyeurism at the heart of the film viewing experience, underlining the dangers of such a psychologically appealing activity.[6] As Stam and Pearson show, Jeff, the immobilized photographer who compulsively spies on his courtyard neighbours in an attempt to relieve his boredom, resembles the cinematic spectator, poised eagerly before the screen in hopes of a narrative which might become an object of pleasure. This analogy between Jeff and the film viewer has an obvious validity (and was indeed noted some years ago by Jean Douchet and François Truffaut, but given real argumentative shape by Stam and Pearson). The analogy, however, also has limitations which emerge when we consider the film's narrative, both the experience it traces and the experience it offers to the viewer.

In his search for different genres of narrative (as these are embodied in the characters he observes in the various apartments across the way), Jeff comes across what he thinks is a murder mystery. When convinced that Lars Thorwald has murdered his wife, Jeff desires to have justice done, a goal he eventually attains by involving his girlfriend Lisa and a detective friend in an investigation that extends to a search of Thorwald's apartment. Jeff, however, is able to trap Thorwald only by provoking a direct confrontation. Thorwald enters Jeff's apartment and pushes him out of the window. Jeff survives the fall, and Thorwald eventually confesses to his wife's murder.

Even this rather brief summary demonstrates, I think, the inadequacy of interpreting Jeff simply as a stand-in for the voyeuristic spectator. The narrative process traces what we might, instead, term Jeff's refusal of the role of spectator, a role defined by what is often simplistically termed a suspension of disbelief. Actually the passivity demanded of consumers of narrative fiction is somewhat more complex. We must not only "forget" that the story which unfolds is an imaginary construct with no claims to truth value (and hence the power to summon us into its own action). We must also invest the story with a carefully circumscribed ability to engage our emotions and intellect. As Christian Metz has suggested, the images on the screen are presences defined by the absences they evoke. Proper spectatorship thus involves a balance between dismissal and acceptance, and requires a distancing from, yet involvement in the diegesis.

As an analogical spectator Jeff experiences an unbalancing of this psychological equilibrium. At first he is indeed very much like a true spectator, searching within the actions he views for the conventional signs which will enable him to fill in an appropriate scheme of action and also to look forward to certain types of closure. Within the framing fiction of *Rear Window*, Jeff turns the raw data of his "reality" into narrative precisely through this desire and this set of expectations (expectations which, based on "peeping" and a socially unconventional curiosity, are continually exposed, especially by Lisa, as aberrations). As Waugh suggests, the metafictional perspective disputes that, epistemologically, our experience of reality is any different from our experience of narrative, thereby decentering the notion of the creative artist: "Metafictional novels . . . show not only that the 'author' is a concept produced through previous and existing literary and social texts but that what is generally taken to be 'reality' is also constructed and mediated in a similar fashion. 'Reality' is to this extent 'fictional' and can be understood through an appropriate 'reading' process."[7] Jeff, in fact, has no need of an author to supply him with the fiction he desires; using the codes of narrative and placing himself in the epistemopsychological position of spectator, he is able to transform the "real" into various texts of pleasure. Jeff, moreover, maintains his distance from the various sources of his gaze, correctly defining to the other characters his interests as engaging (they are nearly an obsession), but uninvolving (they are a function of his immobilization—his enforced release from the more demanding world of work).

The nature of Thorwald's activity, however, necessitates that he abandon this role. Jeff, in fact, makes the decision to enter the diegesis which is of his own construction, thereby assuming the position of character type (i.e., the detective) and giving up that of the subject for whom the story is constructed. Or, to put it another way, Jeff originally had been both the author and the audience of the fictionalized universe in the apartment house across the courtyard. Now he relinquishes his function as audience for that of character and is consequently obliged not only to read the narrative (i.e., through the process of investigation), but also to construct it for a different audience (i.e., Lisa and the detective). As author, however, Jeff's role becomes even more complex because, first, he must convince his new audience that a story can be "constructed" from a proper (and conventional) decoding of the events taking place in Thorwald's apartment and, second, he must convince them in turn to violate the terms of this spectatorship and also "enter" the diegesis to aid his own efforts as detective. The complex relations that result from this series of role shifts account for the tension that develops in the scene where Jeff sends Lisa to investigate Thorwald's bedroom. Here Jeff performs as both detective and author, but resumes his role as spectator, thus providing an analogue (by his personal investment in the outcome of the search) for the viewer's "limited" engagement in the dangers of the fictional enterprise, an engagement which is constructed by the agency of identification. Jeff identifies with Lisa's danger just as we as viewers identify with it. But we, of course, also identify with Jeff's vicarious sense of danger.

The film's ending seizes on just this difference between Jeff's experience and the audience's experience of that experience. For with the other stories in the courtyard Jeff retains his proper relationship as author/viewer. His reward is one of the principal pleasures of the text, a closure that resolves enigmas and signals the end of the code of action. In a bravura sequence, Hitchcock closes out Jeff's other texts with a series of happy endings. Thus Jeff is cheerfully and conventionally dismissed from these stories, his experience in this instance a true analogue for our own (since, presumably, we have kept our seats in the theatre and refrained from any attempt to enter the shadowy world represented on the screen). Having become a character in Thorwald's story, however, Jeff surrenders in this instance the invulnerability of the voyeuristic spectator, who in the unBrechtian cinema theatre cannot announce his presence. As a result, Thorwald, who functions on one level as the villain and on another as a metonymy for the story itself, invades Jeff's private space and threatens him with real harm. We can infer that if Jeff had remained a voyeur, he would not have found himself endangered. Thus it is not accurate to argue that Jeff's predicament embodies a warning about the effects of voyeurism. Instead it spells out the consequences of violating the contract between narrative text and consumer, underlines the diffficulties which might arise from taking a story too seriously. The viewer of *Rear Window*, who remains safe because she or he cannot enter the world of the film, discovers in Jeff both a mirror image and an object lesson.

At the same time, however, Hitchcock's moral point is more complex. Thorwald is a murderer. That is, the decoding of his story demands that it be taken as more than a fiction to be passively and contentedly consumed. Or, to put it another way, Jeff constructs a narrative that generates a rhetoric different from the one he had expected, one which moves him inexorably toward action. And that action, at least in conventional terms, is certainly justifiable. Jeff is no quixotic figure, for in abandoning "proper disbelief" he is not only demonstrating an essential truth about cinematic representation (a process whose imaginariness depends on signifiers which denote "real" events, as Christian Metz suggests). Jeff also, through his conversion into a character, deconstructs the deceptive nature of entertainment, which is not always easily contained by the mechanisms of textual pleasure, but which can shift into the imperative mood, exposing a world whose conflicts can be brought to a satisfactory closure only through active, extratextual intervention. Jeff's response to the call of Thorwald's text, however, is ironically presented by Hitchcock. For this *engagement* merits the dubious reward of another broken leg and, perhaps, a more permanent relationship with Lisa. This constitution of the couple, in fact, effectively marks the distance between Jeff's voyeuristic narcissism (and a consequent desire for the distanced pleasures of "fiction") and an eventual mature commitment to the real. Jeff's voyeurism, in other words, may be seen as an initial stage in a therapeutic project which delivers him to the joys and responsibilities, however ironically undermined, of full adult life.

With Pearson and Stam, then, we may conclude that *Rear Window* is indeed "about" spectatorship; it is thus a metafictional text in the elementary sense that it transforms its own ontology and structures into content. As we can now see, however, the film engages the issue of scopophilia in more complex ways than a global reading that ignores the experiences of characters and viewers might suggest. *Rear Window* is metafictional, but not Brechtian—its thematizing of story-consuming is communicated by a realist narrative (with its compelling enigmas and well-articulated suspense) and inextricably tied to a Catholic moral theme (the disavowal of the spiritual sloth associated with the voyeur's *métier*). The film offers the viewer an essentially Aristotelian experience. We can see this clearly in its narrative design which proceeds, we might say, from two related dislocations: the disturbance of the social order effected by Thorwald's crime and the unbalancing of Jeff's voyeurism which results from it. This fact is important, for it reminds us that Hitchcock's often discussed preference for narrative suspense over narrative surprise must be understood as only a partial elucidation of his storytelling art. As Roland Barthes and others have pointed out, the realist tradition in which Hitchcock worked promoted a narrative in which an initial stasis is unbalanced by a disturbing event. This disturbance is by definition a surprise, though the narrative project of its re-ordering is controlled by the principle of suspense (itself dependent on the viewer's repertoire of expected outcomes, a function of expectation). In the traditional manner of Hollywood storytelling, the two dislocations are satisfactorily re-ordered. Jeff is returned to his apartment safe if not sound, while Thorwald is processed by the machinery of social justice.

Psycho. The formal conservatism of *Rear Window* emphasizes the naturalness of "natural" orders, textual and otherwise; but this formal conservatism exists in a somewhat uneasy balance with the film's thematizing of its institutional basis, a deconstructive project designed to overthrow the "natural," to reveal meaning as the product of human desire and labour. The metafictional structures in *Psycho*, on the contrary, are more radical. Recent work on the film, particularly the studies of Bellour and William Rothman, has emphasized its treatment of voyeurism, especially in the sequences dealing with Norman's observation of Marion and subsequent murder of her in the shower.[8] I would argue, however, that, much like *Rear Window*, *Psycho* exposes not only the psycho-social dynamics of the cinematic institution, but also thematizes the purposes of representation/narration which dominate the workings of that institution. The later film engages the auteur's storytelling project more directly, for its dislocations affect not only the represented world but the viewer's experience of it. *Psycho*, in effect, offers a more Brechtian experience to its consumer, for it deliberately violates the terms of the narrative contract which binds the director to his viewers, promoting a narrative process that refuses the facile operations of closure/disclosure.

The new wave qualities of *Psycho* are not achieved through any obvious or obtrusive overthrowing of institutional regulation; Hitchcock's modernism, I repeat, is metafictional in its intention and effects, tied closely to the realist goals of textual pleasure and invisible enunciation. Instead, the film results from a complex reworking of Hollywood narrative conventions, especially as these take shape within the specific limitations of certain genres. Interestingly enough, this "metagenericism" itself had an institutional base within the spectrum of Hollywood practice in the movement now called *film noir*. It is surprising that *Psycho*'s connection to *film noir* has not been generally recognized; only Foster Hirsch among the various critics who have examined the phenomenon in depth suggests that, like many of Hitchcock's other works, *Psycho* is "richly, demonstrably *noir*."[9] While *Psycho* lacks a number of features often associated with *noir* films (e.g., a claustrophobic urban setting, the machinations of a *femme fatale*), it is very closely connected to some of the thematic and narrative preoccupations of this group of films, as we shall see in some detail. I would argue, in fact, that only within the particular context of *noir* narrative can certain central features of *Psycho* be properly understood. The elusive nature of *film noir* (which was an "invisible category" of Hollywood production) does, however, necessitate some brief remarks on the relationship of the movement to the mainstream practice of Hollywood storytelling.

The critical consensus (unfortunately influenced by auteurist biases) is currently that *film noir* is to be defined strictly by certain elements of visual style which impose themselves on the various types of Hollywood stories.[10] I would argue that the movement is also marked by peculiar types of narrative patterns which establish themselves in opposition to the conventions of Hollywood storytelling; James Damico's pioneering investigation of one of these patterns, what I shall call the *noir* romance, offers some solid evidence that *film noir* is not simply a visual style.[11] *Noir* films were indeed produced and consumed according to the system of genres (thus constituting an "invisible" category of Hollywood film), but they undoubtedly represent a departure from the Hollywood system in that they tended to deconstruct the central elements of those genres or of Hollywood storytelling in general. Or, to put it another way, the presence of ideological strain, to use Pierre Macherey's term, is more obviously a feature of these stories; whereas mainstream Hollywood narrative, so indebted to literary realism, strives toward clear representation, the resolution of ideological contradiction, and a full revelation of the "truth," *film noir* constructs a shadowy world of hidden meanings, a universe where human desire fails to obtain its object, a place where competing discourses are not neatly reconciled in a spirit of social optimism. Naturally *noir* films do not constitute the only Hollywood films that tend to deconstruct the narratological/ideological premises of the studio-constructed world (Douglas Sirk's melodramas, for example, approach the materials of mainstream story in a quite similar fashion).

As Damico has shown us, *noir* romance is an important category of the movement and illustrates nicely its rejection of Hollywood social symbolism. Whereas, as Raymond Bellour and others have demonstrated, the Hollywood film in general relies on the psycho-social imagery of the constituted couple (a function of its construction on the Oedipal trajectory) to provide a sense of ideological closure,[12] many *noir* romances work toward a deconstitution of the couple, a narrative goal that indexes the failure of social forms to either contain or satisfy individual desire. In *Double Indemnity*, perhaps the most influential *noir* romance, the *liebestod* affair of Walter and Phyllis culminates in a scene that features their mutual destruction. It is, moreover, during this same scene that they finally understand that their sexual passion is real love; it is this recognition that prompts them to kill each other. As in many *noir* romances, however, the social protest of this narrative goal is to some extent recuperated by the storytelling machinery of mainstream Hollywood film. *Double Indemnity* does not end with a display of apocalyptic social wreckage, but rather with Walter's confession to his friend and co-worker Keyes, a man who can offer him the consolations of understanding and sympathy even as he lies dying of his wounds. Thus *Double Indemnity* does constitute a couple, but this coupling (with its explicitly homosexual overtones) signifies a mutual comprehension of the dangers embodied in female sexuality and therefore in "normal" social forms. As Christine Gledhill and others have emphasized, *film noir* deals more directly with male fears of female domination than do other categories of Hollywood production, thereby displaying one of the most important social discontents of patriarchy.[13] In general, *noir* narratives are structured by a tension between anti-establishmentarian pessimism and the closure/disclosure mechanisms of classic realism, mechanisms *specifically* designed to contain and reorder threats posed to the natural order of things by the workings of the story. Occasionally, the *noir* elements of social protest are overwhelmed by the conservative workings of the Hollywood machine, but they often figure as unrecuperable dislocations of the struggle towards ideological closure. *Psycho*, I would argue, belongs to this narrative tradition.

Film noir and modernism, therefore, have something in common; both embody critiques of a storytelling tradition based on resolution and suppression. The affinity between the two movements can be seen in films such as *Alphaville* and *The Long Goodbye*, in which, as Larry Gross has persuasively suggested, the radical pessimism of *noir* themes is joined to a Brechtian attack on the Aristotelian logic of mainstream film form.[14] *Psycho* offers a more traditional kind of cinematic experience (hence its financial success in the American market), an experience in which transparent mimesis still plays an important role. But in terms of both narrative and its use of genre conventions, *Psycho* is more a radical text. For, like many *noir* films, it begins and ends with structures derived from mainstream practice, but these exist with (and are undermined by) *noir* patterns that resist such narrative processing. *Psycho*'s metafictionality, in short, lies not so much in a thematizing of the cinema's psycho-social premises (though such a critique is undoubtedly present in the film), but rather in the simultaneous expression and refusal of the enclosed world of realist narration. Thus *Psycho* has much more in common with *The Birds* (where the refusal of the closing process, as Bill Nichols has shown, is even more obtrusive) than with Hitchcock's earlier metafictional efforts (*Rear Window, Vertigo*).

In *Psycho* the experience viewed calls the experience of viewing into question. Thus, in the analysis that follows, I shall be concerned mainly with what might be termed the implied viewer's experience. I shall assume, following Wolfgang Iser, that genre, from this vantage point, is a viewer construct based on inference and access to a repertoire of expectations. As a construct, genre is a flexible *gestalt* which may be modified by the supply of new story information that does not fit the inferred pattern.[15] This is a crucial point. As Roland Barthes has argued, popular narrative is pleasurable in that it caters to repetition compulsion, to the desire for the consumption of the same (yet different) object. Hollywood narrative, as a result, came to depend on a fluid system of genres in order to stabilize production and insure profit at the level of distribution. This means that the majority of Hollywood texts were sold and consumed on the basis of genre; therefore, the genre inferencing which constituted a viewer's reaction to the narrative was normally a stable process, often set in motion by the film's title and advertising (anamnetic elements of genre identification and definition). The *gestalt* thus produced was in no need of further change to accommodate the new information supplied by the unfolding story. As Iser points out, all narrative does continually defeat expectation by generating events that are not *specifically* predictable. This unpredictability, however, does not really constitute "surprise," because the events that occur belong to the *general* repertoire of expected outcomes. This means that any events demanding a radical shift in the *genre* gestalt of a Hollywood film would, on one level, constitute a violation of the implicit contract between film producer and consumer, a contract which specifies the items of exchange (i.e., the discourses of film representation) in terms of iconography, world view, character roles, and plot resolutions. Unlike the ordinary Hollywood film, *Psycho* raises generic expectations only to violate them in order both to express a traditionally *noir* pessimism about the satisfaction of desire (a pessimism indexed by the deconstitution of the couple) and to foreground the suppressive mechanisms of realist narrative.

The film's opening sequences are too well known to require detailed comment, but their function on the level of genre, which has not been much explored, is crucial to the metafictional impact of *Psycho*. The spectacle we first witness belongs to the world of melodrama, for it is the aftermath of desire, a desire which we learn is unproblematically fulfilled except in terms of social containment. And the desire for such containment is identified by means of the dialogue between Marion and Sam as a *specifically* female drive. It is Marion who is uncomfortable with the present illegitimacy of her relationship to Sam; she is unsatisfied by a passion which, although expressed, has not been accorded the cachet of social acceptability. Not surprisingly, the narrative is from this point focused by her actions, and the enigma that arises relates strictly to the dynamics of social engineering. Can Marion remove the financial barrier to marriage with Sam? As Laura Mulvey points out, melodrama (or the woman's picture) is a difficult cinema genre to define, for, like the novel form, it draws on a complex mixture of social discourses. Its most important feature, however, is the establishment of excessive female desire as a problem to be solved by a narrative that re-identifies that desire as acceptable, in the process accommodating the woman within the social order.[16] *Psycho* begins as such a narrative.

Stealing her employer's money is the solution Marion immediately conceives for her problem. Operating within the social conservatism of melodrama, however, the viewer must understand her actions as a different kind of protest, one which, as she recognizes in her own meditations about Sam's probable reaction, has little chance of leading to their marriage. On a deeper level, of course, Marion's theft possesses another meaning: it constitutes a protest against a patriarchal system that esteems the constitution of the couple and flaunts the success of those who have entered into this social bond (Marion's discontents about the system are aroused by her conversation with a co-worker and the flirtatious advances of a vulgar client). For this reason the film's hermeneutic code here becomes somewhat complex. If restoring the money to her employer is a necessary condition for her future marriage (because the criminal act will alienate Sam and make it impossible for them to assume their "rightful" places within the social order), it is not a sufficient condition for such legal constitution of the couple. Marion's action, in short, means that she must make amends for the anti-social expression of her desire for social acceptability and also that she discover some way that her desire may be "lawfully" satisfied. Closure must result, therefore, from a contradictory punishment and rewarding of Marion's desire. The ideological conservatism of these patterns (which discipline the eruption of female desire while rewarding its goal of coupling) typifies those of film melodrama in general. Melodrama, we might say with Mulvey, depends not only on the satisfaction of desire but on the repression/suppression of its excessiveness.

Marion's flight from Phoenix means that some new possibility for the socializing of Marion's desire and its simultaneous chastisement must be generated by the narrative. Her fateful stopping at the Bates Motel certainly holds out this possibility, especially since Norman is a boyishly good-looking version of Sam. As their encounter develops, however, that possibility is eliminated because Norman is not capable of adult sexuality, being held in sexual bondage by his mother. This revelation fixes his function in

the narrative: Norman, in Marion's mind, comes to embody a dysfunctional sexuality which, by contrast, underscores the relative ease with which a
solution might be discovered for her unfulfilled desire:

> *Norman*: Do you know what I think? I think that we're all in our private
> traps. Clamped in them. And none of us can ever get out. We scratch and
> claw, but only at the air, only at each other. And for all of it, we never budge
> an inch.
> *Marion*: Sometimes we deliberately step into those traps.

Norman's socio-biological determinism defines him as a character who
cannot exist in the world of melodrama where, as Marion suggests, human
behaviour not only is controlled by free will but must be subject to moral
self-examination. In expressing a darker *weltanschauung*, with its natural-
ist and Freudian overtones, Norman effectively characterizes himself as an
object lesson (i.e., as a discourse that, by contrast, marks off the psycho-
social premises of the genre world the film is constructing). When Marion
leaves his office, the viewer is made, at least in part, to feel that the object
lesson has served its purpose. Marion will return the money, and, we
expect, the narrative will thereafter discover some mechanism to constitute the couple, erasing the presence of excess desire and its threat to the
social order. Victim of a never to be completed Oedipal trajectory, Norman
will remain behind, no more than a landmark on the road of ruinous
impulse.

At the same time, the film's original audience was encouraged to hold
out some other, contradictory expectations. Trailers and posters for
Psycho had emphasized not only the importance of the Gothic mansion
situated behind the motel, but also the function of a narrative surprise (in
some theatres latecomers were not seated after the beginning of the film).
The film's title and also Anthony Perkins's star billing likewise mitigated
against any dismissal of him by the narrative process. Even for the original
audience, however, the sequences which followed the scene between
Marion and Norman in the office must have proved extremely dislocating.
For these sequences established that Norman's world view is correct, not
Marion's. The aberrant comes to hold sway over the normal, only much
later and rather ineffectually to be subjected to the therapeutic surveillance of the Law. In the process the audience is forced to reject the genre
construct of melodrama as inadequate to their experience of the film.

After Marion leaves the office, the narrative focus surprisingly shifts to
Norman. Marion announces her decision to reform by revealing her true
name to him and by stating that she must "pull out" of the "private trap"
into which she had fallen back in Phoenix. The camera, however, remains
with Norman in the office, seeing him and seeing with him as he uncovers
the hole in the wall through which he watches Marion undress. The self-
reflexivity of the sequence hardly requires comment; Norman's subjective

vision of Marion reminds us that we too have made her the object of our look and desire, that Norman's perverse pleasure is merely a variant of our own. But the narrative focusing on Norman at this point has another meaning which relates to our generic expectations. For the previous scene had written out Norman's desire as dysfunctional, as a drive aborted by his family romance. Only Marion's desire was offered as capable of satisfaction through both the exercise of free will and the acceptance of social regulation as a form of self-correction. Within the horizon of melodrama, then, Norman could only be a dead-ended character, one incapable of bearing the narrative burdens of reform and socialization. Shifting the narrative focus to Norman, however, means that we must abandon such expectations. The world view of melodrama simply cannot accommodate Norman's *noir* alienation and obsessions, his Gothic entrapment by a suffocating past, except as boundaries which mark off by their differences another order of experience.

What is interesting about this juxtaposition of radical pessimism with the centrist optimism of melodrama is that it is, to some extent, a typical *noir* effect. Two brief examples must here suffice. In *Niagara* the narrative contrasts the experience of a happily married couple, whose sexual attraction is restored by a second honeymoon, with that of a couple broken apart by impotence and betrayal. In a climactic scene George Loomis strangles his cheating wife in the honeymooners' bell tower, only later to be swept over the falls by a relentless river that is the very image of a destructive and unrestrainable desire. George's story, however, is contained by the reconstitution of the other couple, the wife barely rescued from sharing George's fate in a dénouement that signifies the fragile claims of the melodramatic world view. In *Mildred Pierce* the opening sequences indict the title character for the murder of her husband and the betrayal of her lover. These *noir* elements, however, give way to a flashback narrative in which she is revealed as the heroine of melodrama, forced by a marital break up to assume the burdens of family support. The film's ending provides but then retracts the satisfactions of melodramatic closure. Mildred is indeed proved innocent, but the guilty party is revealed to be her own daughter, that projection of her social aspirations with whom she has always been obsessed. Mildred is then reunited with her former husband, but the text strains to establish the happiness of this reconstitution by the figure of "a new day dawning" which cannot contain what the night has revealed about the characters' moral natures.

These typical *noir* narratives reveal by contrast the more dislocating threat posed to the melodramatic goal of retrieved social and individual harmony by the death of Marion, which follows directly upon the change of narrative focusing to Norman. As I suggested earlier, *Psycho* begins, in terms of genre, as a melodrama and consequently develops a complex hermeneutic, one which sets the contradictory goals of the satisfaction and chastisement of Marion's desire. Marion's death, on one level, solves the contradiction of this expectation, delivering the heroine to a punishment that obviates any satisfaction of her desire; the narrative, in other words, refuses the goal it had been working toward, in the process baring the device of the goal itself. Marion's death deconstructs the social conservatism of melodrama, but on the level of storytelling and story consuming, it has another effect: underscoring, because it is a surprise, the insufficiency of Aristotelian causality, one of the cardinal principles of classic film realism. Along with Aristotelian causality, the viewer must at this point reject some of the central elements of the ideology of which it is an expression, for we now understand both the contingency of the notion that a free will is capable of effectively reordering existence and the utopianism of the belief that the normality of sexual accommodation prevails over any unrecuperable excess. Marion's death thus reveals the futility of desire in a world now seen to be ruled by unhappy chance and, correspondingly, the insufficiency of plot, a narrative ordering function (keyed to the viewer's desire) which makes provision only for the probable, not the possible.

Believing Marion killed by Norman's jealous mother, we must conclude that our previous estimate of his desire is indeed correct. Like the viewer and Marion, Norman can desire, but his look, like the story itself, offers no guarantee that he might possess the object of that desire. Norman and the viewer are instead trapped within an experience where blind and malevolent chance (working through the ultimate agent of comfort and promised happiness, the mother) has cut out desire itself, deconstituting in *noir* fashion any coupling between Norman and Marion or Sam and Marion. Marion's death, of course, also cuts off the storytelling project itself, so apparently dependent on the tracing of desire, its discontents, and final recuperation. The masterful shot which pulls back from Marion's lifeless eye (a shot crafted, appropriately enough, from stills) images the stasis at which the film has arrived. This apocalyptic scene represents nothing less than the end of both story form and story content.

Having presented its scene of suffering, *Psycho* has in fact no place to go, no genre to follow, unless it assumes the retrospection of the detective story, converting all that we have thus far witnessed into a narrative to be written by the investigation to follow. Norman's reentry into the room and his desire to contain or un-write the murder confirms that the film, having recorded the death of melodrama, will now trace the stages of detection. Hitchcock, having brought the viewer to the recognition of the artificiality of mainstream narrative, retreats from the abyss by proposing another variety of story consuming experience, one which is equally as familiar as melodrama. The device is bared, but not for long. We might compare these elements of *Psycho*'s structure to Buñuel's playful handling of the narrative in *The Discreet Charm of the Bourgeoisie*, a film in which carefully engineered dead-ends are humorously recuperated by the revelation that they are only dreams. Marion's story, in any event, turns out to be the premise upon which the "real" narrative which will write that story is to be based. This switch is enabled by Hitchcock's manipulation of conventional expectations about the murder itself, an event that is represented but not written. Identifying with Marion, we identified with her desire for social accommodation; with her death, our desire becomes epistemological, an urge to discover the meaning of the murder and thereby recuperate the "surprise" with which we have been confronted. In this way the transition from one genre to another is eased.

Because the narrative focus remains at this point with Norman, who busies himself with covering up the traces of his mother's crime, the genre *gestalt* offered by *Psycho* is properly that of the thriller. In its earlier form (*The 39 Steps* is the archetypal example), the thriller problematized the detective story by making the detective figure someone accused falsely of a crime which he then must solve in order to prove his innocence. In the *noir* thriller, like Orson Welles's *The Stranger*, the protagonist becomes a criminal desperate to hide the traces of his wrongdoing and prevent his identification. *Psycho*'s affinities are obviously with this latter type. In any case, the thriller, like the detective story, does ultimately satisfy conservative narrative expectations: the distribution of the labels guilty and innocent to appropriate characters and a restoration of moral order. Watching Norman dispose of Marion's body, our expectation is that the disruption posed by her murder will be "made right" by the surveilling and punishing aspects of the law. The very structure of the film, however, makes problematic the fulfilling of these generic expectations. For, as Geoffrey Hartman points out, the moralistic functions of the detective story depend heavily on a central premise; namely, that the scene of suffering is de-emphasized, emptied of its ideological import, which is that the law itself is necessarily imperfect.[17] *Psycho*, on the contrary, emphasizes the scene of suffering by offering it as a surprise. The detective story also presupposes that the puzzle of the crime may be reduced to a coherent narrative that obeys the laws of science and human nature. In this it conforms strictly to the world view of realist narrative, which resolves its contradictions and enigmas through a full disclosure of their transparent truth. The disclosure process, however, depends not only on a conservative notion of human subjectivity, but also on the repression of any contradictions that the narrative has raised but cannot solve. *Psycho* defamiliarizes the workings of disclosure by refusing to grant these premises.

The sequences which follow Norman's destruction of the evidence are conventional in that they are focused alternatively through the viewpoints of the criminal's agent and of the detectives eager to solve the mystery of Marion's disappearance. In the opening sequences the viewer was made to experience with Marion, sharing her emotional troubles and level of knowledge. Now, however, the viewer's and the characters' experiences are differentiated—the detectives gradually conclude that Marion's absence is to be explained either through sexual desire or greed. Their suspect is a Norman who has either been convinced to shield her from the law (in return for sexual favours) or who has done away with her for the sake of the stolen cash. Having seen her die, the viewer is therefore positioned to regard the investigations of Sam, Lila, and Arbogast with dramatic irony, knowing that their theorizing is based on an Aristotelian logic of human motive whose insufficiency has been demonstrated by the fact and manner of Marion's murder. The enigma which sustains the viewer's interest relates to the horrifying presence hidden in that Gothic mansion. Will our other figures of identification succumb to the same unexpected attack that destroyed Marion? Norman's mother, like Thorwald, thus becomes the horror concealed by the banal (a relationship symbolized by the jarring juxtaposition of the motel, image of a melodramatically conceived sexual excess, and the family home, index of the unshakeable, regressive past). Unlike Thorwald, however, Mrs. Bates is truly monstrous, as the horror film defines monstrosity, for she is a barely glimpsed presence, her hidden nature an important element of the threat she poses. And her mysteriousness is increased by the sheriff's revelation that Mrs. Bates is in fact dead and buried, a revelation that positions a new enigma in the story (i.e., what is the nature of the house's destructive agent?).

Hitchcock's irony effectively places characters and viewers in different genres, the ones in search of an answer to a mysterious disappearance, the others eager for an explanation of a terrifying presence. The elements of closure that the text assembles, however, are equally suited to the resolution of both enigmas. For both detective and horror stories demand not only the restoration of social order, but a disclosing and reassuring explanation of the disturbing events which have put the story in motion.

The anagnorisis scene in the cellar solves the paradox of Norman's mother (who is, it turns out, both dead and alive) and simultaneously answers the detectives' questions about Marion's disappearance. And this scene, predictably enough, leads directly to the sequence at the police station where the psychiatrist writes a full narrative of the crimes and of Norman's obsession. This explanation, however, is deliberately undermined by Hitchcock, its simplistic Freudianism revealed as inadequate. The psychiatrist identifies Norman as the guilty party even though he maintains that Norman has in some sense been taken over by his own vision of the mother he poisoned for her sexual transgression. Who is victim and who is exploiter? The *mise-en-abyme* of Norman's illness, which projects the idea of self into the endless play of difference (the dialectic of the family romance having collapsed under the weight of its own sexual baggage), becomes yet another index of the failure of the melodramatic world view, with its simplistic concepts of subject, object, and desire. In the film's beginning, desire was easily converted into money, and this process assumed a stable series of social roles which could be rearranged by desire, conceived as an objective currency. At the film's end, desire is indexed by the embalmed corpse of Mrs. Bates, a problematic object (subject?) which signifies the impossibility of accommodation except through the collapse of the dialectic (between Norman as Norman and Norman as Mother) which gives it life.

The film, in fact, displays that collapse. In the penultimate sequence, Norman's desire is at last satisfied, for in becoming his own image of his mother he has reached that emotional stasis in which subject and object are one. The scene, in a sense, gives us a constitution of the couple, but this couple, based on psychopathology and Oedipal failure, cannot serve as the microcosm of a restored social order. Lest we view the relationship between Sam and Lila as such a microcosm, Hitchcock, moreover, reminds us that the film is about social apocalypse, not restoration: the film's last sequence shows us Marion's car pulled from the swamp. The image has occasioned a great deal of critical discussion, but its meaning seems clear enough. Such a final emphasis on the suffering which cannot be "made right" by therapeutic intervention or police surveillance effectively undercuts the Freudian/realist emphases on disclosure. Itself a literal "uncovering," this scene constitutes irrefutable evidence of the inability of both social and textual orders to contain what they express. Hitchcock makes us aware that closure/disclosure is a procedure enabled by a suppression which he here will not allow. Thus the two closing sequences of *Psycho* not only reveal the inadequacy of melodramatic concepts of the personality and its discontents; they also undermine the mystifying textual processes that support such social mythology.

If *Rear Window* explores the existential bases of storytelling, making a hero of the voyeur who exceeds, to his social credit but dubious personal benefit, his role as passive consumer, *Psycho* engages the mechanisms of textual pleasure/order more directly and provocatively. The film defamiliarizes the Hollywood system by exposing the flimsy and artificial nature of the generic contract, offering but then undercutting the coherences of puzzle solving and truth telling. Hitchcock's project is, as Robert Stam suggests, a "devious" one; *Psycho* demonstrates the director's rejection both of a facile classic realism and the more obvious antirealism of modernism. In *Rear Window*, Hitchcock thematizes the institutional structures and psycho-social premises of film viewing, creating a metafictional text that tells a story but also tells about story. Like other *noir* films, *Psycho* overthrows the social optimism of Hollywood social symbolism, discovering a deterministic world in which expectations of individual happiness must go down to defeat; *Psycho*, however, goes further than most *noir* films because it challenges the phenomenon of textual determinism as well.

Because Hitchcock was so caught up in the rigors of institutional filmmaking and not inclined to view himself as an artist, it is hardly surprising

that his modernism expresses itself in metafiction. His anti-establishmen-
tarianism takes shape through the industry-wide movement of *film noir*.
While his texts manifest an expressive realist emphasis on the experiences
of characters and viewer, he violates one of the principal rules of mainstream storytelling (thou shall not kill off the main character, source of
identification and expectation), and this turns out to be one of the film's
most commercial features. Or, as Hitchcock himself might have wished it
put, his films are entertainments which reveal the darker realities upon
which such vicarious pleasure must be based.

NOTES

1. Hitchcock's early reputation was made by the series of six thrillers he completed
for Gaumont-British and Gainsborough in the middle and late thirties. His early American
period, including the work done for David Selznick, can be seen as a consolidation of his
ability to work within the thriller genre. With the appearance of the thematic study of this
body of work by Chabrol/Rohmer in 1957, however, attention shifted from the narrative form
of the Hitchcockian film to its purportedly religious content. For further discussion of the
early commercial and critical views of Hitchcock's accomplishment see Maurice Yacowar,
Hitchcock's British Films (Hamden, Conn: Archon Books, 1977).

2. Bill Nichols, *Ideology and the Image* (Bloomington: Indiana University Press,
1981), 131–69 (a chapter based on several previously published articles), and Raymond
Bellour, "Psychosis, Neurosis, Perversion," *Camera Obscura*, nos. 3/4 (1979): 105–32.

3. Robert Stam, "Hitchcock and Buñuel: Desire and the Law," *Studies in the Literary
Imagination*, no. 16 (Spring 1983): 7–27.

4. Patricia Waugh, *Metafiction: The Theory and Practice of Self-Conscious Fiction*
(New York: Methuen, 1984), 6.

5. Robin Wood, *Hitchcock's Films* (New York: A. S. Barnes, 1977). This is a slightly
revised version of the book originally published in 1970.

6. Roberta Pearson and Robert Stam, "Hitchcock's *Rear Window*: Reflexivity and the
Critique of Voyeurism," *Enclitic*, no. 7 (Spring 1983): 136–45.

7. Waugh, *Metafiction*, 16.

8. See Bellour, "Psychosis, Neurosis, Perversion," 105–32, and William Rothman,
Hitchcock: The Murderous Gaze (Cambridge: Harvard University Press, 1982), 246–341.

9. Foster Hirsch, *Film Noir: The Dark Side of the Screen* (New York: A. S. Barnes,
1981), 139.

10. See, in particular, the often-quoted study of J. A. Place and L. S. Peterson, "Some
Visual Motifs of *Film Noir*," in *Movies and Methods*, ed. Bill Nichols (Berkeley: University of
California Press, 1976), 325–38.

11. James Damico, "Film Noir: A Modest Proposal," in *Film Reader*, no. 3 (1978):
48–57.

12. See Janet Bergstrom, "Alternation, Segmentation, Hypnosis: Interview with
Raymond Bellour," trans. Susan Suleiman, *Camera Obscura*, nos. 3/4 (1979): 70–103.

13. Christine Gledhill, "Klute 1: A Contemporary Film Noir and Feminist Criticism," in
Women in Film Noir, ed. Ann Kaplan (London: BFI, 1980), 6–21.

14. Larry Gross, "Film Apres Noir," *Film Comment* 12, no 4 (Jul.–Aug., 1976): 44.

15. Wolfgang Iser, *The Act of Reading: A Theory of Aesthetic Response* (Baltimore:
Johns Hopkins University Press, 1978), 120–31.

16. Laura Mulvey, "Notes on Sirk and Melodrama," *Movie* 25 (Winter 1977–78): 53–76.

17. Geoffrey Hartman, "Literature High and Low: The Case of the Mystery Story," in *The
Poetics of Murder: Detective Fiction and Literary Theory*, ed. Glenn W. Most and William W.
Stowe (New York: Harcourt Brace Jovanovich, 1983), 210–29.

Selected Bibliography

The secondary literature on Hitchcock is probably more extensive than that on any other single filmmaker. The following list is confined to particularly useful book-length works; asterisked titles are represented in the present collection.

*Brill, Lesley. *The Hitchcock Romance: Love and Irony in Hitchcock's Films*. Princeton: Princeton University Press, 1988. Thematic reading arguing for a more positive, romantic, less pessimistic interpretation of Hitchcock's work.

Deutelbaum, Marshall and Leland Poague, eds. *A Hitchcock Reader*. Ames: Iowa State University Press, 1986. Useful anthology of criticism, both original and reprinted, particularly strong on recent trends.

Durgnat, Raymond. *The Strange Case of Alfred Hitchcock: Or The Plain Man's Hitchcock*. Cambridge: MIT Press, 1974. Presents Hitchcock as a supremely talented craftsman whose films lack any overall thematic unity.

Kapsis, Robert E. *Hitchcock: The Making of a Reputation*. Chicago: University of Chicago Press, 1992. Interesting sociological account of the factors influencing the shifting reception of Hitchcock's films.

LaValley, Albert J., ed. *Focus on Hitchcock*. Englewood Cliffs: Prentice-Hall, 1972. Anthology of earlier critical material, including pieces by Rohmer and Chabrol, Wood, and Durgnat.

Leff, Leonard J. *Hitchcock and Selznick*. New York: Weidenfeld & Nicholson, 1987. Interesting account of the making of *Rebecca*, *Spellbound*, *Notorious*, and *The Paradine Case*.

*Leitch, Thomas. *Find the Director and Other Hitchcock Games*. Athens: University of Georgia Press, 1991. Original, wide-ranging study of the films, emphasizing their narrative self-consciousness.

*Modleski, Tania. *The Women Who Knew Too Much: Hitchcock and Feminist Film Theory*. New York: Methuen, 1988. Psychoanalytically informed feminist analysis of Hitchcock's deeply ambivalent treatment of his female characters.

Naremore, James. *Filmguide to Psycho*. Bloomington: Indiana University Press, 1973. Detailed, scene-by-scene formal and thematic analysis.

Rebello, Stephen. *Alfred Hitchcock and the Making of Psycho*. New York: Dembner, 1990. A detailed case history of the making of the film from pre-production to release.

Rohmer, Eric and Claude Chabrol. *Hitchcock: The First Forty-Four Films*. Trans. Stanley Hochman. New York: Frederick Ungar, 1979. Influential study of the films up to *The Wrong Man*, originally published in 1957, which set the thematic agenda for much Hitchcock criticism for the next two decades.

Rothman, William. *Hitchcock—The Murderous Gaze*. Cambridge: Harvard University Press, 1982. Extremely detailed formal analyses of *The Lodger*, *Murder!*, *The 39 Steps*, *Shadow of a Doubt*, and *Psycho*.

Ryall, Tom. *Alfred Hitchcock and the British Cinema*. Urbana: University of Illinois Press, 1986. Unusually detailed account of the social, industrial, and cultural contexts.

Sloan, Jane. *Alfred Hitchcock: A Guide to References and Resources*. New York: G.K. Hall, 1993. An invaluable reference tool.

Spoto, Donald. *The Art of Alfred Hitchcock: Fifty Years of His Motion Pictures*. New York: Hopkinson & Blake, 1976. Intelligent, chronologically organized critical account, primarily thematic in emphasis.

Spoto, Donald. *The Dark Side of Genius: The Life of Alfred Hitchcock*. Boston: Little, Brown, 1983. Thorough and illuminating, if occasionally overly-speculative, biography.

Sterritt, David. *The Films of Alfred Hitchcock*. New York: Cambridge University Press, 1993. Excellent short introduction, with chapters on *Blackmail*, *Shadow of a Doubt*, *The Wrong Man*, *Vertigo*, *Psycho*, and *The Birds*.

Truffaut, François. *Hitchcock*, revised edition. New York: Simon & Schuster, 1983. Book-length interview, concentrating on matters of technique.

Weis, Elisabeth. *The Silent Scream: Alfred Hitchcock's Sound Track*. Rutherford: Fairleigh Dickinson University Press, 1982. Argues for the often overlooked importance of the dialogue, music, and sound effects.

*Wood, Robin. *Hitchcock's Films Revisited*. New York: Columbia University Press, 1989. Reprints Wood's influential 1965 study of the films from *Strangers on a Train* to *Torn Curtain*, together with several more recent and more ideologically informed pieces.

Yacowar, Maurice. *Hitchcock's British Films*. Hamden, Conn.: Archon Books, 1977. Comprehensive, primarily thematic account of all of the British films, particularly useful on those otherwise generally neglected.

Filmography

All feature-length films directed wholly by Hitchcock are listed below. In addition, between 1921 and 1923 Hitchcock designed title cards for Famous Players-Lasky productions; in 1922 he directed an unfinished feature, *Number 13*; in 1923 he co-directed *Always Tell Your Wife* with Seymour Hicks; between 1923 and 1925 he served as scenarist, designer, and assistant director on five films directed by Graham Cutts; in 1930 he directed part of *Elstree Calling*; in 1944 he directed two documentary shorts for the British Ministry of Information; and between 1955 and 1962 he directed 20 television programs.

1926: *The Pleasure Garden*
PRODUCTION COMPANY: Emelka—G.B.A.
PRODUCER: Michael Balcon, Erich Pommer
SCREENPLAY: Eliot Stannard, from the novel by Oliver Sandys
PHOTOGRAPHY: Baron Ventimiglia
CAST: Virginia Valli (Patsy Brand), Carmelita Geraghty (Jill Cheyne), Miles Mander (Levett), John Stuart (Hugh Fielding)

1926: *The Mountain Eagle*
PRODUCTION COMPANY: Gainsborough-Emelka—G.B.A.
PRODUCER: Michael Balcon
SCREENPLAY: Eliot Stannard
PHOTOGRAPHY: Baron Ventimiglia
CAST: Bernard Goetzke (Judge Pettigrew), Nita Naldi (Beatrice), Malcolm Keen (Fear O'God), John Hamilton (Edward Pettigrew)

1926: *The Lodger: A Story of the London Fog*
PRODUCTION COMPANY: Gainsborough
PRODUCER: Michael Balcon

SCREENPLAY: Alfred Hitchcock and Eliot Stannard, from the novel by Marie Belloc-Lowndes

PHOTOGRAPHY: Baron Ventimiglia

CAST: Ivor Novello (the lodger), June (Daisy Bunting), Marie Ault (Mrs. Bunting), Arthur Chesney (Mr. Bunting), Malcolm Keen (Joe Betts)

1927: *Downhill*

PRODUCTION COMPANY: Gainsborough

PRODUCER: Michael Balcon

SCREENPLAY: Eliot Stannard, from the novel by David Lestrange (Ivor Novello and Constance Collier)

PHOTOGRAPHY: Claude McDonnell

CAST: Ivor Novello (Roddy Berwick), Ben Webster (Dr. Dowson), Robin Irvine (Tim Wakely), Sybil Rhoda (Sybil Wakely), Lillian Braithwaite (Lady Berwick), Isabel Jeans (Julia)

1927: *Easy Virtue*

PRODUCTION COMPANY: Gainsborough

PRODUCER: Michael Balcon and C.M.Woolf

SCREENPLAY: Eliot Stannard, from the play by Noel Coward

PHOTOGRAPHY: Claude McDonnell

CAST: Isabel Jeans (Larita Filton), Robin Irvine (John Whitaker), Franklin Dyall (Mr. Filton), Eric Bransby Williams (Claude Robson)

1927: *The Ring*

PRODUCTION COMPANY: British International Pictures

PRODUCER: John Maxwell

SCREENPLAY: Alfred Hitchcock

PHOTOGRAPHY: Jack Cox

CAST: Carl Brisson (One-Round Jack Sander), Lilian Hall-Davis (Nelly), Ian Hunter (Bob Corby), Harry Terry (Showman)

1928: *The Farmer's Wife*

PRODUCTION COMPANY: British International Pictures

SCREENPLAY: Alfred Hitchcock, Eliot Stannard, from the play by Eden Philpotts

PHOTOGRAPHY: Jack Cox

CAST: Lilian Hall-Davis (Minta Dench), Jameson Thomas (Samuel Sweetland), Maud Gill (Thirza Tapper), Gordon Harker (Churdles Ash), Gibb McLaughlin (Henry Coaker)

1928: *Champagne*

PRODUCTION COMPANY: British International Pictures

SCREENPLAY: Eliot Stannard, Alfred Hitchcock (adaptation) from a story by Walter C. Mycroft

PHOTOGRAPHY: Jack Cox

CAST: Betty Balfour (Betty), Gordon Harker (her father), Ferdinand Von Alten (the mysterious passenger), Jean Bradin (Betty's fiancé)

1929: *The Manxman*

PRODUCTION COMPANY: British International Pictures

PRODUCER: Eliot Stannard. from the novel by Hall Caine

PHOTOGRAPHY: Jack Cox

CAST: Carl Brisson (Peter Quilliam), Malcolm Keen (Philip Christian), Anny Ondra (Kate), Randle Ayrton (Mr. Cregeen)

1929: *Blackmail*

PRODUCTION COMPANY: British International Pictures

SCREENPLAY: Benn W. Levy, Alfred Hitchcock (adaptation) from the play by Charles Bennett

PHOTOGRAPHY: Jack Cox

MUSIC: Campbell and Connelly

CAST: Anny Ondra [voice: Joan Barry] (Alice White), Sara Allgood (Mrs. White), John Longden (Frank Webber), Charles Paton (Mr. White), Cyril Ritchard (Crewe), Donald Calthrop (Tracy)

1930: *Juno and the Paycock*

PRODUCTION COMPANY: British International Pictures

PRODUCER: John Maxwell

SCREENPLAY: Alma Reville, Alfred Hitchcock (adaptation) from the play by Sean O'Casey

PHOTOGRAPHY: Jack Cox

CAST: Sara Allgood (Juno), Edward Chapman (Captain Boyle), Sidney Morgan (Joxer), Marie O'Neill (Mrs. Madigan), John Longden (Charles Bentham)

1930: *Murder!*

PRODUCTION COMPANY: British International Pictures

PRODUCER: John Maxwell

SCREENPLAY: Alma Reville, Alfred Hitchcock (adaptation), Walter Mycroft (adaptation), from the novel and play *Enter Sir John* by Clemence Dane (pseudonym of Winifred Ashton) and Helen Simpson

PHOTOGRAPHY: Jack Cox

MUSIC: John Reynders

CAST: Norah Baring (Diana Baring), Herbert Marshall (Sir John Menier), Miles Mander (Gordon Druce), Phyllis Konstam (Dulcie Markham), Edward Chapman (Ted Markham), Esme Percy (Handel Fane)

1931: *Mary* (German version of *Murder!*, shot simultaneously with the English-language version)

PRODUCTION COMPANY: British International Pictures

1931: *The Skin Game*

PRODUCTION COMPANY: British International Pictures

PRODUCER: John Maxwell

SCREENPLAY: Alma Reville, Alfred Hitchcock (adaptation) from the play by John Galsworthy

PHOTOGRAPHY: Jack Cox, assisted by Charles Martin

CAST: Edmund Gwenn (Mr. Hornblower), Jill Esmond (Jill), John Longden (Charles), C.V. France (Mr. Hillchrest), Helen Haye (Mrs. Hillchrest), Phyllis Konstam (Chloe)

1932: *Rich and Strange*

PRODUCTION COMPANY: British International Pictures

PRODUCER: John Maxwell

SCREENPLAY: Alma Reville and Val Valentine

PHOTOGRAPHY: Jack Cox, Charles Martin

MUSIC: Hal Dolphe

CAST: Henry Kendall (Fred Hill), Joan Barry (Emily Hill), Percy Marmount (Commander Gordon), Betty Amann (the princess), Elsie Randolph (Elsie)

1932: *Number Seventeen*

PRODUCTION COMPANY: British International Pictures

PRODUCER: Leon M. Lion

SCREENPLAY: Alfred Hitchcock, Alma Reville, Rodney Ackland, from the novel and play by Jefferson Farjeon

PHOTOGRAPHY: Jack Cox

MUSIC: A. Hallis

CAST: Léon M. Lion (Ben), Anne Grey (Nora Brant), John Stuart (Barton), Donald Calthrop (Brant), Barry Jones (Henry Doyle)

1933: *Waltzes from Vienna*

PRODUCTION COMPANY: Tom Arnold Productions

PRODUCER: Tom Arnold

SCREENPLAY: Alma Reville and Guy Bolton, from the play by A. M. Willner, Heinz Reichert, and Ernst Marischka.

MUSIC: Johann Strauss the Elder and Strauss the Younger

CAST: Jessie Matthews (Rasi), Edmund Gwenn (Strauss the Elder), Fay Compton (the countess), Frank Vosper (the prince), Edmond Knight (Strauss the Younger)

1934: *The Man Who Knew Too Much*

PRODUCTION COMPANY: Gaumont-British Pictures

PRODUCERS: Ivor Montagu and Michael Balcon

SCREENPLAY: A. R. Rawlinson, Edwin Greenwood, and Emlyn Williams, based on original subject by Charles Bennett and D. B. Wyndham-Lewis

PHOTOGRAPHY: Curt Courant

MUSIC: Arthur Benjamin

CAST: Leslie Banks (Bob Lawrence), Edna Best (Jill Lawrence), Peter Lorre (Abbot), Nova Pilbeam (Betty Lawrence), Pierre Fresnay (Louis Bernard), Frank Vosper (Ramon)

1935: *The 39 Steps*

PRODUCTION COMPANY: Gaumont-British Pictures

PRODUCERS: Michael Balcon, Ivor Montagu

SCREENPLAY: Charles Bennett, Alma Reville, and Ian Hay, from the novel by John Buchan

PHOTOGRAPHY: Bernard Knowles

MUSIC: Louis Levy

CAST: Robert Donat (Richard Hannay), Madeleine Carroll (Pamela), Lucie Mannheim (Annabella Smith), Godfrey Tearle (Professor Jordan), John Laurie (Crofter), Peggy Ashcroft (Crofter's wife), Wylie Watson (Mr. Memory)

1936: *Secret Agent*

PRODUCTION COMPANY: Gaumont-British Pictures

SCREENPLAY: Charles Bennett, Alma Reville, Ian Hay, and Jesse Lasky, Jr., from the play by Campbell Dixon, based on stories by W. Somerset Maugham

PHOTOGRAPHY: Bernard Knowles

MUSIC: Louis Levy

CAST: John Gielgud (Edgar Brodie/Richard Ashenden), Madeleine Carroll (Elsa Carrington), Peter Lorre (the general), Robert Young (Robert Marvin), Percy Marmont (Caypor), Florence Kahn (Mrs. Caypor), Lilli Palmer (the maid)

1936: *Sabotage*

PRODUCTION COMPANY: Gaumont British Pictures

PRODUCERS: Michael Balcon and Ivor Montagu

SCREENPLAY: Charles Bennett, Alma Reville, Ian Hay, Helen Simpson, and E.V.H. Emmett, from the novel *The Secret Agent* by Joseph Conrad

PHOTOGRAPHY: Bernard Knowles

MUSIC: Louis Levy

CAST: Sylvia Sydney (Mrs. Verloc), Oscar Homolka (Verloc), Desmond Tester (Stevie), John Loder (Ted), Joyce Barbour (Renée), William Dewhurst (Mr. Chatman), Martita Hunt (his daughter)

1937: *Young and Innocent*

PRODUCTION COMPANY: Gainsborough-Gaumont British

PRODUCER: Edward Black

SCREENPLAY: Charles Bennett, Edwin Greenwood, Anthony Armstrong, Gerald Savory, and Alma Reville, (adaptation) from the novel *A Shilling for Candles* by Josephine Tey

PHOTOGRAPHY: Bernard Knowles

MUSIC: Louis Levy

CAST: Nova Pilbeam (Erica Burgoyne), Derrick de Marney (Robert Tisdall), Percy Marmont (Colonel Burgoyne), Edward Rigby (Will), John Longden (Detective Inspector Kent), Basil Radford (Uncle Basil), Mary Clare (Erica's aunt), George Curzon (Guy)

1938: *The Lady Vanishes*

PRODUCTION COMPANY: Gainsborough

PRODUCER: Edward Black

SCREENPLAY: Sidney Gilliat and Frank Launder, from the novel *The Wheel Spins* by Ethel Lina White

PHOTOGRAPHY: Jack Cox

MUSIC: Louis Levy

CAST: Margaret Lockwood (Iris Henderson), Michael Redgrave (Gilbert), Dame May Whitty (Miss Froy), Paul Lukas (Dr. Hartz), Cecil Parker (Mr. Todhunter), Naughton Wayne (Caldicott), Basil Radford (Charters)

1939: *Jamaica Inn*

PRODUCTION COMPANY: Erich Pommer Productions

PRODUCERS: Erich Pommer, Charles Laughton

SCREENPLAY: Sidney Gilliat, Joan Harrison, and J. B. Priestley, from the novel by Daphne du Maurier

PHOTOGRAPHY: Harry Stradling and Bernard Knowles

MUSIC: Eric Fenby

CAST: Charles Laughton (Sir Humphrey Pengaltan), Leslie Banks (Joss Merlyn), Marie Ney (Patience Merlyn), Maureen O'Hara (Mary, their niece), Emlyn Williams (Harry), Wylie Watson (Salvation), Robert Newton (Jem Traherne), Mervyn Johns (Thomas)

1940: *Rebecca*

PRODUCTION COMPANY: The Selznick Studio

PRODUCER: David O. Selznick

SCREENPLAY: Robert E. Sherwood, Joan Harrison, Philip MacDonald (adaptation), and Michael Hogan (adaptation) from the novel by Daphne du Maurier

PHOTOGRAPHY: George Barnes

MUSIC: Franz Waxman

CAST: Joan Fontaine (the second Mrs. de Winter), Laurence Olivier (Maxim de Winter), Judith Anderson (Mrs. Danvers), George Sanders (Jack Favell), Florence Bates (Mrs. van Hopper), Nigel Bruce (Giles Lacey), Gladys Cooper (Beatrice Lacey)

1940: *Foreign Correspondent*

PRODUCTION COMPANY: Walter Wanger-United Artists

PRODUCER: Walter Wanger

SCREENPLAY: Charles Bennett, Joan Harrison, James Hilton (dialogue), and Robert Benchley (dialogue)

PHOTOGRAPHY: Rudolph Mate

MUSIC: Alfred Newman

CAST: Joel McCrea (Johnny Jones/Huntley Haverstock), Laraine Day (Carol Fisher), Herbert Marshall (Stephen Fisher), George Sanders (Herbert Folliott), Albert Basserman (Van Meer), Robert Bechley (Stebbins), Edmund Gwenn (Rowley), Harry Davenport (Mr. Powers)

1941: *Mr. and Mrs. Smith*

PRODUCTION COMPANY: RKO Radio Pictures

PRODUCER: Harry E. Edington

SCREENPLAY: Norman Krasna

PHOTOGRAPHY: Harry Stradling

MUSIC: Roy Webb

CAST: Carole Lombard (Ann Krausheimer Smith), Robert Montgomery (David Smith), Gene Raymond (Jeff Custer), Jack Carson (Chuck Benson)

1941: *Suspicion*

PRODUCTION COMPANY: RKO Radio Pictures

PRODUCER: Harry E. Edington

SCREENPLAY: Samson Raphaelson, Joan Harrison, and Alma Reville, from the novel *Before the Fact* by Frances Iles

PHOTOGRAPHY: Harry Stradling

MUSIC: Franz Waxman

CAST: Joan Fontaine (Lina McLaidlaw), Cary Grant (Johnny Aysgarth), Cedric Hardwicke (General McLaidlaw), Dame May Whitty (Mrs. McLaidlaw), Nigel Bruce (Beaky), Isabel Jeans (Mrs. Newsham), Leo G. Carroll (Captain Mahlbeck)

1942: *Saboteur*

PRODUCTION COMPANY: Frank Lloyd Productions-Universal

PRODUCER: Frank Lloyd

SCREENPLAY: Peter Viertel, Joan Harrison, and Dorothy Parker, from an original subject by Alfred Hitchcock

PHOTOGRAPHY: Joseph Valentine

MUSIC: Charles Previn and Frank Skinner

CAST: Robert Cummings (Barry Kane), Priscilla Lane (Patricia Martin), Otto Kruger (Charles Tobin), Alma Kruger (Mrs. Van Sutton), Norman Lloyd (Fry)

1943: *Shadow of a Doubt*

PRODUCTION COMPANY: Universal-Skirball Productions

PRODUCER: Jack H. Skirball

SCREENPLAY: Thornton Wilder, Alma Reville, and Sally Benson, from an original story by Gordon McDonell

PHOTOGRAPHY: Joseph Valentine

MUSIC: Dimitri Tiomkin

CAST: Joseph Cotten (Uncle Charlie Oakley), Teresa Wright (Charlie Newton), MacDonald Carey (Jack Graham), Patricia Collinge (Emma Newton), Henry Travers (Joe Newton), Hume Cronyn (Herb Hawkins), Edna May Wonacott (Ann Newton), Charles Bates (Roger Newton), Wallace Ford (Fred Saunders)

1943: *Lifeboat*

PRODUCTION COMPANY: 20th Century-Fox

PRODUCER: Kenneth MacGowan

SCREENPLAY: Jo Swerling, from an original subject by John Steinbeck

PHOTOGRAPHY: Glen MacWilliams

MUSIC: Hugo Friedhofer

CAST: Tallulah Bankhead (Constance Porter), William Bendix (Gus), Walter Slezak (Willy), John Hodiak (Kovac), Henry Hull (Charles Rittenhouse), Hume Cronyn (Stanley Garrett), Mary Anderson (Alice MacKenzie), Heather Angel (Mrs. Higgins), Canada Lee (Joe Spencer)

1945: *Spellbound*

PRODUCTION COMPANY: Selznick International

PRODUCER: David O. Selznick

SCREENPLAY: Ben Hecht and Angus McPhail (adaptation), from the novel *The House of Dr. Edwardes* by Francis Beeding

PHOTOGRAPHY: George Barnes

MUSIC: Miklos Rozsa

CAST: Ingrid Bergman (Dr. Constance Petersen), Gregory Peck (John Ballantine), Leo G. Carroll (Dr. Murchison), Norman Lloyd (Garmes), Michael Chekhov (Dr. Alex Brulov), Rhonda Fleming (Mary Carmichael), John Emery (Dr. Fleurot)

1946: *Notorious*

PRODUCTION COMPANY: RKO Radio

PRODUCER: Alfred Hitchcock

SCREENPLAY: Ben Hecht, based on a subject by Alfred Hitchcock

PHOTOGRAPHY: Ted Tetzlaff

MUSIC: Roy Webb

CAST: Ingrid Bergman (Alicia Huberman), Cary Grant (Devlin), Claude Rains (Alexander Sebastian), Leopoldine Konstantin (Madame Sebastian), Louis Calhern (Paul Prescott), Reinhold Schünzel (Dr. Anderson), Ivan Triesault (Eric Mathis)

1947: *The Paradine Case*

PRODUCTION COMPANY: Selznick International-Vanguard Films

PRODUCER: David O. Selznick

SCREENPLAY: David O. Selznick and Alma Reville (adaptation), from the novel by Robert Hichens

PHOTOGRAPHY: Lee Garmes

MUSIC: Franz Waxman

CAST: Gregory Peck (Anthony Keane), Ann Todd (Gay Keane), Charles Laughton (Judge Horfield), Alida Valli (Maddalena Paradine), Ethel Barrymore (Sophie Horfield), Charles Coburn (Simon Flaquer), Louis Jourdan (André Latour), Joan Tetzel (Judy Flaquer)

1948: *Rope*

PRODUCTION COMPANY: Transatlantic Pictures-Warner Brothers

PRODUCERS: Alfred Hitchcock and Sidney Bernstein

SCREENPLAY: Arthur Laurents and Hume Cronyn (adaptation), from the play by Patrick Hamilton

PHOTOGRAPHY: Joseph Valentine, William V. Skall

MUSIC: Leo F. Forbstein, based on Francis Poulenc's *Perpetual Movement No. 1*

CAST: James Stewart (Rupert Cadell), John Dall (Shaw Brandon), Farley Granger (Philip), Cedric Hardwicke (Mr. Kentley), Constance Collier (Mrs. Atwater), Edith Evanson (Mrs. Wilson), Joan Chandler (Janet), Douglas Dick (Kenneth)

1949: *Under Capricorn*

PRODUCTION COMPANY: Transatlantic Pictures-Warner Brothers

PRODUCERS: Alfred Hitchcock and Sidney Bernstein

SCREENPLAY: James Bridie and Hume Cronyn (adaptation), based on the novel by Helen Simpson

PHOTOGRAPHY: Jack Cardiff

MUSIC: Richard Addinsell

CAST: Ingrid Bergman (Henrietta Flusky), Joseph Cotten (Sam Flusky), Michael Wilding (Charles Adare), Margaret Leighton (Milly), Cecil Parker (Governor), Denis O'Dea (Corrigan)

1950: *Stage Fright*

PRODUCTION COMPANY: Warner Brothers-First National Pictures

PRODUCERS: Alfred Hitchcock and Fred Aherne

SCREENPLAY: Whitfield Cook and Alma Reville (adaptation), from two stories by Selwyn Jepson

PHOTOGRAPHY: Wilkie Cooper

MUSIC: Leighton Lucas

CAST: Marlene Dietrich (Charlotte Inwood), Jane Wyman (Eve Gill), Michael Wilding (Wilfrid Smith), Richard Todd (Jonathan Cooper), Alastair Sim (Commander Gill), Sybil Thorndike (Mrs. Gill), Kay Walsh (Nellie Good), Patricia Hitchcock (Chubby Bannister)

1951: *Strangers on a Train*

PRODUCTION COMPANY: Warner Brothers

PRODUCER: Alfred Hitchcock

SCREENPLAY: Raymond Chandler, Czenzi Ormonde, and Whitfield Cook (adaptation), from the novel by Patricia Highsmith

PHOTOGRAPHY: Robert Burks

MUSIC: Dimitri Tiomkin

CAST: Robert Walker (Bruno Anthony), Farley Granger (Guy Haines), Ruth Roman (Ann Morton), Laura Elliot (Miriam Haines), Patricia Hitchcock (Barbara Morton), Leo G. Carroll (Senator Morton), Marion Lorne (Mrs. Anthony)

1952: *I Confess*

PRODUCTION COMPANY: Warner Brothers-First National Pictures

PRODUCER: Alfred Hitchcock

SCREENPLAY: George Tabori and William Archibald, from the play *Nos Deux Consciences* by Paul Anthelme

PHOTOGRAPHY: Robert Burks

MUSIC: Dimitri Tiomkin

CAST: Montgomery Clift (Father Michael Logan), Anne Baxter (Ruth Grandfort), Karl Malden (Inspector Larrue), Roger Dann (Pierre Grandfort), O. E. Hasse (Otto Keller), Dolly Haas (Alma Keller), Brian Aherne (Willy Robertson)

1954: *Dial M for Murder*

PRODUCTION COMPANY: Warner Brothers-First National Pictures

PRODUCER: Alfred Hitchcock

SCREENPLAY: Frederick Knott, from his play

PHOTOGRAPHY: Robert Burks

MUSIC: Dimitri Tiomkin

CAST: Ray Milland (Tony Wendice), Grace Kelly (Margot

Wendice), Robert Cummings (Mark Halliday), Anthony Dawson (Captain Swann Lesgate), John Williams (Inspector Hubbard)

1954: *Rear Window*

PRODUCTION COMPANY: Paramount-Patron PRODUCER: Alfred Hitchcock

SCREENPLAY: John Michael Hayes, from the short story by Cornell Woolrich

PHOTOGRAPHY: Robert Burks

MUSIC: Franz Waxman

CAST: James Stewart (L. B. Jeffries), Grace Kelly (Lisa Fremont), Thelma Ritter (Stella), Wendell Corey (Tom Doyle), Raymond Burr (Lars Thorwald), Irene Winston (Mrs. Thorwald), Judith Evelyn (Miss Lonelyhearts)

1955: *To Catch a Thief*

PRODUCTION COMPANY: Paramount Pictures

PRODUCER: Alfred Hitchcock

SCREENPLAY: John Michael Hayes, from the novel by David Dodge

PHOTOGRAPHY: Robert Burks

MUSIC: Lynn Murray

CAST: Cary Grant (John Robie), Grace Kelly (Frances Stevens), Jesse Royce Landis (Jesse Stevens), John Williams (H. H. Hughson), Brigitte Auber (Danielle Foussard), Charles Vanel (Bertani)

1956: *The Trouble with Harry*

PRODUCTION COMPANY: Paramount-Alfred Hitchcock Productions

PRODUCER: Alfred Hitchcock

SCREENPLAY: John Michael Hayes, from the novel by John Trevor Story

PHOTOGRAPHY: Robert Burks

MUSIC: Bernard Herrmann

CAST: Edmund Gwenn (Captain Wiles), John Forsythe (Sam Marlowe), Shirley MacLaine (Jennifer Rogers), Mildred Natwick (Miss Gravely), Mildred Dunnock (Mrs. Wiggs), Jerry Mathers (Arnie Rogers), Royal Dano (Alfred Wiggs)

1956: *The Man Who Knew Too Much*

PRODUCTION COMPANY: Paramount-Filmwite Productions

PRODUCER: Alfred Hitchcock

SCREENPLAY: John Michael Hayes, from a story by Charles Bennett and D. B. Wyndham-Lewis

PHOTOGRAPHY: Robert Burks

MUSIC: Bernard Herrmann

CAST: James Stewart (Dr. Ben McKenna), Doris Day (Jo McKenna), Christopher Olsen (Hank McKenna), Bernard Miles (Mr. Drayton), Brenda de Banzie (Mrs. Drayton), Daniel Gelin (Louis Bernard)

1956: *The Wrong Man*

PRODUCTION COMPANY: Warner Brothers

PRODUCER: Alfred Hitchcock

SCREENPLAY: Maxwell Anderson and Angus MacPhail, from "The True Story of Christopher Emmanuel Balestrero" by Maxwell Anderson

PHOTOGRAPHY: Robert Burks

MUSIC: Bernard Herrmann

CAST: Henry Fonda (Christopher Emmanuel Balestrero), Vera Miles (Rose Balestrero), Anthony Quayle (Frank O'Connor), Esther Minciotti (Mrs. Balestrero), Harold J. Stone (Lieutenant Bowers)

1958: *Vertigo*

PRODUCTION COMPANY: Paramount-Alfred Hitchcock Productions

PRODUCERS: Alfred Hitchcock and Herbert Coleman (Associate)

SCREENPLAY: Alec Coppel and Samuel Taylor, from the novel *D'entre Les Morts* by Pierre Boileau and Thomas Narcejac

PHOTOGRAPHY: Robert Burks

MUSIC: Bernard Herrmann

CAST: James Stewart (Scottie Ferguson), Kim Novak (Madeleine Elster/Judy Barton), Barbara Bel Geddes (Midge Wood), Tom Helmore (Gavin Elster), Konstantin Shayne (Pop Liebl)

1959: *North by Northwest*

PRODUCTION COMPANY: Metro-Goldwyn-Mayer

PRODUCER: Alfred Hitchcock

SCREENPLAY: Ernest Lehman

PHOTOGRAPHY: Robert Burks

MUSIC: Bernard Herrmann

CAST: Cary Grant (Roger O. Thornhill), Eva Marie Saint (Eve Kendall), James Mason (Philip Vandamm), Jessie Royce Landis (Clara Thornhill), Leo G. Carroll (the Professor), Martin Landau (Leonard), Philip Ober (Lester Townshend)

1960: *Psycho*

PRODUCTION COMPANY: Paramount-Shamley Productions

PRODUCER: Alfred Hitchcock

SCREENPLAY: Joseph Stefano, from the novel by Robert Bloch

PHOTOGRAPHY: John L. Russell

MUSIC: Bernard Herrmann

CAST: Anthony Perkins (Norman Bates), Janet Leigh (Marion Crane), Vera Miles (Lila Crane), John Gavin (Sam Loomis), Martin Balsam (Milton Arbogast), John McIntire (Sheriff Chambers), Lurene Tuttle (Mrs. Chambers), Simon Oakland (the psychiatrist)

1963: *The Birds*

PRODUCTION COMPANY: Universal-Alfred Hitchcock Productions

PRODUCER: Alfred Hitchcock

SCREENPLAY: Evan Hunter, from the novel by Daphne Du Maurier

PHOTOGRAPHY: Robert Burks

MUSIC: Remi Gassmann, Oskar Sala, and Bernard Herrmann

CAST: Tippi Hedren (Melanie Daniels), Rod Taylor (Mitch Brenner), Jessica Tandy (Lydia Brenner), Suzanne Pleshette (Annie Hayworth), Veronica Cartwright (Cathy Brenner), Ethel Griffies (Mrs. Bundy)

1964: *Marnie*

PRODUCTION COMPANY: Universal-Geoffrey Stanley

PRODUCER: Alfred Hitchcock

SCREENPLAY: Jay Presson Allen, from the novel by Winston Graham

PHOTOGRAPHY: Robert Burks

MUSIC: Bernard Herrmann

CAST: Tippi Hedren (Marnie Edgar), Sean Connery (Mark Rutland), Diane Baker (Lil Mainwaring), Louise Latham (Bernice Edgar), Martin Gabel (Strutt), Bob Sweeney (Cousin Bob), Bruce Dern (the sailor)

1966: *Torn Curtain*

PRODUCTION COMPANY: Universal Pictures

PRODUCER: Alfred Hitchcock

SCREENPLAY: Brian Moore

PHOTOGRAPHY: John F. Warren

MUSIC: John Addison

CAST: Paul Newman (Michael Armstrong), Julie Andrews (Sarah Sherman), Lila Kedrova (Countess Kuchinska), Wolfgang Kieling (Gromek), Ludwig Donath (Professor Lindt), David Opatoshu (Jacobi)

1969 *Topaz*

PRODUCTION COMPANY: Universal Pictures

PRODUCER: Alfred Hitchcock

SCREENPLAY: Samuel Taylor, from the novel by Leon Uris

PHOTOGRAPHY: Jack Hildyard

MUSIC: Maurice Jarre

CAST: Frederick Stafford (André Devereaux), Dany Robin (Nicole Devereaux), John Forsythe (Michael Nordstrom), John Vernon (Rico Parra), Michel Piccoli (Jacques Granville), Karin Dor (Juanita de Cordoba), Philippe Noiret (Henri Jarré), Roscoe Lee Browne (Philippe Dubois)

1972: *Frenzy*

PRODUCTION COMPANY: Universal Pictures

PRODUCER: Alfred Hitchcock

SCREENPLAY: Anthony Shaffer, from the novel *Goodbye Piccadilly, Farewell Leicester Square* by Arthur La Bern

PHOTOGRAPHY: Gil Taylor

MUSIC: Ron Goodwin

CAST: Jon Finch (Richard Blaney), Barry Foster (Bob Rusk), Barbara Leigh-Hunt (Brenda Blaney), Anna Massey (Babs Milligan), Alec McCowen (Inspector Oxford), Vivien Merchant (Mrs. Oxford), Billie Whitelaw (Hetty Porter), Clive Swift (Johnny Porter)

1976: *Family Plot*

PRODUCTION COMPANY: Universal Pictures

PRODUCER: Alfred Hitchcock

SCREENPLAY: Ernest Lehman, from the novel *The Rainbird Pattern* by Victor Canning

PHOTOGRAPHY: Leonard J. South

MUSIC: John Williams

CAST: Karen Black (Fran), Bruce Dern (George Lumley), Barbara Harris (Blanche Tyler), William Devane (Adamson), Ed Lauter (Maloney), Cathleen Nesbitt (Julia Rainbird), Katherine Helmond (Mrs. Maloney)

Rental and Other Sources

Hitchcock's films generally, and more particularly those which receive particular attention in this volume, are widely available on videotape, laserdisc, and 16mm.

Blackmail is available on 16mm from Biograph Entertainment, Budget Films, Em Gee Film Library, Ivy Films, Kit Parker Films, and Swank Motion Pictures.

The Man Who Knew Too Much (1934 version) is available on video and laserdisc from Image Entertainment and on 16mm from Biograph Entertainment, Budget Films, Em Gee Film Library, Ivy Films, Kit Parker Films, and Swank Motion Pictures.

The 39 Steps is available on video and laserdisc from Voyager and Janus Films and on 16mm from Biograph Entertainment, Budget Films, Em Gee Film Library, Films Incorporated, Ivy Films, and Kit Parker Films.

Notorious is available on video and laserdisc from Voyager and Janus Films and on 16mm from Ivy Films.

Rear Window is available on video and laserdisc from MCA/Universal Home Video and on 16mm from Swank Motion Pictures.

Vertigo is available on video and laserdisc from MCA/Universal Home Video and on 16mm from Swank Motion Pictures.

North by Northwest is available on video and laserdisc from MGM/UA Home Video and Voyager and Janus Films.

Psycho is available on video and laserdisc from MCA/Universal Home Video and on 16mm from Swank Motion Pictures.

DISTRIBUTORS

Biograph Entertainment, Ltd.
2 Depot Plaza, Suite 202B
Bedford Hills, NY 10507
Telephone: 914–242–9838

Budget Films
4590 Santa Monica Blvd.
Los Angeles, CA 90029
Telephone: 213–660–0187

Em Gee Film Library
6924 Canby Ave., Suite 103
Reseda, CA 91335
Telephone: 818–981–5506

Films Incorporated
5547 North Ravenswood Ave.
Chicago, IL 60640
Telephone: 800–323–4222

Image Entertainment
9333 Oso Avenue
Chatsworth, CA 91311
Telephone: 800–473–3475

Ivy Films
725 Providence Rd., Suite 204
Charlotte, NC 28207
Telephone: 704–333–3991

Kit Parker Films
P.O. Box 16022
Monterey, CA 93942
Telephone: 800–538–5838

MCA/Universal Home Video
70 Universal City Plaza
Universal City, CA 91608
Telephone: 818–777–1000

MGM/UA Home Video
2500 Broadway St.
Santa Monica, CA 90404–3061
Telephone: 310–449–3000

Swank Motion Pictures, Inc.
201 South Jefferson Ave.

St. Louis, MO 63103
Telephone: 800–876–5445

Voyager and Janus Films
1 Bridge St.
Irvington, NY 10533
Telephone: 800–446–2001

Index